White Lives

How are we to understand race at the beginning of the twenty-first century? How do concepts of 'race' intersect with gender and class?

White Lives reconsiders white identities through white experiences of race. Exploring race, alongside class and gender, Bridget Byrne analyses the flexibility of racialised discourse in everyday life, while simultaneously arguing for a radical deconstruction of the notions of race these discourses create.

Byrne focuses on the experience of white mothers and their young children, as a key site in the reproduction of class, race and gender subjectivities. Through this, she offers a unique perspective on both the experience of motherhood and ideas of white identity. Her analysis is multilayered, looking at local and private spaces but also considering national and public debates concerning race.

This accessible and revealing book will appeal across disciplines to students studying sociology, anthropology, geography, race and ethnicity and cultural studies.

Bridget Byrne is a lecturer in Sociology at the University of Manchester.

For Sara and Khalid

White Lives

The interplay of 'race', class and gender in everyday life

Bridget Byrne

Routledge
Taylor & Francis Group

LONDON AND NEW YORK

First published 2006
by Routledge
2 Park Square, Milton Park, Abingdon, Oxon OX14 4RN

Simultaneously published in the USA and Canada by Routledge
270 Madison Ave, New York, NY 10016

Routledge is an imprint of the Taylor & Francis Group

© 2006 Bridget Byrne

Typeset in Sabon by Prepress Projects Ltd
Printed and bound in Great Britain by Antony Rowe Ltd,
Chippenham, Wiltshire

British Library Cataloguing in Publication Data
A catalogue record for this book is available from the British Library

Library of Congress Cataloging in Publication Data
A catalog record for this book has been requested

ISBN10: 0–415–34711–4 (hbk)
ISBN10: 0–415–34712–2 (pbk)

ISBN13: 9–78–0–415–34711–2 (hbk)
ISBN13: 9–78–0–415–34712–9 (hbk)

Contents

Acknowledgements

This book has been some time coming and there are many people who have read parts or even most of it. In particular, I would like to thank Annie Whitehead who encouraged me from the start. Thanks also to Niamh Moore and Khalid Nadvi who have been reading and commenting on the research almost from the beginning to the very end. Thanks also to Les Back, Jane Cowan, Suki Ali, Bev Skeggs, Fiona Ross, Eva Mackey, Justin Byrne, members of the Feminist Theory Reading Group at Sussex (in particular Charlotte Adcock, Jude Redaway, Cate Eschle, Jo Littler, Andrea Hammel, Niamh Moore and Paramjit Rai) and participants at various conferences who have commented on parts of the work. I would also like to thank colleagues at Manchester, in particular Laura Doan, Tej Purewal, Virinder Kalra, Nick Thoburn, Paul Keleman, Sheila Rowbotham, Helen Woods and Darren Waldron.

Thanks also to the Byrne and Nadvi extended families and to my friends both inside and outside academia.

I would like to thank all those who gave up their time and were prepared to open some of their lives to me through the interviews. Pursuing interviewees can be a tiring and stressful process, but it was always heartening to receive so much generosity. Not only did many women welcome me into their homes and were prepared to be interviewed and taped, but they also went to some lengths to introduce me to their friends. I hope I have given their accounts the respect they deserve.

This book is based on research funded by the ESRC.

1   Knowing 'whiteness'

One of the difficulties of being an academic researcher is knowing how much detail to go into when people ask you about your work. This book is based on research on a subject which, for many of the people I chatted to, had very little concrete meaning: that of white experience and identities. This was particularly true for white people who had no reason to think that their own experience or identities were racialised in any way. In these casual conversations, I found that a common response to the idea of studying 'whiteness' was to suggest that the really interesting whiteness was somehow 'out there', somewhere else, preferably far away. So it was often suggested that I should study whiteness in South Africa, in Zimbabwe or in the development aid donor community. All of these would indeed be very interesting and important contexts for understanding how 'race'[1] structures identity and interaction. Nonetheless, this book is focused on a context which, for many of those making these suggestions, was not 'out there' but very much at home and perhaps too close for comfort – that of middle- and working-class white mothers of young children living in south London.

These conversations can tell us something about whiteness and white identity. There is often a tendency when thinking about whiteness (and perhaps most other social phenomena) to look to the extreme and to that which is seen as 'different'. Thus, many people can recognise the interest in understanding whiteness in a situation where white people are in a minority (therefore different) and/or who exercise extreme power (as in the recent history of apartheid) or hold extreme views (far-right groups were also popular suggestions). But the 'normalness' of whiteness in Britain does not hold so much interest. The assumption often is that 'we' (everyday white people in Britain who are not politically racist) cannot be interesting as 'race' has nothing to do with us.

This book sets out to examine the racialised experience of a particular group of white women, living in a specific location and at one moment of their lives. It takes a group of white people who have not been selected as extreme examples – people who would consider themselves as 'normal' or 'average' people – but still asks how they are raced. That is, how are their experiences, sense of selves, ways of thinking, speaking and doing shaped by ideas of race and racist structures and relations. Thus, it requires hearing and seeing 'race' in contexts where it is not explicitly felt as present. When one white woman (interviewee) talks to another white women (interviewer) about schooling or national identity or living in London, the ways in which they are 'doing' 'race', just as they are doing class, sexuality and gender, will not necessarily be referred to or even understood. But this book tries to trace some of the ways in which this talk is shaped by racist processes that produce raced bodies, imaginaries and ways of being and relating to others. Those who have been positioned as non-white are more likely to have their lives scrutinised for the effects of 'race', but this book asserts the importance of applying similar attention to the lives and identities of those who are positioned as white. As Ruth Frankenberg argues:

> To speak of whiteness is, I think, to assign everyone a place in the rela-tions of racism. It is to emphasize that dealing with racism is not merely an option for white people – that, rather, racism shapes white people's lives and identities in a way that is inseparable from other facets of daily life.
>
> (Frankenberg 1993: 6)

However, it is also important to heed Sara Ahmed's warning that merely marking whiteness (which is itself an act that is only new to white people) does not achieve anti-racist aims: 'putting whiteness into speech, as an object to be spoken about, however critically, is not an anti-racist action, and it does not necessarily commit a state, institution or person to a form of action that we could describe as anti-racist' (Ahmed 2004: 12). Rather than making claims for moving 'beyond race' or for successful anti-racism, Ahmed argues that work on whiteness should 'be about attending to forms of white racism and white privilege that are not undone, and may even be repeated and intensified, through declarations of whiteness, or through the recognition of privilege as privilege' (Ahmed 2004: 58).

Nonetheless, I argue that to mark what is frequently (at least to white eyes) unmarked – the racialised nature of white experience – is part of a process of decentring whiteness. It is a crucial counter to racism, or at least a condition for better understanding its workings. The intention is not to reify – or essentialise – something called whiteness, but to show how the practices, subject construction and identities of people positioned as 'white' are racialised. An important way to avoid essentialising whiteness is to ac-knowledge that it is not a singular experience and to examine the different ways in which whiteness or 'white' people are produced. In particular, I am interested in exploring how class and gender intersect with whiteness and how identities are produced in specific times and places.

To examine whiteness requires going beyond questions of white con-sciousness or as Helen (charles) (1993: 99) puts it, whether white people know that they are white. White people's conscious appreciation of their 'whiteness' may well be limited. They may only feel, or be conscious of being, white in the presence of racialised others (and perhaps even then only when they feel that they are in a minority). But I will argue that whiteness is more than a conscious identity, it is also a position within racialised discourses as well as a set of practices and imaginaries. As such, it plays a part in constructing the identities that white people *do* express. It may underpin notions of being a 'woman' or a 'Londoner' or 'British'. Thus, I want to show how white people are positioned within processes of racialisation, even when they may not explicitly articulate their 'whiteness'. This further implies the need for a model of identity that goes beyond 'identity politics' and addresses *processes of identification*, as will be explored in Chapter 2. I will suggest that 'race' needs to be understood as the product of a range of discourses and practices, which construct how people see, understand and live difference as racialised. 'White', 'black' or 'Asian' subjects are produced through the operation of racialised discourses and practices. But these processes of racialised subject construction do not occur independently of gender and class. Rather, 'race', class and gender intersect in complex and changing ways to produce different subjects and subjectivities. These intersections which produce subjects are also located within specific contexts – time and place matter. The ways in which whiteness works will be different in Britain and South Africa. It will also be different in Hackney and Hampstead, or New York and Nebraska.

Accordingly, this book sets out to examine not just white experience, but particular gendered and classed articulations of white experience. The book is based on material gathered from interviews with white women who were living in south London (predominantly Clapham and Camberwell) and who were bringing up young children. I set out to consider a series of questions through the interviews: how do class, 'race' and gender construct the lived experience of white women living in London?; how do they talk about and imagine racialised differences?; how are their practices as mothers racialised, classed and gendered?; do they encounter particular issues around 'race', class and gender with their children?; how are they bringing up children who are also raced, classed and gendered subjects?; do they live and move around geographies in London and in England which they see as raced, classed or gendered?; if they account for their lives, producing a narrative of their self, how are these racialised, classed and gendered?; do they have a sense of a collective, national identity?; do they feel English or British?; and how are these identities raced, classed and gendered?

The interviews that resulted provide rich material for examining the interplay of 'race', class and gender both in the constructions of the women's sense of self and in their everyday lives. By examining the interviews with mothers living in specific areas of London, I am able to explore in depth how subjectivities and experience are constructed by 'raced', classed and gendered discourses and how they are produced in particular contexts. The women were encountered at a particular time in their lives when they were engaged in specific practices of mothering young children. This led them to interact with their local areas in particular ways. While much of their focus was on the domestic and their family, they were also forming local friendships with other mothers and engaged in sometimes fraught negotiations with public institutions, particularly schools.

The next chapter, 'Troubling "race"', will explore the question of identity, identification and 'race'. This chapter introduces the study by placing it in the context of its intellectual roots/routes – that of a response to black feminist calls for the need to examine white racism. The chapter then goes on to examine other work carried out in what might (problematically) be called the field of 'white studies'. Thus, it begins to address the question of the politics and problematics of studying whiteness.

Why look at whiteness? Critiquing white feminism

Examination of whiteness from within the study of 'race' has come from different perspectives, as will be explored below, but the particular entry point for this research was the critical interventions of black feminists whose work draws out both the classed and the gendered nature of processes of racialisation. From the 1970s to 1980s, black[2] feminists in both Britain and the US voiced critiques of white feminists who lacked an analysis of racism. They pointed to the acute irony of a movement such as feminism, which claimed to stand for inclusivity and universal sisterhood but, in fact, was making black women invisible. The central position given to experience within feminism did not include an awareness of different racialised experiences. The struggle for the right to have a voice (like that of political representation) often did not include consideration of who was being silenced in the process.[3] Black feminists contested the agenda set, and approach taken, by white feminists on a variety of issues, including motherhood, abortion, childcare, rape, sexuality, equality, family, contraception and welfare rights (Amos and Parmar 1984; Mohanty 1988). White feminist campaigns were criticised for failing to examine or account for different experiences of, and interests in, these issues. For instance, calls for sexual liberation had a very different significance for black women who had historically, and in current popular culture, been constructed as promiscuous and already sexualised. White feminists also failed to examine how white women's supposed sexual 'purity' was often constructed through contrast with the sexualisation of black women. Or how white women's vulnerability was constructed through the representation of black men as violent and threatening. It was also argued that, when white feminists did write about black women, it was in a stereotyped and patronising way, presenting them as passive victims and voiceless Third World subjects (see Amos and Parmar 1984; Mohanty 1988; Carby 1992: 222).

Similar critiques were also made by lesbian and working-class women who felt that their experiences and positions had been ignored by white middle-class heterosexual feminists who then, in turn, failed to understand why some women did not respond to the call for universal sisterhood. Thus, black feminist critiques arose at a time when a range of challenges was being made to 'mainstream' feminist practice and theory. Part of the problem was that, with its 'single "mistress narrative" of gender domination' (Frankenberg and Mani 1993), much white feminism had omitted to analyse how some women might be positioned as oppressors of others, rather than merely as the oppressed (see C. Hall 1992; Ware 1992). With the singular focus on patriarchy, white feminists had not developed the conceptual tools for understanding complexities of racialised, classed and gendered power and oppression (see Anthias and Yuval-Davis 1983; Barrett and McIntosh 1985; Bhavani and Coulson 1986). As bell hooks argues: 'we still do not have the language paradigms for white women to be able to express "this is how I am privileged" and yet "this is how I am oppressed"' (Childers and hooks 1990: 63).

These questions shifted the theoretical and political terrain of feminism in general. This was not merely a case of rethinking the nature of feminist campaigns, for instance around violence or reproductive rights, or of including studies of black women's lives as well as those of white women. These debates raised the question of difference in such a way as to fundamentally disrupt feminist categories, in particular the unitary concept of 'woman'. If there were so many differences and conflicts of interest between women – on the basis of class, 'race', ethnicity and sexuality – then how could a singular 'woman' or even 'women' ever be theorised or mobilised? They also raised epistemological questions about knowledge and standpoint (see Hill Collins 1990). These challenges prompted a reconceptualisation of the self, highlighting how the formation of identity through the process of 'othering' was more complex than merely being an opposition between man/woman, but was also – and already – white/black, heterosexual/homosexual. Thus, black feminists stressed the need to understand and analyse the mutually constitutive, intersecting axes of race, class and gender. There needed to be an analytical frame that could incorporate the complexities of power and subject production and developments in politics that recognised these complexities based on shifting identities and necessarily shifting coalitions and negotiated alliances. As Chandra Talpade Mohanty writes: 'sisterhood cannot be assumed on the basis of gender; it must be forged in concrete history and political practices and analysis' (Mohanty 1988; see also Reagon 1983).

An important part of this process of coalition building involves feminists positioned as white acknowledging and examining the particularity of their own experience – or else being complicit in racism:

> Racism requires a perspective of deviance. It speaks (implicitly or explicitly) from a position of the dominant white group. A racist perspective is composed of two elements: first, the failure to own the particularity of white-ness; second, the failure to acknowledge that, in a racist context, a 'white' voice stands in a relationship of authority to a 'black' voice.

> To 'see' deviance instead of difference means to take the experience of the dominant group as the implicitly or explicitly universal standard or norm.
>
> (Aziz 1995)

Thus, black feminists pushed white feminists to explore their relationship to, and complicity in, racism. They also asked white people to regard themselves not as in the position of the unmarked norm, but as racialised and classed. While much black feminist work examined hitherto ignored and unexplored aspects of black experience and identity, there was also the suggestion of the need to examine white experience and identities as racialised rather than normative. These challenges raised the need for an increasingly complex conceptualisation of identity. 'Identity politics' proved to be an uneasy and often unproductive terrain, often characterised by reductive analysis. But the question of identity and identification would not go away so easily.

The calls by black feminists for the examination of whiteness and white racism fed into a wider 'turn' to whiteness within academia. The following section gives a broad overview of this heterogeneous body of work.

White studies?

What Mike Hill calls the 'critical rush to whiteness' (Hill 1997: 3) has resulted in a range of different research projects that are now being clustered into something which is sometimes called 'white studies'. This has inevitably led to different approaches to the characterisation and categorisation of this newly emerging 'field'. Hill, echoing feminist periodisation, identifies first and second 'waves' in work on whiteness. The first wave is that which identifies whiteness as something that is both invisible and impermanent. The second wave is, according to Hill, characterised by 'epistemological stickiness and ontological wiggling immanent in whiteness' where whiteness becomes something identified and singled out for critique, but also avoided – by those who critique whiteness and yet are also 'identifiably white' (Hill 1997: 3). Ruth Frankenberg divides work in the field into four different, albeit overlapping, approaches: historical approaches, which map out the 'salience of whiteness to the formation of nationhood, class and empire'; sociological and cultural studies, which 'examine the place of whiteness in the contemporary body politic in Europe and the US'; those who study the performance of whiteness by subjects 'whether in daily life, in film, in literature or in the academic corpus'; and, finally, those which examine racism in movements for social change (Frankenberg 1997: 2–3). Frankenberg's account stresses the interconnected nature of the different areas she outlines but therefore tends to downplay the theoretical differences that may be implicated in the different approaches.

In contrast, Alastair Bonnett identifies two broad and potentially conflicting tendencies within the new area of 'white studies'. The first tendency incorporates the analysis of whiteness within a class analysis of racialisation, while the second 'stresses the plural constitution, and multiple lived experiences of whiteness' (Bonnett 2000a: 139). Bonnett points out that the former position, of which Theodore Allen and David Roediger (Allen 1994; Roediger 1994) are prime examples, has tended to focus on the development of whiteness within American capitalism. They, along with the contributors to the journal *Race Traitor* (Ignatiev and Garvey 1996), call for the 'abolition' of whiteness: 'The journal takes its stand on two points: first, that the "white race" is not a natural but a social category and, second, that what was historically constructed can be undone' (Garvey and Ignatiev 1997: 346). This places them within Hill's 'second wave' of white studies, which critiques and seeks to avoid (or abolish) whiteness. There are, however, serious limitations with the exclusively class-focused analysis that is unable to develop the links between racialised formations and modernity, rather than simply capitalism (Bonnett 2000a: 141; see also Gilroy 1992a; Goldberg 1993). It also leads to reductionist accounts of subjectivity where individual's 'loyalty' to the 'white club' (Garvey and Ignatiev 1997) is bought solely through mechanisms of class privilege. This approach rules out more complex psychological processes of formation of identity and the self. These are more likely to be explored within what Bonnett characterises as the second tendency within white studies.

It is interesting that all these different characterisations of 'white studies' tend to include works that were written no earlier than the 1970s and are generally concentrated in the late 1980s and 1990s. The majority of the writers included within this body of work would also appear to be white. This demarcation of a 'field' is problematic and, I would argue, to be avoided, serving as it does to erase a considerable body of black writing on whiteness. bell hooks has written of the extensive knowledge that black people build up about whiteness and white people (hooks 1997: 165). David Roediger has collected several contributions by black writers on whiteness, ranging from 1854 to the 1990s, into an edited book (Roediger 1998). Yet those who seek to review the literature within 'white studies' tend to ignore much of this work, apart from obligatory references to, and quotations from, James Baldwin and Frantz Fanon. The editors of *Off White: Readings on Race, Power and Society* respond to the risk that 'understanding whiteness could surface as the new intellectual fetish' by arguing:

> we (arrogantly? narcissistically? greedily? responsibly?) believe that maybe this should be the last book on whiteness, that we should get back to the work of understanding and dismantling the stratified construction of race/colors, rather than one group at a time.
>
> (Fine *et al.* 1997: xii)

While one is tempted to add 'naively' to their interrogatory list, I think it would be more correct to see their plea as misplaced. Rather than seeing whiteness as involving the study of 'one group at a time', I would argue that it can only be analysed within a framework of racialisation. If a field of 'white studies' exists at all, it is at most a subset of other concerns around 'race' and identity. It would be preferable to avoid the idea of a distinct field or area of study altogether. The project of studying whiteness should be seen as an integral part of understanding the 'stratified construction of race/colors'. This involves a relational rather than the self-contained analysis that is suggested.

There is a risk that, in the field of 'white studies', which is dominated by concerns arising from the situation in the US, the importance of contextualising any discussions around 'race' and identity will be overlooked. Frankenberg stresses how the collection that she has put together 'break[s] new ground' because the texts 'emphasise and document how whiteness is always emplaced, temporally and spacially' (Frankenberg 1997: 21). Ruth Frankenberg's own ground-breaking study, *White Women, Race Matters: The Social Construction of Whiteness*, provides one potential model for this research. It is an exception to the tendency in Britain (discussed below) to study working-class youth. Frankenberg interviewed women from varied class backgrounds and of a wide age range living in California. She adopted a broadly life history approach with the women, many of whom had been active in anti-racist or feminist activism. Her research established the importance of examining the accounts of white women to explore the construction of whiteness. However, there are several important methodological and theoretical differences in my approach. A key one is that my research takes different women living in specific geographical areas, but also at a particular common moment in their lives – that of being mothers of young children. Thus, the study focuses on those issues, such as schooling and parental socialising, that were particularly significant to the women at this specific moment in their lives. It also enables a thoroughgoing examination of the ways in which talk about questions such as to which school to send your child and, more broadly, socialising children can be highly raced as well as classed and gendered. In addition, in this research, as will be explored in Chapter 4, I also examine the ways in which production of the self is narrativised and raced. As Frankenberg herself argues, context is extremely important. What 'whiteness' means and how it is experienced will vary considerably, not only over time and between Britain and the US, but also between London and Cornwall. The debates that arise in these different situations cannot be transported between them without adaptation. Therefore, in the following discussion, I focus on a range of research undertaken in Britain, which constitutes one important context of this book.

Examining the white in the Union Jack

Much of the research on everyday experience of 'race' in Britain has focused on urban young people.[4] In the case of considering white experience as racialised, much of this too has focused on urban-based young people, especially working-class men. This line of research has its roots in both cultural studies and ethnography. There has been a gradual shift in this kind of research from a focus on inter-racial friendships and cultural interchange to examination of those who use explicitly racialised discourses and are often self-identified racists. Focusing on language and semiotics, in particular the usage of Creole among both black and white young people, Roger Hewitt produced some of the first research in this area in his in-depth study of friendship patterns in two areas of south London (Hewitt 1986). This study focused specifically on the white end of inter-racial friendships because of his interest in understanding racism and contexts where racism appeared to be absent. This focus on inter-racial friendships and cultural exchange in the form of language led to an emphasis more on synchronicity between youth cultures and less on the perpetuation of racism. Les Back, cautioning against 'projecting romantic and utopian desires on to the accounts and interpretations of the culture of young people', set out to 'examine how the formation of identity, racism and multiculture is manifest within everyday life' (Back 1996: 6). In his in-depth study of two different estates in south London, Back explored the different racialised discourses of community utilised by black and white young people as well as the formation of their social identities and experience of racism. His research findings suggested that, where young people grew up in more racially mixed areas, 'profound and rigorously syncretic cultural dialogues took place between black and white young people' (Back 1996: 247). Back found that young whites, in adopting black idioms of speech and vernacular culture, were marking their 'vacation' of concepts of whiteness and blackness. However, this did not eliminate all expressions of racism, particularly against those positioned as non-black racial others, in this case Vietnamese youth.

A shift in focus in the research on white youth came with the realisation that, not only was racial harassment increasing rather than decreasing through the 1980s and 1990s, but that it was as much, if not more, a feature of white suburbs than racially mixed inner city areas (Hesse 1997; Nayak 1999). As Back writes:

> what became clear by the early 1990s was that some of the most violent forms of racism were found in the outlying suburban districts. The English suburbs were no less complex in their social composition but what was striking was the degree to which quintessential middle-class images of English gentility and the 'good life' converged with violence, xenophobia and crude racism.
>
> (Back 1998: 67)

The imperative became to 'explain the complexities of young white men's experience without reducing them to caricatures of violent thuggery' (Back 1998: 60).

Phil Cohen has done extensive empirical research on racism within a policy framework of trying to improve anti-racist initiatives. In 1997, he argued for 'rethinking racism and the way racism speaks the body' (Cohen 1997a: 246). Cohen places his analysis of 'race' within a history of labour. Positing 'race' as 'labour's "other scene"', he argues against economically reductionist accounts of 'race', bringing in psychoanalytic perspectives. Nonetheless, his analysis is confined to white working-class masculinity and, despite recognition of 'non-class – i.e. gender or generational – positions' (Cohen 1997a: 258), class remains the main motor of his analysis. His focus on labour poses problems for an attempt to think through the inter-relations of gender and 'race', as well as class.

Because of the predominance of men as perpetrators of racist violence, the analysis of racism and racists is often confined to young men. As the following explanation of Cohen's decision to focus on boys shows, it is clear that it is also relevant that the majority of those who have published work in this field are men:[5]

> We considered whether to try to involve girls in the group. We decided against it for several reasons. Firstly, as is evident from the tape, the girls on the estate had been cast in the role of passive supporters rather than activists. We neither wanted to reproduce this position in the group, nor as men did we feel adequately equipped to explore the connection between these girls' subordination and their racist views. Secondly, it was the boys who were responsible for the racial harassment and we were under considerable pressure to do what we could about that. So although we were not entirely happy about it, we decided to opt for all boy groups, with a mental footnote to the effect that we would keep an eye and ear open for the sexual dynamics of working-class racism.
>
> (Cohen 1997b: 148–9)

Other researchers have examined white girls' racialised identities and relationships to racism when undertaking research on white youth racism. Back, for example, in *New Ethnicities and Urban Culture: Racisms and Multiculture in Young Lives*, acknowledges some of the problems faced by a man undertaking research with adolescent girls (Back 1996: 24–5). Nonetheless, his work does deal with both male and female identities in some depth. However, when he comes to writing more exclusively about racism using the material from his book and another research project, masculinity becomes the sole focus, as his footnote explains: 'Both of these ethnographic projects have involved discussion of the position of young women, class and gender relations. The focus here is on male youth because of their involvement in overt forms of racist action and violence' (Back 1998: 60). In contrast,

Hewitt's study of Greenwich is explicitly examining racist action as embedded within social relations: 'we believed that perpetrators of racist harassment probably did not behave in a social vacuum. It was somehow either allowed or even encouraged by others and there was something in the local community that enabled it to happen' (Hewitt 1996: 2). However, although he does quote girls' racist comments and attitudes, it is 'exceptional' girls who tend to be the main focus of attention given to girls: 'Where the full exceptions to the general flow of racism were found, they were almost always girls and not boys' (Hewitt 1996: 28).

Vron Ware cautions against confining analysis of racism to 'almost pathological male-on-male violence' (Ware 1997: 293), not least because this will distort strategies to counter racism. She argues that:

> One of the dangers with this approach is that, if racism (and fascism) is seen to be something that white working-class men do to black working-class men, many people may feel either unconcerned or intimidated in the face of it. Instead, the fact that the imagery of racism is largely male dominated, and a working-class phenomena, . . . ought to ring alarm bells about the importance of gender and class in analyzing the continuing appeal of white supremacy.
>
> (Ware 1997: 290–1)

Ware suggests that, not only should women's actual involvement in violent and fascist practices be examined, but also that 'female racism' should be explored, particularly women's involvement in sustaining and promulgating racist beliefs. In addition, Ware argues that there needs to be a better understanding of the 'codes and styles of masculinity and femininity that express ideas about cultural superiority and difference [. . .] if we are to break through the surface tension of everyday life in order to analyze how gender figures in the psychological construction of whiteness' (Ware 1997: 307–8).

Ware's argument that we need to understand practices of racism beyond and around those of extreme violence should be extended to include not only women, but also a class analysis that goes beyond the idea of a 'popular racism' confined to working-class culture. Working-class male whiteness is frequently constructed within public discourses as itself deviant or, as Ware argues, 'pathological'. In general, analysis of elite racism has been confined to state action (in particular immigration, police and social policy[6]) and cultural production (film, literature, media[7]). The racialised nature of the everyday for the middle classes and their own expressions of racism has received much less attention. Yet Back, for instance, found that some of the 'most crude forms of popular racism and ethnocentrism' that his young black research subjects were exposed to was from middle-class peers at university (Back 1996: 168). This finding, of the impact of middle-class racism, suggests the need to examine the construction of whiteness from a more central location. This book is concerned with formations of whiteness that remain more firmly at the centre of public discourses of class, gender and 'race'. In these constructions, whiteness tends not to be an explicit, proclaimed identity as is sometimes expressed within certain working-class discourses. Rather, whiteness functions as a silent or unmarked norm, which serves to exclude and marginalise others, and yet is critical to the construction of the white metropolitan subject as normative.

This research attempts to address the intersections of 'race', class and gender in normative constructions of whiteness. It examines the accounts of women, both working and middle class, who would not identify themselves as racists, and who are also not engaged in what Back identifies as the 'liminal space' of some youth cultures (Back 1996: 244). Through these accounts, it is possible to examine a different range of racialised, classed and gendered practices from those of young people which were also taking place in different locations. As will be explained in more detail in Chapter 3, this research involves interviews with a selection of women who are located in particular places (in two areas of London) at a particular moment of their lives. All the women interviewed were mothers of young children. The fact that they were occupied with bringing up their children meant that they were engaged in a specific range of activities, located in spaces that include both domestic and public locales.

Through their experience as mothers and through their children, the interviewees also have a specific range of concerns, which involve negotiating classed, raced and gendered discourses. Therefore, these women offer very different experiences and configurations of whiteness than those most often researched. They offer the possibility of exploring how racialisation plays a part not only in the construction of self, but also in practices of mothering. The women's accounts also suggest the need for a range of approaches to analyse racialised identities and experience. Rather than focusing on the production of discourse in interactional settings, this research has involved in-depth interviews on an individual basis, in which interviewees were asked to reflect on their sense of self, on their past as well as their present activities. These more reflective interviews proved to be a rich source of material on how 'race', class and gender figure in the practices and imaginaries of both middle- and working-class white women living in London.

Summary of the book

The next chapter, 'Troubling "race"', is concerned with questions of identification, taking identities to be discursive constructions, never complete and always in production. Examination of processes of identification require an understanding of both how subject positions are constructed (including through racialised, classed and gendered discourses) and how individuals come to occupy those subject positions. It is in this context that the chapter sets out an approach to studying the salience of 'race' within identifications and in the everyday, while at the same time destabilising the category of 'race' itself. It argues that Judith Butler's combination of Foucauldian and psychoanalytic approaches to gender has important implications for the analysis of 'race' and particularly for an understanding of the intersections between 'race', class and gender. Thus, 'race' is proposed to be performative – that is, that the concept itself, and its lived nature, is produced through the reiteration and recitation of racialised and racialising discourses. The chapter further argues that a range of perceptual practices – especially those centred around the visual – are particularly important to the construction of 'race' and in the repetition of racialised discourses.

In the final introductory chapter, 'Talk, tea and tape recorders', the context of the fieldwork is given. This chapter gives a thumbnail sketch of the areas where the study took place. It also raises questions of power and accountability in interviewing and fieldwork, as well as a further consideration of the politics of research on whiteness.

Chapter 4, 'Narrating the self', explores the production or non-production of a narrative of self in four interviews. This chapter will suggest that the production of a narrative of self is not inevitable and requires a sense of coherence and difference, both of which may be produced through racialised discourses.

Questions around racialised performativity are taken up in Chapter 5, 'Seeing, talking, living "race"'. In discussions with mothers about children's attitudes to 'race', the question of perceptual practices is discussed as well as the extent to which 'race' is a subject that white women prefer to ignore or avoid. This chapter also examines aspects of the white imaginary, with a particular focus on gendered responses to blackness, which mix both fear and desire. It also explores the ways in which London is experienced as a racialised place and produces racialised subjects.

Chapter 6, 'In search of a good 'mix'. 'Race', class and gender and practices of mothering', moves from the realm of the imaginary back towards questions of practice. This chapter examines the practices of mothering of a group of middle-class women based in one area of London. The chapter focuses on two aspects of mothering –social activities of mothers and children, and choices around schooling and education. It explores the processes of inclusion and exclusion which are both classed and raced.

Collective identities are explored in Chapter 7, 'How English am I?'. This chapter examines the different ways in which interviewees positioned themselves in relation to a concept of Englishness that is both classed and raced. This chapter will explore not only how constructions of Englishness are related to constructions of the self, but also how, for some of these women, a key metaphor for explaining their relationship to national identity was that of the domestic.

Several themes run through this book and are taken up in different ways in the various chapters. They concern not only the way in which lives are lived, but also the ways in which selves are narrated and imagined. In order to understand the formation of whiteness, it is important to explore how individuals construct themselves and live their lives in relation to the spaces and localities in which they live. The self is constructed through a process of interpellation into a range of discourses and the way in which they are located in a particular time and place and within a biographical trajectory. As the material discussed in these chapters shows, this is a highly complex process. By focusing on the particularly gendered experience of mothering, the material also illustrates the extent to which these racialised and classed processes are also gendered.

2   Troubling 'race'

Introduction

Despite longstanding academic and activist insistence that 'race' is a social construction devoid of any inherent or essential meaning, the ontological status of 'race' remains in question. As Howard Winant (2000: 185) writes: 'contemporary racial theory ... is often "objectivistic" about its fundamental category. Although abstractly acknowledged to be a sociohistorical construct, race *in practice* is often treated as an objective fact: one simply *is* one's race'. Paul Gilroy (2000: 37) argues that 'we have entered a period where "race" and raciology are in crisis and ripe for abolition and that "race" should be approached as an afterimage – a lingering effect of looking too casually into the damaging glare emanating from colonial conflicts at home and abroad'. Both Gilroy and Winant raise important questions for those who seek to analyse processes of racialisation, including the construction of 'whiteness'. At what point are racism and raciologies to be opposed or countered, not by examining their impact on people's lives but, rather, by finding new ways of seeing and speaking about the body and the self? When will 'colour blindness' not mean evasion of processes of exclusion in which one is positioned as privileged, but instead be a reflection of a new era of seeing and visualising the body? Gilroy makes a timely call for the need to radically question and even perhaps move 'beyond' race. Yet this book argues that there remains a need to analyse the powerful impact of 'race' on the construction of identity and experience in everyday life, particularly in the hitherto often neglected area of white lives. This chapter suggests an alternative route towards the objective of fundamentally unsettling 'race' as an ontological category through attention to the performativity of 'race'. That is, the examination of the production of the concept of 'race' through discursive practice and, in particular, ways of seeing difference.

The concept of 'race' has a long and controversial history. The central contention in this book is that 'race' as an idea and as a lived experience is socially and discursively constructed. That is to say that 'race' has no biological basis – it is not a 'natural' or inevitable way of categorising or regarding human beings.[1] This does not mean, however, that 'race' does not have a real

impact on human experience. The enduring power of race as a way of divid-
ing people means that it continues to have effects: 'although we might say
there is no such thing as race as the intrinsic property of bodies, this does not
mean that race does not exist, as an effect of the very way in which we think,
know and inhabit the world' (Ahmed 2002: 47). Drawing on the work of
Judith Butler on the construction of sex and gender categories and identities
and gender performativity, this chapter examines the possibility of using the
concept of performativity to move away from essentialist notions of identity.
It argues that 'race' needs to be understood as an embodied performative.
That is, that the repeated citation of racialised discourses and, importantly,
the repetition of racialised perceptual practices produces bodies and subjects
that are raced. What is critical here is that these practices *produce* the idea
of differences, rather than being an effect of them. 'Race' is in the eye of the
beholder. Thus, this chapter will discuss the shifting nature of perceptual
practices that produce racialised seeing, as well as the ways in which subjects
are positioned as visible or invisible within racialised schema.

Deconstructing, de-essentialising and troubling 'race'

Judith Butler is concerned with the ways in which the body (and therefore
the experience of the body) are discursively constructed. Butler grants
neither sex nor gender a material 'reality' (which is not to say that there
is no material body, only that it is not experienced prior to or outside of
discourse). The construction of gender (and hence the establishment of the
norms of sexual difference) is achieved through the continual reiteration and
'performance' of particular discourses:

> gender proves to be performative – that is, constituting the identity it
> is purported to be. In this sense, gender is always a doing, though not a
> doing by a subject who might be said to preexist the deed . . . . There is
> no gender identity behind the expressions of gender . . . gender is per-
> formatively constituted by the very 'expressions' which are said to be its
> results.
>
> (Butler 1990: 24–5)

What is the impact of racialising this formulation? Can we do so without
reserving primacy for sexual difference? Butler points out that assuming
the primacy of sexual difference is what marks psychoanalytic feminism as
white 'for the assumption here is not only that sexual difference is more
fundamental, but that there is a relationship called "sexual difference" that
is itself unmarked by race' (Butler 1993a: 181). There may well be problems
in trying to translate too closely Butler's formulations on gender to race.[2]
Nonetheless, it is important to trace how 'white', 'black' or 'brown' bodies
and identities are produced and how they are produced as gendered. If we
were to consider racialising Butler's position, it would become: 'there is no

racial identity behind the expressions of race . . . race is performatively constituted by the very "expressions" which are said to be its results'. What does
it mean for 'race' to be performative? What kind of 'doing' and 'expressions'
does this involve? What processes of identification are being proposed? How
do subjects come into being, by what process of subjectification? What are
the possibilities for agency within discourses or in creating new discourses?
Butler herself certainly believes that her concepts can and should be applied
to 'race' and opposes those who grant a primacy to sexual identification
above other and, in particular, racial identifications. She argues that: 'though
there are clearly good historical reasons for keeping "race" and "sexuality"
and "sexual difference" as separate analytic spheres. There are also quite
pressing and significant historical reasons for asking how and where we
might read not only their convergence, but the sites at which one cannot be
constituted save through the other' (Butler 1993a: 168).[3]

So, how can we understand racialised and sexed bodies and identifications?
Butler contends that bodies are materialised as 'sexed' through a normative
process: 'the regulatory norms of "sex" work in a performative fashion to
constitute the materiality of bodies and, more specifically, to materialise the
body's sex, to materialise sexual difference in the service of the consolidation
of the heterosexual imperative' (Butler 1993a: 2). For Butler, 'sex' is 'one
of the norms by which the "one" becomes viable at all, that which qualifies
a body for life within the domain of cultural intelligibility' (Butler 1993a:
2). This embodiment, through a normative process, is inextricably linked to
subjecthood. This is not merely a matter of social inscription, but involves
psychic processes that govern the formation of the subject and circumscribe
the domain of liveable sociality (Butler 1997a: 21).

Without occupying the site of the subject, the individual has no means by
which to speak or be spoken about. Yet, at the same time, this production of
a subject is a violation, it involves loss and repression, which in turn impacts
on the psyche. The individual is therefore the sum of the subject and the
psyche and is in the process of constantly rearticulating itself as a subject.
This process of the reiteration of the individual as a subject is discussed by
Judith Butler in *The Psychic Life of Power*. She describes the ambiguous and
contradictory processes of subject formation. Although it is 'a power *exerted
on* a subject, subjection is nevertheless a power *assumed by* the subject, an assumption that constitutes the instruments of that subject's becoming' (Butler
1997a: 11). The operation of the psychic involves powerful forces of desire
and repulsion. Subjects develop passionate attachments to their positionality,
even though it inevitably involves foreclosure and the loss of other possibilities and ways of being. It is normative discourses that shape the kinds of
subjects that emerge and the identifications that they make. For Butler, '[t]he
forming of a subject requires an identification with the normative phantasm
of "sex" and this identification takes place through a repudiation which produces a domain of abjection, a repudiation without which the subject cannot
emerge' (Butler 1993a: 3).

However, is 'race' also a norm through which bodies, and subjects, are rendered culturally intelligible? How are subjects constructed not just through the reiteration of gendered norms but also racialised ones? How are gendered norms racialised? How are the psychic processes of subjection racialised? Can one talk of the regulatory apparatus of whiteness (or, as Hall calls it 'compulsive Eurocentrism'; Hall 1996: 16) as well as that of hetero-sexuality? Butler discusses the ways in which a fetus and baby are 'girled'. But, just as one cannot enter social processes as an intelligible individual without being a girl or a boy, one cannot be a person without having a, similarly embodied, racial identity. Indeed, one is a white/black/Asian/mixed-race girl or boy, and the gendering is racialised as the racing is gendered. The fact that there are numerous possible descriptions of race – rather than the neat duality of male/female – does not mean that it is somehow less obligatory or coerced. If one's race is not obvious, it will be searched out, and different definitions will be applied across different cultural and temporal contexts, as illustrated by Linda Martin Alcoff:

> When mythic bloodlines which are thought to determine identity fail to match the visible markers used by identity discourses to signify race, one often encounters these odd responses by acquaintances announcing with arrogant certainty "But you don't look like . . ." or then retreating to a measured acknowledgement "Now that you mention it, I can sort of see . . ." to feel one's face studied with great seriousness, not for its (hoped for) character lines, or its distinctiveness, but for its telltale racial trace, can be a particularly unsettling experience.
>
> (Martin Alcoff 1999: 31)

For Butler, regulatory schemas function as 'historically revisable criteria or intelligibility which produce and vanquish bodies that matter' (Butler 1993a: 14). They achieve their power through citation: 'the norm of sex takes hold to the extent to which it is "cited" as such a norm, but it also derives its power through the citations that it compels' (Butler 1993a: 134). This repeated, compulsive citation of the norm is what Butler terms performativity. The terminology here is awkward. By performativity, Butler does not refer to a voluntaristic, self-conscious acting, but practices that serve to enact and reinforce sets of regulatory norms.[4] She defines performativity as 'not the act by which a subject brings into being what she/he names, but rather, as that reiterative power of discourse to produce the phenomena that it regulates and constrains' (Butler 1993a: 2). Through performativity, subjects repeatedly re-enact the discourses through which they are constructed.

Minnie Bruce Pratt, a white woman writing in 1984 about her struggle to challenge her own racism and anti-semitism, gives an account of some different experiences of being interpellated as a white woman. This account is interesting because of the way in which it can be read to suggest ways in which whiteness is performative. Pratt is compelled to act in certain ways that are constructed as racialised and thereby serve to emphasise and reinstate her whiteness. She is hailed as a white woman and can only respond as a white woman. Pratt first gives an example of a comforting, positive (as she sees it) recognition and speaking. Walking in an area in Washington in which white people are relatively rarely seen, she reports being acknowledged and accepted:

> When I walk by, if I lift my head and look towards them and speak, 'Hey', they may speak, say 'Hey' or 'How you doing?' or perhaps just nod. In the spring I was afraid to smile when I spoke, because that might be too familiar, but by the end of the summer I had walked back and forth so often, I was familiar, so sometimes we shared comments about the mean weather. I am comforted by any of these speakings, for, to tell you the truth, they make me feel at home.
>
> (Pratt 1984: 11)

But other encounters are less comfortable and are more painfully and explicitly racialised. She gives the example of encounters with the janitor who works in her building:

> When we meet in the hall or on the elevator, even though I may just have heard him speaking in his own voice to another man, he 'yes ma'am's'me in a sing-song: I hear my voice replying in the horrid cheerful accents of a white lady: and I hate my white womanhood that drags between us the long bitter history of our region.
>
> (Pratt 1984: 12)

The way she is acknowledged, the way she responds, both inform each other and draw on different norms and ways of being. They suggest different ways of being a middle-class white woman, drawing on different discursive and historical circumstances. To step out of these citations of the norm is painful, where it is possible at all: 'By the amount of effort it takes me to walk these few blocks being as conscious as I can of myself in relation to history, to race, to culture, to gender, I reckon the rigid boundaries set around my experience, how I have been "protected"' (Pratt 1984: 13).

Pratt's account gives some insight into the regulatory regimes that positioned her and shaped her sense of self and her practices. It is shaped by her gendered positioning, which means that she fails to live up to her father's expectations. She describes being taken as a child to the roof of the courthouse in the centre of her town by her father and being too scared to climb on to it: 'But I was *not* him: I had not learned to take that height, that being set apart as my own: a white girl, not a boy' (Pratt 1984: 16). Her relationship to the town is also constructed through her whiteness:

> I was shaped by my relation to those buildings and to the people in the buildings, by ideas of who should be working in the Board of Education, of who should be in the bank handling money, of who should have the

guns and the keys to the jail, of who should be *in* the jail, and I was shaped by what I didn't see, or didn't notice, on those streets.

(Pratt 1984: 17)

Writing about her adult life, Pratt vividly describes living within a pattern of repeated practices that only make sense within a certain regulatory regime and which, through repetition, also serve to shore up certain norms. The market place she is referring to had been a place of auctioning slaves:

> Every day I drove around the market house, carrying my two boys be-
> tween home and grammar school and day care. To me it was an impedi-
> ment to the flow of traffic, awkward, anachronistic. Sometimes in early
> spring light it seemed quaint. I had no knowledge and no feeling of the
> sweat and blood of people's lives that had been mortared into its bricks:
> nor of their independent joy apart from that place. What I was feeling
> was that I would spend the rest of my life going round and round in
> a pattern that I knew by heart: being a wife, a mother of two boys, a
> teacher of the writings of white men, dead men. I drove around the
> market house four times a day, travelling on the surface of my own life:
> circular, repetitive.
>
> (Pratt 1984: 21–2)

Pratt is describing these experiences from a position in which she is no longer repeating them or at least not in the same way. In becoming a lesbian, she discovered what it felt like to be outside the norm: 'I had learned that I could be either a lesbian or a mother of my children, either in the wilderness or on holy ground, but not both' (Pratt 1984: 26). This new positioning had led Pratt to challenge the way she was positioned not only as a woman but also as white. This is not just a matter of external imposition but also involves internal processes for Pratt.

Pratt might perhaps express more optimism than Butler about the ability self-consciously to change one's identity and positioning (for a critique of Butler's approach to agency, see McNay 1999). Nonetheless, I think that this highly personalised account does help to draw out some of the concerns of Butler's work. Pratt's work suggests the need to re-examine that which is unseen and unquestioned in experience and subject construction. She also accounts for some of the functioning of discursive construction of norms and their regulation through practice. The following section will take up the question of racialised perceptual practices, examining in detail one of the ways in which race is performative.

Perceptual practices and the performativity of 'race'

Pratt's account begins, as I have said, with a description of the different ways in which she is hailed and spoken to, as well as of her fears of how she might be spoken of. She also writes of different ways of seeing and being seen.

Pratt writes of the need to expand her 'constricted eye', 'an eye that has only let in what I have been taught to see' (Pratt 1984: 17). This account of the 'constricted eye' is key here because it alerts us to the importance of what is seen and not seen in racialised visual schema. It could be argued that visual differences are to 'race' as Butler argues that sex is to gender. Butler argues that sexual difference is never simply a function of material differences, but is marked and formed by the discursive practices of gender: 'gender is not to culture as sex is to nature; gender is also the discursive/cultural means by which "sexed nature" or "a natural sex" is produced and established as "prediscursive", prior to culture, a politically neutral surface *on which* culture acts' (Butler 1990: 7). So, for 'race', racial discourses serve to construct the visible differences on which they themselves are based. It is through raced categories that visual differences become apprehended. In this way, seeing or perceiving of visual differences is constructed as 'prediscursive', neutral or inevitable. Thus, 'race' has to be understood as produced through a particular discursive history – a history that is specifically western, linked to both imperialism and notions of modernity: 'Racist culture has been one of the central ways modern social subjects make sense of and express themselves about the world they inhabit and invent (Goldberg 1993: 9). Above all, 'race' is a particular way of seeing, and then categorising, difference. It requires both that differences are defined and that a particular kind of seeing the human body is learnt, and then that those differences are placed in a hierarchy of power and value.

This way of placing humankind into different groups first emerged in the sixteenth century and was systematised in the late eighteenth and early nineteenth centuries, coinciding with the rise of western colonialism and imperialism as well as the development of western science (Goldberg, 1993: 255). It is important to note this particular trajectory of western concepts of 'race', in order to understand what distinguishes this way of marking and seeing difference from other ways of grouping humans in different societies. Even where a language of 'race' is being deployed in non-western or in non-modern contexts, caution should be exercised in directly translating the concept. Alastair Bonnett (2000b: 8) argues that 'the modern idea of "race" is distinctive because it emerged from modern attitudes towards nature and politics. In other words, it is the product of European naturalist science and European colonial and imperial power'. While there may have been ideas of 'colour-coded' identity and discrimination in premodern contexts (Bonnett draws on examples from China and the Middle East), these identities were not 'reified into a natural attribute.

> Modern European white identity is historically unique. People in other societies may be seen to have valued whiteness and to have employed the concept to define, at least in part, who and what they were. *But they did not treat being white as a natural category nor did they invest so much of their sense of identity within it.* Europeans racialised, which

is to say naturalised, the concept of whiteness, and entrusted it with the essence of their community. Europeans turned whiteness into a fetish object, *a talisman of the natural* whose power appeared to enable them to impose their will on the world.

(Bonnett 2000a: 20–1, original emphasis)

Western science proceeded through processes of categorisation of the 'natural' and reliance on visual evidence. So, in the 1700s when Linnaeus established practices of classifying animals and plants, this process was extended to humans, and the idea was introduced that there were different species or races of humans, established by visible criteria. These different races were increasingly placed in a hierarchy of value, with visible physical differences linked to different innate characteristics of personality and ability. Western ideas of 'race' are a product of these perceptual practices, coupled with an imperial imperative to establish superiority over others as critical to rule.

Racial imagery involves the identification and separation of various visually identified somatic features: skin tone; hair colour and texture; nose, eye, ear and hand shape; genitalia; body shape, etc. These multiple (and flexible) visual signs are then characterised into types and inserted into racialised hierarchies, with the category white invariably placed at the top of the 'racial family tree'. Yet at the same time, 'race' is about more than visible differences. Howard Winant writes of 'the slow inscription of phenotypical signification [which] took place upon the human body in and through conquest and enslavement, to be sure, but also as an enormous act of expression, of narration' (Winant 2000: 188). The narrations that produce racial difference are not solely confined to the visual. Racial differences may also be constructed by other practices of perception and embodiment (for instance, aural and vocal practices) (see Cohen 1988: 15). Nonetheless, it is clear that the visual plays a key role in racial narrations. Despite the discrediting of racial science, racist structures and the discourse of 'race' with its shifting perceptual practices remain in contemporary society. Richard Dyer argues not only that 'sight has been a privileged sense in Western culture since the middle ages', but also that racial imagery is central to the modern world and is never 'not in play' (Dyer 1997: xiii and 1).

However, 'race', although the product of European naturalist science, has never been fixed as a discourse or observational practice. There has rarely been agreement between 'racial' scientists about the number or definition of the different racial groups. The signification of, and even visual sensitivity to, different types is historically and geographically contextual. Few people would be able to identify the 'Irish ear' or 'Irish pug nose', which was once a marker of the 'primitive nature' of the Irish. Indeed, for most people, 'the Irish' would not constitute a group who were anything other than unproblematically white, although this has not always been the case (Ignatiev 1995; see Dyer 1997: 12). As Sander L. Gilman notes, in America of the 1880s,

'Looking Irish was one further category of difference that was written on the body and signified a poor character and bad temperament' (Gilman 2001: 97). Equally, the process of identification of 'race' may be uncertain – leading to a need to 'fix' a person's 'race'. Despite the function of the visible as a key signifier of 'race', the visibility of 'race' is not always clear or evident. There are unsettling and unclear borderlands[5] between racial identifications, as the quote from Linda Martin Alcoff above illustrates.[6]

Nonetheless, the link between the 'Irish ear' and the alleged Irish 'primitive nature' points to the functioning and efficacy of racialised perceptual practices. Racialised seeing involves not only the observation and identification of visible somatic differences, but also the attachment of significations to those differences. The visual becomes embedded in the symbolic. The flexibility and malleability of the practices and significations account for their durability and efficacy. Gilman describes how, at the beginning of the nineteenth century, as Jews in Europe shed their different clothing and different ways of wearing their hair, the discourse of science created new ways of visually identifying and understanding their difference. New bodies for the Jewish man and women were created that marked their difference. New practices of observing the body identified Jews as having differently shaped eyes and eyelids, which in turn were seen to signify how they saw the world differently from non-Jews, and large hands were discovered as an irrefutable demonstration of alleged grasping, material attitudes. The more the Jews came to look like their neighbours, the greater the impetus to identify them as physically, biologically different (Gilman 2000).[7] The different meanings attached to visible differences depend on how they are inserted into racialised ideologies. Therefore, Matthew F. Jacobson argues that we need to trace the 'complex process of social value *become* perception' (Jacobson 2000: 238).

Racialised discourse has long been concerned with reading into the 'black body' traits of the primitive and symbolic associations with darkness, which in turn constructs white bodies as 'pure', 'enlightened' and 'civilised'. Signs of blackness or non-whiteness have long been studied and categorised. David Goldberg writes of the role modernity and science have played in producing 'racial knowledge', particularly in the fields of anthropology, natural history and biology (Goldberg 1993). The rule of law in nation states has also been instrumental in identifying who is black or non-white (for example see Domínguez 1986). Yet whiteness itself has often seemed to evade categorisation. This is partly a result of the difficulties in actually pinning down the notion of 'race'. As mentioned above, even the most highly racialised discursive formations have difficulties in deciding how many 'races' there actually are (see Gilroy 2000). As a consequence, whiteness is difficult to contain within a single 'race' defined in any other way than it not being some other 'race' (or more commonly by it somehow not being racialised). Certainly, the idea of the 'Aryan race' cannot include all who are generally considered 'white'. So whiteness becomes an absence – an absence of colour or of other signs of racial degeneracy. White people are those who do not have 'one drop' of black blood, or who do not fail the apartheid 'pencil test'. As a result of this gap between whiteness and its physical attributes, Richard Dyer argues that, within racialised discourse, white people are not reducible to their bodies in the same way as black people are: 'white people are something else that is realised in and yet is not reducible to the corporeal, or racial' (Dyer 1997: 14). The meaning of whiteness for Dyer is contained in that which is beyond the body. This means that whiteness has a complex relationship with the visible: 'whites must be seen to be white, yet whiteness as race resides in invisible properties and whiteness as power is maintained by being unseen' (Dyer 1997: 45). However, the question of being seen or unseen relates closely, as Dyer suggests, to questions of power.

The power plays involved in seeing race and racialised positioning also encompassed class and gender differences. Alastair Bonnett (2000b) argues that, in the late nineteenth century and early twentieth century, Victorian bourgeoisie imaginatively aligned the working class with non-whites as well as, at times, positing them as a distinct racial group. Bonnett argues that, as the nature of capitalism changed, so too did the racial status of the working class, who could then be included in, and assert their inclusion in, whiteness. The extent to which women were truly included within whiteness has also varied historically. The racial tree of superiority was frequently imagined as a male one, with white, heterosexual European man at the pinnacle of civilisation and racialised privilege and culture. Yet white women were also essential for reproducing this superiority and had therefore to be assigned a place. This was particularly true in colonial contexts where racialised divisions were particularly critical to the social and political ordering of society. Ann Laura Stoler argues that 'the very categories of "colonizer" and "colonized" were secured through forms of sexual control that defined the domestic arrangements of Europeans and the cultural investments by which they identified themselves' (Stoler 1997: 345). At times, white women might be regarded as vulnerable to intellectual and moral weaknesses and in need of protection and direction and, in particular, protection from black sexual aggression.[8] At other times, women were given a more central role in the protection and reproduction of civilisation, particularly with regard to the maintenance and regulation of domestic space (see C. Hall, 1992; Ware, 1992; McClintock, 1995).

The question of visibility and invisibility is crucial to an understanding of perceptual practices of 'race', as it raises the question of power and relationality. Perceptual practices involve both seeing and being seen – or not being seen. The fields of the visual and visibility function in different ways according to how and where subjects are positioned. Above all, as David Goldberg discusses in his elaboration of Fanon's writings on visibility and invisibility, these are dynamic, ever-changing processes of power: 'visibility and invisibility are not simply states or conditions of being. Rather they characterise, express, reflect, or they are the effects of strategic relations' (Goldberg 1997:

82). The implications of being seen or unseen depend on the context. They also depend on what one is being seen as – an individual with subjecthood or as a mere exemplar of the 'race'.

The idea of whiteness as racially unmarked is of course only held by those positioned as white. bell hooks, in the context of teaching, found that her white students: 'have a deep emotional investment in the myth of "sameness", even as their actions reflect the primacy of whiteness as a sign informing who they are and how they think' (hooks 1992: 167). Those positioned outside the dominant norm may not regard whiteness as invisible. Whiteness, in terms of the power exercised by whites, has long been visible and an object of analysis for those who are positioned as black. As hooks writes: 'black folks have, from slavery on, shared with one another in conversations "special" knowledge of whiteness gleaned from close scrutiny of white people' (hooks 1997: 165; see also Roediger 1998). It might be more appropriate to say that whiteness functions as an, albeit large, 'blind spot' for white people in a 'racially saturated field of visibility' (Butler 1993b: 15).

Thus, in examining racialised perceptual practices, questions of visibility and invisibility are central, but they cannot be analysed without reference to the play of power. We have to ask who is seeing, who has the ability to assert certain practices of seeing as much as who is being seen. Who is endowed with subjecthood and to whom is it denied?

Conclusion

This chapter has explored processes of identity and subject construction. While the work of Judith Butler is largely focused on gender identity, I have argued that her elaboration of discursive construction, performativity and the interplay of the normative and the abject are equally pertinent to understanding 'race'. Despite the resurgence of biological examinations of 'race' (for example Herrnstein and Murray 1994; Entine 1999), it is, I would argue, largely accepted that essentialised notions of 'race' have been scientifically, politically and philosophically repudiated within the intellectual arena. Nonetheless, as Paul Gilroy points out, it remains a concept to which academics and anti-racists are deeply attached. Gilroy himself, speaking to academics working on 'race' and ethnicity, calls for a 'frank confrontation with our own professional interests in the reification of "race"' (Gilroy 1998: 841). The liberal paradox that David Theo Goldberg describes as 'race is irrelevant but all is race' (Goldberg 1993: 6) potentially holds sway for intellectuals as much as wider modern society. This chapter has argued for the concept of 'race' to be fundamentally questioned or 'troubled'. At one level, it could be argued that this is what work that might loosely fit into 'race studies' has been doing for the last half-century.[9] However, I would argue that what is needed is a deconstruction of racialised discourses, practices and identities at a more profound level than the majority of previous approaches. Rather than question or disrupt the characteristics attributed to visible differences, we need to expose the actual construction of these differences themselves, which serve to make categories of 'race' somehow prediscursive. At the same time, there needs to be vigilant reflexivity to ensure that the study of 'race' does not result in the confirmation and reification of the concept. 'Race' cannot be dismissed as merely ideological and nor does the simple statement that it is 'socially constructed' suffice. The nature of the construction needs to be examined more closely.

I have argued that perceptual practices lie at the heart of the construction of 'race'. Racialised discourses are dependent on the construction of visible differences and perceptual practices, which make the apprehension of 'racial' differences seem inevitable and prediscursive. These discourses and practices also work to render racialised subjects visibilised or invisibilised in different ways. The challenge raised in this book is to acknowledge the salience of 'race' in people's lives without re-endowing the concept itself with 'respectability' and essential meaning. Indeed, at one level, this study is trying to argue for further examination of the impact of 'race' on lives that are often considered to be untouched or 'unblemished' by 'race' – that of people positioned as white. Minnie Bruce Pratt's narration of her life provided an example of the power of the performativity of whiteness in constructing subjectivity and identity with her vivid portrayal of compelled and repeated enactments and internalisations of both gendered and racialised discourses.

In this chapter, I have suggested ways in which 'race' might be more seriously 'troubled' or destabilised than has been achieved by more orthodox social constructionist approaches. By emphasising the constructed nature of 'race', examining how its various meanings are created historically through discourse and practice and by suggesting its contradictory, ambivalent nature, I have tried to set up an approach that will make it possible to examine racialised lives and experience in such a way that does not merely serve to reinstate or reify the concept of 'race'. But the question remains as to how 'whiteness' should be conceptualised. I take 'whiteness' here to mean that which is constructed as the racialised norm (but is paradoxically often perceived to be non-racialised or unmarked). It is therefore a relational position, constructed through opposition to that which is 'other', rather than a fixed set of physical attributes. It should be clear that whiteness needs to be approached as a historicised and contextualised construction. It is produced in a series of instances where discursive and psychic processes lead to identifications with subject positions that are constructed as the norm, the neutral, the centre, which is defined by and through a construction of a racialised other. These moments of construction are at the same time gendered and classed.

People are positioned as white through a range of discourses and practices. They also identify as white, responding to the ways in which they are positioned discursively and within racialised performativity. They 'see' themselves as white. These practices are never fixed, but are constantly reinvoked with shifting definitions. Nonetheless, the focus of this research is on the accounts of a set of women who were positioned and identified relatively unproblematically as 'white'. The interviews will be examined in various ways in order to examine some of the practices, discourses and processes of subjection that combine to produce white, female subjects. Although I asked the women about their perceptions and experiences, the analysis of this requires different readings of their accounts. In the following chapters, I will look at how the women negotiated questions of seeing and talking about 'race' in their everyday lives and particularly in their practices as mothers. I will also explore some of the different ways in which 'race' and racial tropes, such as the threatening young black man and the racialisation of location, were imagined. I will examine how some of the women produced or failed to produce a narrative of the self and how these accounts were racialised, gendered and classed. The mothering practices of the interviewees are explored in a further chapter and, finally, the question of collective, national identity is examined. The next chapter explains the approach I took in finding and talking to the women I interviewed. It also gives a sense of the context in which the study took place and how the process of analysis was undertaken.

3   Talk, tea and tape recorders

White people generally do not spend much time thinking about whiteness or how their experience and identities are racialised. When I designed this project, I assumed that an interview that consisted entirely of questions around 'race' and whiteness would not yield much 'material' beyond the interesting question of silences and erasures. Instead, I opted to take a more indirect approach, which also had the advantage of opening up interview conversations to questions of the social imaginary and narrative. This chapter will give an overview of the approach taken to the fieldwork part of the research. It will: explain why a particular group of women – mothers – was chosen for the interviews; give a sense of the areas (Camberwell and Clapham) where they lived; explain how I made contact with the interviewees; convey a sense of the interview process and the subsequent analysis of the interviews.

There were a number of interconnected reasons for choosing to talk to mothers[1] of preschool and primary school-aged children. Mothers have a particular relationship to processes of identification, having experienced a fundamental identity change of becoming mothers, which is both personally and socially very significant. Yet they are also conscious that this is just one identity among others that are important to them. Thus, motherhood offers an avenue into discussions of the ambivalent processes of identity construction and performativity. In addition, mothers are continually involved in identity work with their children. They are crucial in providing the material circumstances and introducing the discourses and practices that shape the identities of their children. In a child's progression through mother-and-toddler groups, playgroups, nursery, childcare and, most significantly, primary school, many choices are made, involving important decisions about child development: who you want your child to socialise with; what social and practical skills you want them to obtain; what experiences you want them to have; and how they should be educated. Mothers are well aware of the role that they play as well as the other forces that act upon their children (education, media, other people, etc.). As mothers, they both have a particular relationship to the domestic and are involved in negotiating with public institutions, particularly the education system.

A further set of reasons for choosing mothers revolved around the fact that children in Britain, and particularly in London – the area of study – are growing up in a society that is often more racially or ethnically mixed than that of their parents' childhoods. So talking to parents who are aware that their children's lives are very different from what they themselves experienced is one route into exploring the racialisation of everyday life and the imaginary. Children may also play a role in bringing their parents more directly into contact with people of different races and cultures, as well as different classes (at least for those attending state nurseries and schools). Through encounters at playgroups, the school gate and other arenas, parents may develop social relationships with people from different social groups from those they usually meet in their working or social life. Finally, being with and bringing up children brings one into a different relationship with one's own sense of self and with memories of childhood and development. Thus, talking to mothers offered a very specific route into reflections on their own childhoods and histories.

Having decided to interview mothers, I had to select specific areas in which to work and locate interviewees. My initial criteria was that I wanted to interview white women who were living in areas that were not exclusively or predominantly 'white'. Yet at the same time, I wanted to interview women living in areas where 'race' was not a highly contentious or politicised local issue. The next section gives a thumbnail sketch of the areas.

Camberwell and Clapham

The majority of the interviewees lived in Camberwell and Clapham, which are two discrete areas of London lying approximately three miles from each other. Camberwell lies less than three miles from the centre of London in the large inner city borough of Southwark. Rates of unemployment were relatively high at the time of the study, 18.2 per cent for the borough as a whole in the 1991 census. The same census recorded that 76 per cent of the borough were 'white (UK)' with the largest other ethnic group being black Caribbean at 7 per cent. However, this borough covers a wide variation of different areas, with Dulwich in the south, an extremely prosperous and suburban area. Camberwell itself is an area with relatively higher levels of social deprivation and a higher percentage of ethnic 'minorities', largely African Caribbean and African. Camberwell does not have a central focus, or a large shopping centre, although there is a small triangle, Camberwell Green, at a very busy crossroads, which functions as a central landmark. The housing in the area is mixed, ranging from high-rise and low-rise council estates and considerable housing association accommodation to large Georgian town houses. The area did not have a strong or cohesive public identity. There was, for instance, no single source of employment that could form the basis of a sense of community. Some of the interviewees from Camberwell had been born in the area, their parents having been early occupants of the high-rise estates. However, most had only more recent histories in the area. Those middle classes who live in Camberwell have a reputation for being relatively 'bohemian', prepared to live in what is regarded as an inner city rundown area and benefit from cheaper house prices. This reputation is strengthened by the presence of a local arts school. Indeed, several of the interviewees and/or their partners were involved in theatre or the arts.

Clapham spreads over quite a large area of London with Clapham Common at its symbolic centre. It is dissected by the border between two boroughs, Wandsworth and Lambeth, which have different images in public and political discourse. The former was a Conservative council throughout the Thatcher years, and the latter is regarded as a Labour stronghold. Clapham has good communication into central London by bus, tube and rail. A significant proportion of housing in Clapham consists of good-sized Victorian terraced houses in the leafy roads that fan out from, or lie parallel to, Clapham Common. There are also low-rise and some high-rise council estates. In the public social imaginary, Clapham is a middle-class area, characterised by winebars, restaurants, delicatessens, small shops selling expensive and fashionable gift items or exclusive toys and clothes boutiques. Clapham's reputation is indicated by a tongue-in-cheek article in a London paper where it pictured a typical resident of Clapham who was described as:

> smug, married-with-kids thirtysomething Caroline. At the weekend she protects herself from the [. . .] chill by muffling up in lots of fleece. Smokes Marlboro Lights. Works in PR and admires former PR girls Julia Carling and Sophie Rhys Jones for their dress sense and social piggy-backing abilities. Husband does Something In the City.
>
> (*Evening Standard* 2000)

However, the area is, as might be expected, not so homogeneous. The ward in which the majority of the middle-class interviewees lived is largely white with (in the 1991 census) 79 per cent of the population white, 13 per cent black and 3 per cent Asian.[2] In 1991, it was estimated that almost 23 per cent of the population of the ward were professional and managerial workers and 40 per cent were other non-manual workers. However, the neighbouring ward to the east presents very different statistics with a population of 55 per cent white, 35 per cent black and 3 per cent Asian and 6 per cent 'other'. This neighbouring ward (which is not in Clapham, but neighbouring Brixton) has only 11 per cent of the population estimated to be in professional classes and 29 per cent in other non-manual work. An estimated 45 per cent of the population are semi-skilled and unskilled manual workers. One of the interesting aspects of this area, as will be explored later, was that the interviewees (particularly the middle-class ones) lived in areas that they perceived and were reinforced in public discourse to be largely white and middle class. But when they encountered other conceptions of area, such as those presented by school catchments, they were confronted with a very different social make-up.

Finding interviewees

For the main study, I interviewed 25 women over a period of 9 months, between June 1997 and March 1998, with ten respondents interviewed twice.[3] The interviewees were contacted through a variety of means. Initially, I made contact through nurseries, where the organisers were asked to give out a sheet explaining that I wanted to interview parents about 'social identity, particularly race, ethnicity and national identity (but issues of class and gender are also important to me)'. This was the least successful method of contacting people. I also spent time at some playgroups and one o'clock clubs[4] (after having obtained permission from the local authorities). At the clubs, I would chat with women and ask if I could come to interview them at a later date. Some initial contacts were also made through friends or members of my family who knew mothers in the two areas and arranged for me to interview them. I also asked interviewees if they could put me in touch with any of their friends or neighbours. This was the most productive way of contacting interviewees and, as a result, I ended up with at least two groups of women who had multiple interconnections, in that they were friends or neighbours with other interviewees or their children went to the same schools.

The overlapping nature of the sample of interviewees indicates the way in which there is no attempt to achieve statistical representativeness. Nor can the interviews be necessarily regarded as representative of the interviewees' lives. They are analysed at a particular moment in which certain representations of their subjectivities were produced. Nonetheless, as I have argued above, these particular moments of motherhood provided rich material on identity and subjectivity, as well as racialised, classed and gendered practices. The inter-relations between women in the same groups enrich the sample as it offers a multilayered perspective on a relatively small geographic area. I was able to interview several women who saw each other regularly in the same streets. They used the same libraries, swimming pools, shops, nurseries, playgroups and schools. In some interviews, the women used very similar discourses and referred to discussions that they had had with other interviewees or referred to the experience of others. As will be clear, the majority of the interviewees are middle class, although there were differences in their occupations, outlooks, material circumstances and backgrounds.[5] This was at least partly the product of the way people were contacted, as I found that middle-class interviewees were more likely to introduce me to other potential interviewees. This may be a result of the different ways that social networks function, but I suspect is more due to the fact that middle-class interviewees found the interviews a more positive experience than others and were more likely to be prepared to invest in the research process (class differences in the interview process will be discussed more fully later in the chapter). In any case, in examining dominant identities or experience, the middle classes seem an appropriate place to start. They will be the direct focus of some chapters, in particular Chapter 6 on the practices of motherhood, which examines the production of classed as well as raced and gendered identities.

Who is white?

Given that 'race' is a construction and far from fixed, there can be no hard and fast rule of who fits into racial categories. As was discussed in the previous chapter, historically, who is included in the term 'white' has been the result of contestation and alteration.[6] This raises questions of how one defines whiteness in terms of conducting empirical research. Although there exist several unclear borderlands between racialised categories, such as the inclusion or exclusion of certain ethnic groups, or 'mixed race' within the category 'white',[7] many people fit and would place themselves within the category 'white' in an uncomplicated way. I was looking for people who would be viewed by the (black, Asian or white) person in the street as 'white'. This proved to be a straightforward process with most of the interviewees assuming that they were positioned as white. An exception was Jessica,[8] a Jewish woman living in Clapham who was suggested by a friend of hers, who resisted being categorised as white: 'I am conscious of not actually being white . . . quite often [. . .] I am conscious of being Jewish' (Jessica, Interview 41).[9] However, in the main, this study is concerned with those who are positioned in what you might call a 'zone of comfort' firmly within the category 'white' rather than those who, for reasons such as religion or national identity, may lie nearer the shifting boundaries of whiteness. For instance, they were all (except for Jessica) from Christian backgrounds, whether practising or not. They were also all British born. The question of national identity will be considered directly in Chapter 7, 'How English am I?'. However, it is worth noting here the inter-relations between racial, ethnic, religious and national identities. In the case of whiteness and Englishness or Britishness, they generally serve to shore each other up. Englishness and whiteness can be mutually re-enforcing (see Parekh 2000).

The interviews

Excepting one, all the interviews took place in the interviewees' homes. Meeting in people's houses provided intimate locations for the interviews. This domestic space was likely to have an impact on the nature of the conversations, which generally took place over kitchen tables or on sofas over a cup of tea. Barring the tape-recorder, the interviews had some of the feel of a relaxed conversation and, indeed, the interviews were often embedded in or interspersed with more social chat (and sometimes lunch). While the interviewees may not have participated in an interview before, the encounters would in other senses have had a familiar feel, echoing social occasions. In some cases, children were present at the interviews, but the interviews had generally been arranged at times when the children would be out or otherwise occupied (for example, eating, playing with friends and watching television). Although the children sometimes provided dramatic background noise for the taped interviews, they did not generally inhibit the interviews. The relaxed and social feel to the interviews was one feature and advantage of the 'snowballing' method of meeting interviewees, as we often had some common point of reference – I knew or had met a friend or neighbour of theirs or I had spent time in the playgroup or club where they spent time. I tried to maintain this conversational feel through the interviews, giving space for people to have time to think about their answers, come back to issues later and ask questions themselves.

All the interviews that I undertook were relatively relaxed and friendly affairs. Although they were inevitably an intrusion into very busy lives, many respondents appeared to enjoy the interviews, and some said as much. As Heather put it to me at the beginning of her second interview:

> I remember thinking it was interesting, it raised lots of issues that I hadn't ever thought of particularly, because you don't – you just poddle along, and you don't, you know, get that opportunity to spend that time kind of reflecting on a bit of self-analysis.
>
> (Interview 27)[10]

For many of the interviewees, the interview process was more relaxed than they expected it to be, with some commenting that they were surprised by the way it felt more like chatting than interviewing. This was partly due to the fact that, although I had a tape-recorder which would be turned on at the beginning of a session and would have to be turned over occasionally, I made no notes and kept a mental note of areas to be discussed.[11] The interviews also had a conversational feel to them because I would sometimes offer my own experience in response to what they had said. However, I would not want to suggest that the interviewees somehow 'forgot' that they were in an interview situation. But rather, that it was a situation in which they felt relatively relaxed. Emma, for instance, decided to turn the questioning around:

Emma: I'm dying to ask about you, but we're not supposed to are we? (laugh)

BB: No, you can ask whatever you like about me.

(Interview 16)

This exchange resulted in a 10-minute 'interview' in which she asked me where I was from, what I thought about class, how old I was and about my qualifications. This giving of information about oneself follows good feminist practice (see Oakley 1981). However, these occasions were relatively rare. As Ribbens points out, in some situations, the attempt of the researcher to place herself and give personal information may be seen as an imposition rather than as a welcome offer of friendship: 'After all, is not part of the research exchange that I have expressed an interest in hearing about the interviewees' lives' (Ribbens 1989: 584). In general, the focus was on letting the interviewee speak, as Madeleine (who was particularly interested because her work involved doing qualitative interviewing) remarked on:

> I find it really fascinating actually, and really interesting. It's really interesting as well, your kind of style [. . .] Because there are times when you just don't say anything and I think, 'oh well I'll just carry on with that, I'll try and think of something to say about that' which is brilliant because I really lead people when I interview them.
>
> (Interview 44)

However, while it would be tempting (and in some cases no doubt accurate) to paint a picture of interviews that were relaxed, enjoyable and even gave the interviewees space and time from which they might feel they benefited, this would be to ignore those other potentially less harmonious aspects or experiences of interviewing.

There has been some consideration by feminist writers of the impact of class and 'race' differences on the interviewing situation (for instance see Edwards 1990; Cannon *et al.* 1991; Reay 1996). My own experience in conducting this research was that differences of class or 'race' did have an impact on the atmosphere and outcome of an interview, but that what the impact would be was unpredictable. The majority of the interviews were of course conducted with white women and differences of 'race' between myself and the interviewees were not at issue. However, I did conduct three interviews with women who would not position themselves as white. Edwards (herself white) writes that, in interviewing black women:

> I realised that rapport was easier after I had signalled not a non-hierarchical, non-exploitative, shared-sex relationship, but rather an acknowledgement that I was in a different structural position to them with regard to race and did not hold shared assumptions on that basis.
>
> (Edwards 1990: 486)

Setting up this understanding in the interviews I undertook with women who were not white was relatively straightforward, given the subject matter, and I found that this did provide a context for informative and relaxed interviews. Hope, a black woman, for example, responded to my thanks at the end of the interview by saying (perhaps surprised herself) 'That's all right Bridget, I enjoyed that actually'. She also told me that she had checked with the (black) nursery co-ordinator who had given her the sheet requesting interviews whether or not I was white: 'I asked, I asked [laugh] but I gathered, if you know what I mean, I thought it must be a white woman who's doing it'. Hope also expressed more interest in the end result of the interview than any other interviewee: 'Especially as a white woman, do you know what I mean, as a white person, I want to see what [you're getting at], you know' (Hope, Interview 5).

In this interview, Hope constantly referred to herself and put her experience in the context of being 'a black woman' and also explicitly positioned me as 'a white woman'. In contrast, in interviews where there was a class difference between myself and that of the interviewees, this was not dealt with so explicitly, either by me or by the interviewees. In only a very few situations did class constitute the kind of context-setting, explicit identity that people would refer to themselves as either 'a middle-class woman' or 'a working-class woman'. Without this explicit positioning, it was difficult to acknowledge class position. Mariam Fraser discusses how class may not be amenable to a politics of visibility because of the way in which people may be reluctant to identify as working class (Fraser 1999: 126). In fact, this was impossible for those who adopted very strongly class-blind discourses. For example, Rosemary, a working-class woman, is signalling in the following extract that she is not 'posh', but in such a way that discourages further discussion of class. She is responding to a question about whether issues of class or race come up with her children much:

> No we don't talk about that. I mean class, personally, we're the same as everyone, you know. You either like us or you don't. But we get on with everyone, there's not any people that we say 'oh no, we don't get on with them, no they're too posh, no they're this colour, that colour'.
>
> (Interview 14)

This first interview with Rosemary was markedly more stilted and awkward than with other people, which was not helped by a time pressure, as she only had a short time for the interview, and the audience provided by her children. But I certainly felt that class played a large part in her reticence. The second interview was more relaxed. However, in both interviews with Rosemary, she seemed to feel the most conscious, among all the interviewees, about the presence of the tape-recorder. In the first interview, she asked me to switch off the tape-recorder (so she could express more forcefully some of her views of 'Africans'). In the second interview, in the middle of an account of a difficult pregnancy, she asked the tape-recorder 'do you want to hear that?'. This seemed to be referring to someone superior to me, perhaps an assumed male supervisor (who would not want to know gynaecologically related medical details) and who could absorb some of the awkwardness of the situation – even though I had told her that no-one else would listen directly to the tapes, although I might quote from them.

Other working-class interviewees did talk more explicitly about class differences. However, in contrast to the conversations with Hope, in which we were both happy to refer to my positioning as a white woman, in these discussions of class, my own middle classness was not mentioned. Which is of course far from saying that it was not present in the conversations and influenced the questioning and responses. In addition, class influenced the style of interviewing and responses. Middle-class interviewees tended to produce longer replies to the questions and be more likely to adopt a narrative style where they might have strayed off the immediate focus of the question.[12] Working-class interviewees tended to reply more briefly, leading to a more conventional question and answer session in which there was less scope for the concerns of interviewees to emerge. Class was certainly present in the interviews with middle-class women, in contributing to the assumption of certain shared experiences, views and positions that made the interview more relaxed. This would have worked in a similar way to shared white identities. For instance, in the following extract, Madeleine referred to our common middle classness:

> I think class is really, class is one of those things. I don't know if you had this experience when you were growing up, but class is one of those things which people use in arguments against you, like 'you can't have an opinion on this because you're middle class'.
>
> (Interview 9)

This is not to say that there weren't differences between myself and other middle-class interviewees. As mentioned above, interviewees would have surmised my class position from my accent, my educational status, my modes of speech and ways of being. But they also knew, generally without the need to question, that I did not, at the time, have children. While I obviously conveyed this through the way in which I phrased and asked questions, I admit that I found their ability to assume my childless status rather mysterious. I do not know what assumptions they made about my sexuality, although it is likely that the majority of the interviewees assumed I was heterosexual. Coupled with the fact that I was often younger than the interviewees, the fact that I myself was not a mother put them in a position of explaining their experiences to me. There was also a difference in financial position between myself and several of the interviewees, which I was certainly conscious of and they may also have been. For instance, on one occasion, an approach to the co-ordinator of a private nursery in Clapham turned into an attempt on her behalf to recruit me to do babysitting for her. Of course 'middle class' is far from a homogeneous category, and minor distinctions become oversignificant in the context of social class.[13] I did not practice middle classness (or womanhood) in the same way as many of the middle-class interviewees or even necessarily share their common knowledge.

These differences make questions of power and control in the research process more complex than is sometimes suggested. It could be argued that, at the time of the interview, it is the interviewee who has the most control over the situation. As a researcher, I felt a deep sense of gratitude that someone had not only consented to give me an interview, but had given their time, invited me into their house and were willing to talk frankly. This inhibited my ability to ask what I perceived might be more difficult questions, or to press the interviewees to expand on answers when they adopted defensively short answers or where there were inconsistencies. At the same time, one could argue that it doesn't make good research practice to antagonise, upset or irritate interviewees. An example of how my reticence led to gaps in the material occurred in the case of Helen, who had two young daughters, one about 6 months old and the other almost 3 years old. In the first interview, Helen told me that these children both had the same 'mixed-race' father, who was not the person she was now living with and who was bringing up the children with her. In the second interview, when she was giving a narration of her life, she presented her current relationship as beginning soon after university with no suggestion that it had ever been interrupted. Given this strong narrative of a single relationship, I felt that it would be raising a sensitive issue to ask about the father of her children, and in this case felt unable to broach the question.

Although there were times when I felt somewhat inhibited in the interview, the interviewee may equally feel inhibited or unable to refuse to answer a question that is put directly. Nonetheless, there are many ways to resist or divert questions in such a way that they become difficult to ask again. I would not like to suggest that this was a big problem in the research. What was remarkable to me was the extent to which interviewees were willing to open themselves to questioning and to share confidential information, different experiences and their sense of themselves. At the same time, some of the resistances and silences are in and of themselves important to this research. Indeed, Chapter 5, 'Seeing, talking, living "race"', shows how this happened around the subject of 'race' itself. But the point I want to make here is that power or control at this stage could be argued to be relatively equally balanced. This stands in marked contrast to the situation once the fieldwork is completed and the analysis begins. Therefore, it was perhaps particularly appropriate that Rosemary (as mentioned earlier) reserved a sense of deference to the tape-recorder. She was perhaps aware that I would be the person listening to the interview, but the question was what I, as the distanced listener and researcher, rather than the woman sitting in her living room, would make of and do with what she said.

There have been many claims made within feminism for the emancipatory potential of qualitative research (for example see Oakley 1981). However, these formulations can be problematic where they lack analysis of the shifting dynamics of power in a research process. They also potentially overemphasise the development of a relaxed rapport, even friendship, with research subjects, which ignores divisions and differences between women (those who validate interviewing in these terms generally assume that it will be women, not men, who are interviewed). In addition, they fail to address the situation in which the researcher is interested in researching an area that the interviewees may not consider significant or, more importantly perhaps, where there is a need to analyse the interview in a way with which the interviewees would not necessarily agree. Here, issues of power become critical as, whatever her friendly demeanour, the researcher assumes the power to analyse and interpret the material. It may not always be possible, or desirable, to include interviewees or participants in research in the processes of analysis.[14]

It is not necessarily in the interests of feminism for researchers to restrict their interpretations to that of the interviewees. Some level of abstraction and interpretation is essential in order to link the account of the individual to processes outside her immediate social world. Accounts may also need to be read 'against the grain'. Thus, there remains the dilemma that presenting an alternative perspective on an interviewee's account of her life or a particular aspect of her life may cause emotional distress:

> The performance of a personal narrative is a fundamental means by which people comprehend their own lives and present a 'self' to their audience. Our scholarly representations of those performances, if not sensitively presented, may constitute an attack on our collaborator's carefully constructed sense of self.
>
> (Borland 1991: 71)

There is a high risk that my research might be seen, by respondents if not by myself, as 'an attack' on their 'sense of self'. The nature of my project is to mark that which is often unmarked to the subjects themselves, and this is likely to disrupt self-perceptions. This was not an interactive research process, where research subjects are able to control the processes. Nonetheless, this does not mean that I do not have ethical responsibilities towards the women that I interviewed. The first involved being as open as possible to the interviewees about who I was and what was the nature of my research; the second is to ensure the anonymity that I had promised them; the third is to do my utmost to be faithful to the accounts that the women gave me. This does not mean that I have not allowed myself to analyse them, but that I have tried to be sensitive to the complexities of what the interviewees say and how they say it. It is this third responsibility that has involved the most careful, and sometimes painful, work.

It is at the stage of analysis where questions of power and control shift unequivocally from a relationship between the researcher and the researched to rest solely with the researcher. The process of analysing and interpreting the interviews is necessarily subjective. As Parker and Burman argue, 'to offer a reading of a text is, in some manner or other, to reproduce or transform it' (Parker and Burman 1993: 159). It might be possible at this point to argue that enough of the interviewees' accounts are present in the book to allow readers to come to their own conclusions about what the interviewees were saying, and this is indeed a common argument. However, while there is inevitably room for alternative interpretations, this argument would be somewhat disingenuous given the high degree of filtering and framing of the accounts in the main body of the book. Therefore, the rest of this section is concerned with explaining some of the processes of analysis in dealing with the interview material in order to set the context for what follows.

Analysing the interviews

All the interviews were transcribed. This in itself is an act of distilling an in-the-flesh interpersonal encounter with all the different non-verbal communications that involves, set in a particular place, to a textual reproduction devoid of tonal and phrasing subtleties. The interviews are rendered fairly simplistically, without techniques used for conversational analysis (for example see those used by Jennifer Coates 1996: x–xiv), as this was not logistically possible. This more technical form of rendering a conversation also has the disadvantage of being relatively difficult to read, providing another barrier to getting a sense of what is being said. I have tried to convey a limited sense of the tone given – by noting in italics where particular emphasis was given to words or phrases and noting other expressions, such as laughter. Initially, I used a computer package (the unfortunately named NUD*IST) to analyse the material, but found that this limited the analysis in various ways, for example by breaking the narrative flow within individual interviews.

As a result of these conclusions, I took each interviewee individually and analysed her interviews, producing an account of each interviewee with an individual biography and analysis of the interview. In these profiles or summaries, I tried to establish a picture of who the interviewees were, the ways in which they thought, the discourses they used in different contexts and the assumptions they worked with. In this way, an attempt was made to examine the performativity of race, class and gender in the interview encounter. I explored how they approached questions of 'race', class and gender, what account they gave of their lives, of their childhoods, their experiences of motherhood and how they went about bringing up their children. Each interviewee was written up and, in these accounts, I drew on my impressions of the interviewees when I had met them, how they spoke and other aspects of the encounter that are not caught on the transcribed text. I examined the way they represented their selves, in particular examining how some produced narratives of their lives in the interviews while others did not. Those interviewees who had given second interviews were particularly interesting in this context. In these interviews, a life history approach was used as a device to open up the space for interviewees to produce an account or narrative of their selves. The interest here is less directly in the life history itself, but more in the different modes that the interviewees used to generate meaning and an account of self. The question of silences and avoidances in the interviews was also important. What did interviewees discuss willingly, and what did they avoid? How are questions of power and difference alluded to without being mentioned directly? Once this process was completed for all the interviewees (with individual summaries sometimes running to over

10,000 words), I then felt in a much stronger position to explore similarities, differences and resonances across cases, as well as to analyse some interviews in even more depth.

The rest of the book is the product of this analysis, based on an in-depth knowledge of the accounts that the interviewees gave. In order to explore how their experiences were racialised, classed and gendered, and how discourses are reproduced within interviews, it was necessary to approach the analysis in many different ways and at different levels. What emerged as a result of the analysis was sometimes different from my impression during and immediately after the interviews. At times during the fieldwork, I felt that the interviews were 'boring' or yielding little useful material. However, my impression of what was significant within interviews changed considerably once the analysis had been completed. What might have seemed empty of content could emerge as a series of complex evasions or silences. Not only content, but also form is important. But more significantly, whereas I sometimes feared that there would be nothing to discuss but silences and evasions, close attention to the interviews revealed the degree to which the accounts were in fact explicitly classed and raced. In addition, repetitions and resonances between different accounts can be frustrating when conducting interviews, but become fascinating for identifying common discursive constructions and important features of a social imaginary.

The citation of racialised and classed discourses is sometimes so ubiquitous that it takes careful reading to 'see' or 'hear' it. And of course, in this case, the 'seeing' and 'hearing' is done by an individual who is limited by having a subject position similar to those whose accounts she is analysing. I do not want to enter here into debates around the benefits or otherwise of 'insider' and 'outsider' status, as these have perhaps been overworked and have the risk of essentialising the notion of community, which one can only be either inside or outside. It is, however, fair to say that, after studying and working in the area of development studies, and influenced by the black feminist writers mentioned in Chapter 1, I was politically drawn to the idea of rejecting the position of being the white researcher who 'knows' and studies 'the other'. I have not chosen to research myself, but have chosen to research those who are quite like myself. This, however, has various pitfalls, not least of which is that white people are long trained in colour blindness[15] – that is, the inability to see the impact of racist processes on their lives and the lives of others. Thus, a white researcher is unlikely to be the most adept analyst of whiteness and white privilege. Despite this, in order to conform to the individualistic goalpost structured within the academy, I have produced a sole-authored text and taken the authoritative position suggested by the word 'author'. This inevitably reduces the politics and potential of the work as bell hooks argues:

> One change in that direction that would be real cool would be the production of a discourse on race that interrogates whiteness. It would just

be so interesting for all those white folks who are giving blacks their take on blackness to let them know what's going on with whiteness. . . . First of all, let's acknowledge that few nonwhite scholars are being awarded grants to investigate and study all aspects of white culture from a standpoint of 'difference'.

(hooks 1990: 54–5)

I do not wish to labour the point of *mea culpa* and take up the role of the anguished white academic, but I raise it here to highlight the position from which this work is written. Nor do I propose to give what has become known as a 'reflexive account' of the self of the researcher. Beverly Skeggs (2002: 360) critiques the 'tendency to think that the problems of power, privilege and perspective can be dissolved by inserting one's self into the account and proclaiming that reflexivity has occurred in practice'. Skeggs (2002) and Adkins (2002) also caution against the ways in which writing the self into research accounts can rely on the fixing of others. As Sara Ahmed writes: 'Studying whiteness can involve the claiming of a privileged white identity as the subject who knows . . . we cannot simply unlearn privilege when the cultures in which learning take place are shaped by privilege' (Ahmed 2004: 40). Readers need to take account of the limitations of the position and adjust their reading accordingly.

4 Narrating the self

Introduction

> We lived in a tiny little village with a dead end, you had to turn right
> to get to the village, and it had the river at the bottom, [. . .] so quite a
> few holidaymakers and things . . . And then there was just a little village
> school which only had about 50 children altogether, maybe. Which is
> actually closed down now. So we just went there, and I think probably
> all the time I was at school, you know, it was quite a sort of idyllic little
> set-up in a way, sort of playing with kids in the village, and we had a
> lot of freedom from when we were really, really young, and then out
> on bikes and things when we were eight for half the day, and stuff like
> that. And then I just, I don't know, I presume I took the 11-plus and I
> obviously failed, I'm sure I must have taken the 11-plus at that time, so
> I just went on to my local high school. Which was just two miles away.
> So once again, that was sort of very local.
>
> (Sally, Interview 22)

In the above extract, Sally began telling me a version of her life story. This
was a long and involved account, and it largely unfolded without prompting. Her opening had all the drama of a well-crafted story, beginning with a
dramatic flourish, which set up one of the major themes of her account, that
of escape: 'we lived in a tiny little village with a dead end'. She was drawing
me into the story of how she managed the transportation from this 'tiny little
village' to London where the narration took place. Sally set up a particular
relationship to the past in this opening. She placed the events firmly in the
past – even the school no longer exists – and she took the position of analysing and passing judgement on it: 'it was quite a sort of idyllic little set-up in
a way'. The ambiguity of the qualification of 'in a way' again suggests that
there was a story to be told. At the same time, she showed how distanced
she was from the events. She cannot remember whether or not she took,
or passed or failed, her 11-plus – something that would have presumably

been of significance at the time. Her vagueness about these events seemed to demonstrate that they were of little importance to the Sally of the time of the interview. She was separating herself from the child who took (or did not take) the exams. In the narrative, Sally presented an ambiguous relationship between her present self and her past selves. On the one hand, Sally often distanced herself from the events and the person who experienced them. For example, she continually speculated on what this character did or felt (for instance, seeing a man with pornographic magazines 'probably did scare us') but without claiming ownership of the memories. Yet, at the same time, Sally was constructing a narrative for her younger self that tried to make sense of where she was at the time of the interview, for instance by demonstrating her difference from her family from a young age.

This negotiation between the self of the present and the self/selves of the past is an inherent part of telling one's life story. To be asked about one's life is, to some extent, to be asked to give an account of one's self. It is also to produce an account that is explicitly or implicitly a story, an act of creation. In telling the story of her self, the narrator claims the position of the subject for her fictionalised self and accounts for her subjectivity. This book is concerned with how white subjectivities are produced through the working of racialised, gendered, sexed and classed norms. By asking interviewees to give an account of their lives, I was opening up an avenue to examine processes of subjection. Producing a narrative of one's life, representing one's self, involves to a certain extent repeating processes of subjection. One must construct oneself as the subject of the story and, in doing so, claim intelligibility and agency. The fiction of the whole coherent self is created, but it can also be undermined in the telling. This chapter will ask to what extent providing a narrative of the self involves individuals positioning themselves as raced, classed and gendered subjects.[1] In particular, it will examine the extent to which whiteness is produced in the accounts.

Donald E. Polkinghorne describes 'self-narratives' as the ways 'individuals construct private and personal stories linking diverse events of their lives into unified and understandable wholes. These are stories about the self. They are the basis of personal identity and self-understanding and they provide answers to the question "Who am I?"' (Polkinghorne 1991: 135). Approaching these accounts as narratives suggests acknowledgement of the constructed, flexible and fictionalised nature of the process of accounting for the self. However, this still leaves the question of what is involved in constructing a 'unified and understandable whole' out of the diverse events of a life. Is this inevitable or, indeed, always possible to achieve? What is behind the posing and answering of the question 'Who am I'? How does an individual come to occupy the site of the subject implied by such a question? What 'enabling violations'[2] does this involve? What is claimed and enabled by taking up this position as a speaking subject, and what is repressed? Paul Ricoeur stresses the importance of an 'examined' or 'recounted' life:

> We never cease to reinterpret the narrative identity that constitutes us, in the light of the narratives proposed to us by our culture. In this sense, our self-understanding presents the same features of traditionality as the understanding of a literary work. It is in this way that we learn to become the *narrator* and the hero *of our own story*, without actually becoming the *author of our own life*.
>
> (Ricoeur 1991a: 32, original emphasis)

For Ricoeur, this occurs through emplotment, which draws multiple incidents into a single story: 'the recounted story is always more than the enumeration in an order that would be merely serial or successive, of the incidents or events that it organises into an intelligible whole' (Ricoeur 1991a: 21). Yet Ricoeur also argues that individuals may go through 'dark nights of personal identity' where they experience a sense of 'nothingness of permanence identity' – or one might argue an absence of a narrative self (Ricoeur 1991b: 199).

It is clear that we are 'post' the Enlightenment subject. The conception of the subject as fixed, unique and rational has been fatally undermined by a succession of challenging theories, including psychoanalysis, Saussarian linguistics, Foucauldian discourse analysis and feminism.[3] However, the question remains as to what subject we are left with. Jane Flax cautions against the restrictions in theorising subjectivity:

> Our abilities to imagine such subjectivities are impeded by the positing of false alternatives. Some postmodernists confine all talk about subjectivity to critiques of the split Cartesian rationalistic subject or of the unitary, authentic 'true self'. On the other hand, critics of postmodernism and some postmodernists reduce all descriptions of a decentered subject to a fragmented one that lacks any agency or organisation. None of these constructs are appealing or plausible. Their juxtaposition and the limits of the arguments demonstrate how difficult it is to imagine subjectivity outside Enlightenment ideas of it. The unitary self and the fragmented one are simply mirror images; neither represents an alternative to the subjects Enlightenment discourses construct.
>
> (Flax 1993: xii)

We may try to 'imagine' subjectivity as multiple, precarious, contradictory, in process and undergoing constant reconstitution, but it is a complex operation to speak of it as such and even more difficult and potentially dangerous to feel it as such: 'the subject may be the effect of discourses, institutions and practices, but at any given moment the subject-in-process experiences itself as the "I", and both consciously and unconsciously replays and resignifies positions in which it is located and invested' (Brah 1996: 125). This chapter treats the narrative accounts of four individuals as moments of reiteration of processes of subjection, the narrativisation of the self as a performance of subjecthood. By creating the subject of a narrative, explaining who she is and who she is not, as well as by accounting for how she came to be, Sally, in the first case study, recited processes of subjection. However, for the others, the norms and conventions of narrative did not conform with their experiences of subjection; either because they did not experience an easily retold sense of themselves, or because they wished to present themselves as so inevitable and conforming to dominant norms that there was no story to tell. Discourses of 'race', class and gender are all implicated in these different renderings of the self.

A story to tell

Sally – transformation of the self

Sally's narrative of her self was produced in the second interview that I undertook with her. In the first, she had already spoken about her children and how she felt about being a mother and living in London. This had also involved talking to some extent about her childhood and life history. In this interview, I said that I wanted to go back over her life in a little more detail, and suggested that she might want to begin chronologically. She stuck to this approach throughout a long account. This was not always the case in the interviews I undertook. Some interviewees would specifically say that they were not going to take a chronological approach or others would begin at a beginning, but then make links back and forth in time as the story unfolded. I think the chronological approach appealed to Sally as it enhanced particular aspects of the story that she was seeking to tell. The main thrust of her narrative was to establish her difference from her family and to account for the changes in her life and values. Sally's account charted, in Raphael Samuel's words, 'progress from darkness to light. Here the past serves as a kind of negative benchmark by which later achievement is judged, and the narrative is one of achievement rather than loss' (Samuel and Thompson 1990: 9). Both interviews with Sally were littered with phrases that emphasised transformation: '[I] forged my own identity'; '[I] grew up in a vacuum'; '[studying sociology] presented me with another side of things . . . [and] was quite a big change for me, at that stage'; 'I looked back and thought that it was very narrow'; 'just going out into the big wide world, leaving my little tiny village'; 'I had different experiences and I had my eyes opened up in a different way'; 'I feel like having come from the other side'; 'I've gone beyond it'; 'I came from not knowing anything and being very sheltered'; 'it does feel like I've come from one world into another in a way'. In the account, Sally allocated both her background and her current situation certain racialised, classed and gendered features. In this way, through the account, she occupied different subject positions governed by different norms and discourses. Class and 'race' in particular became tropes that marked or dramatised the ruptures in her life story. Her account also suggested the social availability of certain accounts of classed and raced transformation (see Lawler 2002).

Sally grew up, as she said in the extract quoted at the beginning of the chapter, in a small village. She described her family as one that had problems, particularly in communication, many of which she associated with a working-class background:

> I would say though that the kind of set-up I come from, I wouldn't . . . for me personally, I wouldn't just say oh that's quite a dysfunctional family. I would say, that's got lots of working-class stuff running through it, personally. Do you know what I mean, about things like education, not necessarily . . . especially at that time maybe, not necessarily being a priority and seeing how one thing might lead on to another.
>
> (Interview 22)

The problems with the family were focused particularly around Sally's father: 'my dad was just terribly restricted by this awful difficulty he had in just relating'. There is a suggestion in the account that at least some of these problems with her father were related to gender and sexuality. Her father was represented as at times domineering: 'he was really controlling, and he was the sort of person, you'd be watching something on TV and he would come and turn the TV over', but also as a protective figure, willing to drive long distances to pick her up, for instance, when she needed him to. In contrast to the domineering father, Sally's mother was presented as largely passive and lacking agency. Sally described how her mother failed to intervene in the worsening dynamic between the father and children in an effort to protect her relationship with her father. Rather than describing her mother as a role model, or as someone who played an active role in shaping her behaviour, Sally suggested that she and her sisters developed in opposition to her mother:[4]

> I think we're quite a force to be reckoned with, me and my sisters. We're all sort of strong-minded, quite loud and assertive, and my mum just isn't like that. You know, like now, she wouldn't dare do lots of things if one of my sisters was coming round.
>
> (Interview 22)

The main protagonists in the earlier part of the narrative were Sally and her sisters. They were sometimes described (as above) as if they formed one unit. Again, the sisters acted as one when they decided to leave home:

> So, then things went really wrong, and one day there was an argument about something [. . .] and we put our viewpoint and we ended up getting into an argument with my dad, and he said, 'well, if you don't like

it, get out' or something. And we just looked at each other, the three of us, and we had absolutely nowhere to go and we just said: 'let's do it'. And it was like we'd finally . . . I mean, I'm not saying we weren't stroppy teenagers because we probably were, you know, [. . .] And so we just got up and left at that stage. And then over the years, we kind of drifted back at times, but that was it. We were off.

(Interview 22)

At certain points, there was no clear distinction between Sally's stories and her sisters. For instance, it is notable how in the following extract the protagonist in the narrative shifts, without need for explanation, from Sally to her sister:

Yes, so school . . . I think I was quite good in primary school in terms of . . . it was really small and I was really happy there, and I used to quite get into it. [. . .] . . . I just really loved going. My little sister used to run away out the garden to get to the village school. My mum . . . sometimes she'd go out and Susie would be gone, and then Susie would be found at the school, or the school would 'phone and say: 'she's fine, she can sit at the back of the class', and that was because she was bored without us two.

(Interview 22)

This accords with what has been identified as a 'female' form of narrative by Isabelle Bertaux-Wiame:[5]

the men consider the life they have lived as *their own* as a series of self-conscious acts, with well-defined goals; and in telling their story they use the active 'I', assuming themselves as the subject of their actions through their very forms of speech. Women, by contrast talk of their lives typically in terms of relationships, including parts of other life stories in their own.

(quoted in Thompson 1988: 155–6)

Sally's narrative swung between these 'male' and 'female' forms, which marks in some ways a desire to stress a growing difference and independence from her sisters. Sally talked of 'taking on a different role' to her sisters in her childhood and described how they now have very different outlooks on life. In the following description, Sally gave herself and her sisters distinct subject positions and subjectivities. She was also suggesting that, as well as now living under different material conditions (Sally did not have the resources to do the travelling they do or send her children to private school), she and her sisters had different identifications with normative discourses of 'race', class, heteronormativity and gender:

In that way there was always something a bit different about me to my sisters, because my sisters now live a very . . . I mean, in a way, I wouldn't say they're kind of . . . they got together . . . the two that are closest to me have definitely got together with people who are from middle-class backgrounds, with middle-class aspirations, and they have very good lifestyles. They travel abroad a lot, they have private educations for their kids and things. So . . . but at the time, I . . . but within that they're very . . . they've still, I would say, got very narrow views about most things, sort of quite homophobic and underlying racist and quite a lot of sexist kind of stuff that to me seems unbelievable. They'll look at their watch and say 'I must get home to get so-and-so's tea', and yet they're only 30-year old women. I mean, that to me just seems amazing that people would think like that at that age, but they just do. So . . . but I from a young age, was really quite different, I think, and then *the fact that I then went on to do what I did*, but I was always the sort of . . . I think from a young age I was the sort of . . . I don't know, my sisters wanted to take me out to pubs and things and sit with those kind of rugby types who, if you're a woman, you're supposed to sit on a bar stool and laugh at their jokes. And I would actually question quite a lot of what they'd said. But that was probably when I had come back from Spain more. And I was doing my A levels.

(Interview 22, emphasis mine)

Sally set up various differences between herself and her sisters. She suggested that their whiteness, their middle classness and their gender meant very different things to them and led to the performance of different norms. She presented them as having an unquestioning relationship to dominant norms and acting out racism, sexism and homophobia in their everyday lives. The account was one of rupture. Sally always felt different, and then 'went on to do what I did'. She did not explain what this was. The rest of her narrative suggests various possibilities. It might be because she went on to further education, or that she got involved with alternative and oppositional culture in the form of squatting organisations (mentioned but not elaborated on in her narrative), or her relationship with a 'non-white' man and the two children she had with him, or that she does not have a husband or career to provide the material resources for the middle-class lifestyle they led. In various ways, she had established her difference from her sisters. At the same time, for Sally, there was also the fear that this transformation had not been fully achieved. For instance, when she described her decision to leave her college course because she had become pregnant, it was clear that she feared there was an inevitability in her situation which represented an inability to 'escape':

I don't think that sat very well with me because I was probably only the first person in my family that had ever done a degree, and it really felt when I was pregnant I'm sure there was part of me that just felt this is so kind of *predictable and expected*, do you know what I mean? And yet I . . . I think there was part of me that wanted to kind of make it work and see how far I could take it.

(Interview 22, emphasis mine)

In the narrative, Sally was presented as struggling to be a different subject, expressed and established through different actions and ways of being. But the intervention of events, such as getting pregnant, means that she feels she was drawn into reperforming certain classed and gendered norms. The creation of subject positions is not a free or voluntaristic process. It is produced through accessing available material and discursive resources. Sally's narrative had established some of the ways in which her subjectivity had been formed in childhood. She had suggested ways in which her life was affected by class and gender as well as 'race'. In her first interview, she described the way 'race' influenced her viewpoint as a child:

> But I think I was brought up *really* looking at things through white eyes. I think it was quite, in some ways it was quite a racist kind of upbringing. There was a *lot of* suspicion, a lot of, in a way, yeah, there was kind of outright derogatory remarks. And it was very much seen as something which was *totally* alien to us. We were really *white* English, you know in terms of our food and everything I think.

(Interview 7, emphasis Sally's)

The fact that she characterised the outlook of her childhood in this way indicates that she had moved away from this position. This raised the question that is set up in the narrative itself of how Sally came to have such an altered outlook on life. On the one hand, Sally suggested, as already mentioned, that she had been different from her sisters for a long time (although she had difficulty pinpointing exactly when or perhaps how). It is interesting that, in the following extract, the signifiers of difference are classed (classical music) and racialised (reggae):[6]

> I can't remember when but there was some stage when I knew I probably felt a bit different to my sisters in a way. I remember sort of I'd spend a lot of time in my room. I did at some point, maybe around the age of 16 or so, I did develop an interest in sort of music and reading and stuff, which I've still got now. Classical, pop, reggae, I started to get into all that. Maybe more so a bit later actually.

(Interview 22)

Yet, at the same time, Sally did not claim sole agency or essentialness for her difference. One of the things that set Sally apart from her sisters was a very important friendship with a woman. She described meeting this friend as a key turning point in her life. It occurred when she was working abroad:

I met somebody who just sort of really changed my life really, it was amazing. Which is Emily and Ellen's aunt, which is how I met their dad, and that literally did set me on another path. But she was . . . there I was in Spain working on my tan, and wearing my bikinis and thinking oh Spain, it's nice, but I'm off to Australia, then I'm going to America, [. . .] I was kind of, in a way, I was very kind of quite directional in terms of I wanted to travel, but I was so kind of . . . you know, I wanted to meet a rich man, to rescue me, you know, it was all that kind of stuff going on. And then I . . . then one day, Joy breezed in and I always remember 'cos I was sitting with all these ex-pats. And Joy breezed in. And she lived opposite me in the winter. She'd only come in between college and university, but she started talking about things that obviously I might have thought, well, she's obviously a complete lunatic or it doesn't mean anything. But for some reason, it was very strange. For a start, I got on brilliantly with her and felt really close to her, and . . . but she just had completely different priorities in life. She'd come from something *so* different. And she'd just started to question some of the things that I was about, and some of the things that I wanted, do you know what I mean? And she really influenced me. And when I came back from Spain, I actually decided I think while I was in Spain that I wanted to come home, do some O and A's and . . . I don't know if I knew what I wanted to do at that stage, but I thought I'd like to go home and do something. I'd like to go to college again. And I definitely see meeting her as a real, real changing point in my life. Up until then I'd probably met people who were into quite similar things to me. And probably hadn't even really thought that much about direction and values and things like that really. I mean, it was just a case of, you know, you were a bit like one of those little wish things that just blows through life.

(Interview 22)

There is little that Sally could have done in this narrative to make the entrance of Joy more dramatic: 'I met somebody who just sort of really changed my life, really, it was amazing!'. Instead of the hoped-for man 'rescuing' her, this woman 'breezed in' to her life and completely transformed it. In the narrative, Sally relinquished a sense of her own agency to Joy, who transformed her from 'one of those little wish things who blows through life' into someone with 'direction and values'. This could read like the beginning of a lesbian coming out narrative, but it is not sexuality or sexual orientation that marks Joy out. Yet Joy was clearly different – Sally said that she might have thought that Joy was 'a complete lunatic'. The clue is in the juxtaposition of Joy with the 'ex-pats'. It was Joy's racial positioning and their friendship that prompted Sally to question her values and certain aspects of her life and to set a distinction between Joy and her sisters:

I think I'd started to have that questioning with Joy. And Joy wasn't white either. Her dad was African. So yeah, I was very . . . and in that way there was always something a bit different about me and my sisters.

(Interview 22)

Meeting Joy was presented as marking a distinct rupture from Sally's family; she offered a different way of being, which Sally jumped at. When she returned to England some months later, the change in her priorities was made clear: 'the day I flew back she actually picked me up from the airport and I went and stayed with her family for 2 weeks, I didn't even bother to go home'. In the account, there continued to be an apparently unconscious parallel narrative of desire as the narrative followed the forms and conventions of a romance. The transgression of racialised norms was heightened by this echo of the transgression of heterosexual norms. This engagement with difference, or the other, was clearly marked as liberatory for Sally. In her essay 'Eating the other, desire and resistance', bell hooks has written about the 'idea that racial difference marks one as Other and the assumption that sexual agency expressed within the context of racialised sexual encounter is a conversion experience that alters one's place and participation in contemporary cultural politics' (hooks 1992: 22). Within the narrative, Sally's friendship with Joy was indeed presented as a 'conversion experience', which offered her the possibilities of change and liberation:

She breezed in that day . . . and she just came in like a bit of a breath of fresh air because she was my age and she was on a similar level, and then we just got chatting, and she had a similar thing with me. She just thought I was totally wonderful as well, I mean, it was very . . . for a while we were really stuck up each other's backsides . . . we just thought we were absolutely, you know, wonderful, I think in a way, or we couldn't quite believe either of us that we'd met this other person who we just thought was really great, you know. And it's probably been like that ever since although it's really de-intensified as we've got older and, you know, got on with our own lives. But it was very intense, but nicely I think. I think at one stage it wasn't nice; it was almost like I'd almost relied on Joy a little bit too much. It was like I wanted something from her, probably some direction with my . . . who I was I'd say, more than where I was going. So that was quite interesting. For a time, I think we probably purposely needed a bit of space. But now we're just on a really, really nice . . . for the last few years, we've been on a really nice level again, 'cos this was about 13, 14 years ago, when I first met her. 13 years ago, I suppose.

(Interview 22)

The figure of Joy played a key role in Sally's story of herself. By entering into Sally's life, she had enabled her to be something that she was not previously. Sally attributed herself only very limited agency in this story. Her teenage desire for a man to rescue her appears to be merely replaced by the figure of Joy. The significance of Joy's racial positioning was ambiguous in Sally's account. On the one hand, as we have seen above, the fact that Joy 'wasn't white' was part of the reason why Sally began to question the assumptions that she was brought up with. At other points, Sally herself denied that Joy's racial positioning meant anything to her:

> The thing that struck me that was really different about her was mainly her pace of life, and her self-confidence and the way that she did things. I can't ever remember being aware of the whole colour thing with that particular family. I mean, they're very, very London, quite Cockney sort of . . . you know, it's much more to do with London, it sort of feels like now than it did to be a total cultural difference. And it could have been that I was aware of the colour thing, of course it could, but no, it wasn't like that.
>
> (Interview 22)

Sally presented the differences that excited her in Joy as being nothing to do with 'race'. Yet at the same time, she mentioned characteristics such as energy ('pace of life') and spirit (self-confidence) that are often attributed to (and desired in) the racial other (hooks 1992; Dyer 1997). Part of the difference that Joy offered to Sally was not just racialised but also classed. Through her influence, she decided to go back to studying. Through Joy she met a group of people who were involved in alternative squatter and anarchist culture in London and who had very different class positions from Sally's own and the friends she had had before. Sally contrasted her working-class background and its 'narrowness' with that of her middle-class friends. She constructed a discourse of 'coming home', naturalising the shifts she has undergone in her life along the line of having been a square peg in a round hole:

> It's like a real coming home feeling, that all of that narrowness just doesn't make sense. And actually to be very open to learning new things all the time and having different experience, I suppose, and not being shut off to things that are really important. So, after a while, yeah, it was a real . . . it felt really like the right place for me to be.
>
> (Interview 22)

These different performances of class or a different position felt for Sally as though she had achieved naturalness or found her inner core. For Butler, the nature of the performative is that it produces feelings of naturalness: 'I argued that gender is performative, by which I meant that no gender is "expressed" by actions, gestures, or speech, but that the performance of gender produces retroactively the illusion that there is an inner gender core. That is, the performance of gender retroactively produces the effect of some true or abiding feminine essence or disposition, so that one cannot use an expressive model for thinking about gender' (Butler 1997a: 144). What is interesting in Sally's narrative is that she needed to account for how she achieved this feeling of her inner core only once she had undergone a transformation. This sense of rupture led her to articulate her subject position in a narrative that was framed around tropes of sameness and difference. Through exposure to difference, of both class and 'race', she had found a 'home', a place where she could at least approximate sameness. This enabled her to mark her differences from her family, in both who she was and what she did. She was 'doing' motherhood differently from her mother and womanhood, whiteness and middle classness differently from her sisters. One of the means by which this rupture and transformation was achieved was through the trope of the transforming encounter with the other. As a result of these encounters, Sally felt that she now occupied a position where she felt comfortable with herself and her whiteness (and the 'non-whiteness' of her children whose father is black). Her account ended with a presentation of a subject who had found completeness and 'home':

> I have a lot of friends who are from completely different ethnic backgrounds to me. A lot of black friends who . . . and obviously once you start being open to people on a much more human level and get to know people . . . and then obviously my children aren't white anyway. I think I came from not knowing anything and being very sheltered to then, meeting friends and things. So I suppose I feel quite comfortable with where I am as a white person really.
>
> (Interview 22)

Sally is an example of someone who has a clear narrative of the self. She set out this narrative chronologically and established its different geographic, social and political contexts. Her story had a cast of characters whose importance to herself and her development were made clear. Sally clearly enjoyed this narrative mode, was an accomplished story-teller and felt comfortable talking about her life with me. The account is interesting not only because it demonstrates how the story of a self can be told, but also because of the way in which the account is gendered, classed and racialised. Part of the story that Sally wanted to tell was about how she had come to feel 'comfortable' with her whiteness and how she had responded to classed positioning and experiences. She talked less directly about gender. Nonetheless, it is clear that many of the events she was describing – for instance leaving college to have a baby and single motherhood – were gendered in significant ways. It is also interesting how 'race' provided a signifier of change in Sally's narrative. She accounted for her changing subjectivity and altered subject position through encounters with others. Therefore, in various ways, Sally's interviews provide rich material for examining how individuals may narrativise the self and how these narratives can be classed, gendered and racialised.

However, Sally's account was not typical of the interviews I undertook. Many of the interviewees, I would argue for various reasons, did not provide a narrative of the self in such a straightforward manner as Sally. In different ways, other women did not have a story to tell. Marie-François Chanfrault-Duchet points out that what she describes as 'real' narratives are rarely produced. This is partly due to interviewers refusing to give up control of the situation and allowing the narrator's account free flow. But Chanfrault-Duchet also notes that 'some interviewees may be unable to present herself (himself) as the subject and hero of a narrative aiming to communicate an experience laden with signification' (Chanfrault-Duchet 1991: fn. 8).[7] What does it mean that a person is unable to present him- or herself as the subject of a narrative? Clearly, this is not to say that individuals do not have a subjectivity or even necessarily that they lack a position from which to speak. In the following three examples, I suggest different reasons why narratives were not produced in some interviews. In the first, the case of Madeleine, I suggest that she found it difficult to occupy a single subject position that is required, however momentarily, in order to present a coherent self. In the second, Deborah, I argue that she had constructed herself as a subject who was so normative that there was little sense in presenting, in the words of Chanfrault-Duchet, 'an experience laden with signification'. Finally, Rosemary appeared to be unable to construct herself as the active subject of a narrative.

Where there is no story

Madeleine: 'Where do I fit in?'

Madeleine appeared on the face of it to be very similar to Sally. She was of a similar age, living relatively close to Sally and was also a single mother of a mixed-race child. She was relaxed and articulate in the two extensive interviews she gave me and seemed happy to talk. Yet, the way she talked about her life was very different. Most notably, her account lacked the narrative thrust of Sally's account. Whereas Sally produced a story that told of her progressive development from one subject position to another, Madeleine did not have such a coherent story to tell. When I asked her what had been the significant turning points in her life, while she was able to name some, they did not make much sense to her in terms of providing a narrative:

> The key turning points in my life? [laughing], ah, right. Um key turning points? Well, having a child is probably the biggest thing that's ever happened to me and has changed my life really radically . . . and since I've had her, I don't think there were necessarily any key things since I've had

her, just endless crises one after another [laugh]. I think probably when I was eleven and I went to public school which was different from everybody I knew, that has probably changed the course of my life slightly.

(Interview 44)

The lack of a clear narrative is underlined by the fact that Madeleine did not provide an account that followed a chronological order. This is not to suggest, however, that Madeleine was in some sense inarticulate or confused, but that she did not view her own life experience in a way that enabled the production of a narrative in this way. One way to understand this is to examine Madeleine's relationship to or experience of normative discourses. At one level, Madeleine's various positionings as white, middle class and heterosexual would seem to suggest privilege and recognition within normative discourses. Yet she did not feel that she could fit straightforwardly or easily into those positions. In her childhood, whiteness was a largely unquestioned norm, although the presence of others was acknowledged:

I mean when I grew up in a suburb in London, I didn't know anybody black at all and maybe there were a few Asian families, but there *certainly* weren't any Caribbean families kind of thing. So it was something I grew up, I didn't grow up around people of other colours. That was when I was living in *England* of course. So, but you know, my mum was always, she talked to me about race so it was always 'we will be terribly *nice* when we *meet* people of different colours' [laugh].

(Interview 9, emphasis Madeleine's)

Her mother's attitude clearly fitted into a liberal discourse of tolerance, which retains white as the norm, and subject, which is defined by its tolerance and kindness to 'others', who are distinguished in gradations of otherness: 'there *certainly* weren't any Caribbean families'. Later in life, Madeleine had come to reflect on this position, particularly prompted by a relationship with a West Indian boyfriend who had pointed out some of the ways in which her position was marked by whiteness, and therefore had a problematic relationship to blackness:

I had a boyfriend for a while who was Jamaican who lived with us for, oh, a year or so. And . . . he was very . . . active on all sorts of race issues [. . .] And he would point out to me . . . I think I really learnt from him that it's not about, . . . that you just have to listen to what other people, you might not think you're being racist, you might not think you have an attitude, but you really have to actually sit down and listen to what somebody says to you. If somebody comes to you and says 'look you're making me feel in a particular way because of this' that you're not even aware of or 'I can't sit down and watch that film with you because it makes me really uncomfortable because there are no black people in it at all and you aren't aware of that. And that isn't an issue for you yet it's a really big issue for me'. . . So that was quite, um, I don't know, I'd never thought of myself as a racist person, I'd always thought of myself as someone who was very open. And I think being with him I had to accept that just the way I'd been brought up and my culture there were things that I did that were actually very racist, without me intending them to be.

(Interview 9)

As a result, Madeleine was now much more aware of how the social world in which she operates was racialised – even to the extent that it had become something of an issue (although not very significant) with her current partner: 'a white bloke who's from the home counties and he thinks I'm really over the top about it [race]'. This was not always an easy awareness to have. Madeleine echoed Minnie Bruce Pratt, who (as discussed in Chapter 2) writes of the 'amount of effort it takes me to walk these few blocks being conscious as I can of myself in relation to history, to race, to culture, to gender' (Pratt 1984: 13):

. . . I don't know, I suppose I'm more sensitive about it. I suppose because I've *had* to look at all those issues in such minute detail. I'm really aware that I might be being racist without intending to [laugh]. It's made me really un-relaxed about the whole thing [laugh]. Yeah um . . . I think that's definitely it, because I've had to . . . because it's been such an issue, I'm very very aware of it now and I wouldn't have been so aware of it before, I'd have been more relaxed about it.

(Interview 9)

This sensitisation towards her own racialised positioning did not perhaps fit so readily into a transformative story as Sally's account of classed transformation. Stories of 'becoming aware of one's whiteness' are not (yet?) so established as those of moving from a working-class to middle-class position (see Lawler 2002). In terms of class, Madeleine had the experience of confounding expectations, those of her parents and perhaps her own. She described herself, and particularly some of the attitudes she has passed on to her daughter, as middle class:

I always think that the thing that makes me middle class is the fact that, one, I had a good education, and two, I have that kind of belief that I might be poor at the moment, I won't always be poor, because I'm clever, because I can, because I never think: 'I can't take that opportunity because that's not meant for me'. You know, anything is open to me . . . and I don't know whether that's necessarily . . . kind of a classic middle-class attitude, but I think that's probably something that, that's what she gets from me. That's the kind of class thing that she gets from me . . .. Not that she's got to break out of something, but that she deserves something that is hers to take . . .

(Interview 9)

So, middle classness for Madeleine, apart from education, meant a state of mind where you are an active agent who is capable and confident of your abilities. All choices and opportunities are, and should be, available to you. Yet at the same time, Madeleine had transgressed class norms by, perhaps inadvertently, closing off choices and opportunities. She had decided at the last minute not to take up a place at university and went to live in a squat with her boyfriend. She had had a child as a single mother and, as such, found herself placed in a politically problematised social category:

> There's definitely been times when it's been a problem and there's been times when I haven't necessarily wanted to volunteer that information. Which was really in the last 3 or 4 years of the Tories being in. And there was kind of Peter Lilley and Michael Portillo and everything is single mothers' fault [laugh]. And it's quite amazing in retrospect how much that affects your self esteem and how you value yourself. If the whole of society is just saying, you're useless.

(Interview 44)

Madeleine was now trying to understand just how and why she had transgressed class norms and now found herself in a position where she lacked not only the material resources that were required to perform middle classness, but also the sense of agency and, in particular, control of the future that she saw in her friends:

> And I do wonder now actually . . . now that my, now that I'm kind of in my 30s and my friends are, some of them obviously, not all of them, but some of them have now bought flats and are in stable relationships and you know. I mean very few of my friends have *had* children. But you know that when they do, they'll make a decision to do it and they'll have it with the partner that they've had for a long time, and I just think, what happened to me then? [laugh] what is it about my, I don't know, I just don't really understand when I look back, why I didn't have that. You know there's meant to be that thing, isn't there about how middle-class people are supposed to have, they're into long-term planning, they put money away for a rainy day and they make decisions based on long-term things. And I just think that I've never had that and I just think that it's so ridiculous. And yet I've really shaped, you know, my life now is quite tough because of that. And um, I don't know, I don't know anybody else that I kind of went to school with, or I grew up with or that I've been friends with for a long time that's kind of taken the same path as I have, at all [laugh]. In fact, I hardly know *anybody*, I mean, obviously

there's all the other mums at Yasmin's school, you know many of whom are very young, single parents, um, and I have *nothing* in common with them at all.

(Interview 44)

Madeleine did not interpret this altered class position, as Sally did, as an 'escape' from narrowness or a transformation of the self. Instead, Madeleine expressed a sense of regret at the way her life had developed. She was experiencing the loss of status and security involved in falling outside dominant class and gender norms. The discourse that Madeleine used to describe this position was that of 'sensibleness'. She repeatedly described the lives of others as 'sensible', clearly implying that her life and particularly the choices she had made were, at least in the eyes of her parents and others around them, not sensible. She contrasted her position with that of her brothers, affirming and then denying the importance of being 'sensible' and 'successful':

And he was never the bright one, I was always the really bright one [laugh]. But he was the one who kind of made sensible decisions. Oh, no, no, no, that's not true, he's the one who's had making lots of money as his priority, so he has had the successful lifestyle now.

(Interview 44)

The gendered aspect to being 'sensible' was also underlined by her joke about her mother regretting sending her into 'temptation', where boys were present. She was explaining why she had been sent to a public school:

My mum and dad really wanted me to go to a co-educational school, and there wasn't one in our area. Although, you know, we were living in the countryside, so there were good schools, it was absolutely fine, they were just good girls' schools. So that was the main reason behind it [laugh]. I think my mum regretted that ever since, sending me where there might be boys [laugh].

(Interview 44)

Madeleine's relative lack of narrative did not come from an absence of events in her life that were significant to her. But the turning points in life served as points of disjuncture which disrupted a sense of coherence in self, rather than pegs on which to hang a story. She appeared set on one course, then jumped to another. She has experienced living outside normative discourses, but did not have a narrative of 'I was always different', as Sally had. In a situation where she had an ambiguous relationship to the nature of her subject position, it was difficult for Madeleine to present her self in a storied narrative. I do not wish to present Madeleine as a confused, incoherent or somehow dysfunctional individual. This would be a total misrepresentation. She had a busy life in which she 'juggled' bringing up her daughter and working as a self-employed researcher. She was also comfortable and easy with herself in many situations. Madeleine suggested that she was comfortable moving round different locations in London; however, she also explained that she was less easy in social situations where she felt that she was being categorised, by either class or 'race':

Madeleine: ... I think actually it's one of the things that I'm not particularly good at and I'd like to be better at. I'm not necessarily as outgoing as I'd like to be in ... I'm absolutely fine talking one-to-one with people. But if there's a group situation and I feel somebody's making, being a certain way with me, or whatever. And I'd like to be, just you know ... go and chat and sort things out or whatever.

BB: A social situation?

Madeleine: 'Um [affirmative] ... and I'm much more likely to not do anything and clam up or close up and probably people think, oh she's just looking down her nose at us or whatever, you know.

(Interview 9)

She had at times felt a similar discomfort at being positioned as a mother:

Madeleine: I don't know if I ever really saw myself as a mum, really to be honest. I didn't enjoy it very much when she was little. I was quite young, ... it wasn't something I'd decided I wanted to do ... um ... and I found it very hard to identify with other mums [laugh] ... yeah, yeah ... and I found it very hard to kind of relax about it and ...

BB: Be as a mum in those places?

Madeleine: yeah ...

(Interview 9)

So Madeleine's account has shown some of the ways in which processes of subjection are seldom clear cut. Individuals can be pulled in different directions and can feel a lack of fit with the way they are being positioned and available discursive resources. This affects the ways in which they can narrate their selves and understand their own lives. In a similar way, Sara Ahmed writes of 'the impossibility of adequately naming myself for the demands of representation is symptomatic of the impossibility of the racially marked and gendered subject being addressed through a singular name' (Ahmed 1997: 155). Madeleine's account suggests how this can also be true for those positioned as white.

Deborah: a natural progression

Madeleine seemed to lack a narrative flow in her interview because it was difficult for her to accommodate her sense of self into one story. In contrast, it appeared that others did not produce a narrative because they presented such coherent unified selves that there was no real story to tell. One example of this was Deborah, a middle-class journalist and writer living in Clapham. For her, the question of turning points did not strike a chord because, as she said: 'It's difficult to say what's just a natural progression and what's a turning point'. The version of her life and self that she presented to me in the interview is one of inevitability and predictability. The events she mentioned tend to focus on her working life, and the choices she makes are presented as natural within their particular context. Her wholly normative position may only be possible to maintain by remaining silent on other aspects of her life. To some extent, the interview resembles a curriculum vitae, charting progress from college to work. This is signalled in the first thing that comes to mind when I asked a question about turning points:

BB: So, one way I have started it off with other people is to say, other
           than perhaps becoming a parent, what are kind of key turning
           points in your life?
Deborah: It's really difficult to say. I guess, going right back would be col-
           lege, because that was just a difference.
BB: And that involved leaving home?
Deborah: Yeah [questioning], but I mean I went to college in London, and
           I lived in London so it didn't really feel very much like that. I did
           leave home; I think its more, I don't know, just the independ-
           ence of the way you're taught and the way you're treated I guess
           is completely different. I guess, that was my turning point. And
           also learning so much more about a particular thing . . . oooh,
           what else?'

(Interview 40)

From the outset, Deborah was clearly defining the life and the self that she was going to talk about. 'Going right back' means that she was marking the beginning as being adulthood – going to college, reaching independence and being treated with more respect. Her childhood was marked as off limits, or not significant. Previous events that might have been given importance in other people's accounts – such as the periods spent living abroad in her child-hood, her parents' divorce when she was 13, her father subsequently leaving the country – are not part of the picture of herself that she was presenting. By marking this separation between the child and the adult, there was no narrative produced that might lead to an explanation of how she came to be the person she was. Her subjecthood was presented as an unquestioned thing that just was, rather than something that requires a story to explain it.

Deborah: Maybe I think maybe going freelance and buying my flat were
           probably turning points. Buying my flat was a big turning point,

but it depends what you mean by turning points. Because, did it change things? No it didn't. But it was a significant event.

BB: It didn't change things in? It didn't change your sense of yourself or . . .?

Deborah: Not really because I don't think. *I think I'd always I expected to be . . . I'd never been anything other than independent, . . .* I think turning points for me would have been being restricted. Rather than those things happening. I don't mean by that that I took it for granted, I mean it was all very exciting and I was very pleased about it and I was worried about the mortgage all that kind of thing. But it wasn't the sort of be all and end all, I didn't think that 'when I am such and such an age I will have a mortgage, I will be doing this and this' and 'then I am going to get married' and all that kind of thing. Because I never ever felt like that about it, *I just wanted to do you know, what I wanted to do really*, and get a lot out of what I wanted to do, that was an ambition for me. So yeah, it was exciting but I wouldn't necessarily say that it changed my sense of myself.

(Interview 40, emphasis added)

For Deborah, her subjectivity was something that she considered to be autonomous from outside forces, her desires were not shaped or produced, they just were: 'I just wanted to do what I wanted to do'. This contained circle of desire and action was also supported by the belief that she had, by and large, achieved what she had wanted to do. Later in the interview, there was again the suggestion that life for Deborah began at adulthood. She began by saying 'I'm sort of in touch with most of the people I have met during various parts of my life really'. This again emphasised her sense of coherence and completeness. But when I asked if this included school friends, she realised that she was not thinking of them:

No. I don't see anybody from school. I suppose I just think of my life as starting when I went to college really, maybe it's I'd rather forget school. I think perhaps people are like that. I guess I didn't have much in common with the others I went to school with. I mean we all got on fine at sixth form, but she lived near me and she still lives where my mother used to live, and I sort of hear of what she's doing.

(Interview 40)

Here, we see that Deborah's sense of self as totally whole and coherent was constructed on some omissions and forgetting. It is not clear what Deborah would rather forget and, in the interview, I took the cue not to ask more about it. Some of what she was suggesting, though, was the wish to move away from particular classed and gendered ways of being. In Deborah's account, the school treated its pupils as gendered subjects who should not have high ambitions:

> Careers advice was just hilarious, it was 'you can be a nurse' (there was no 'you can be a doctor or a surgeon'), 'you can be a nurse or a secretary' – and then if you asked about something, like, 'well I want to be a brain surgeon or something', 'oh dear, well you'll have to come back in a week when we've got the information'. I mean they were very helpful but they didn't really set their sights very high for girls.

But fellow pupils also demonstrated by example the perils of other forms of gendered and class behaviour, such as early pregnancy, which she wished to avoid: 'we'd see a lot of the girls who'd left after O levels, walking around with, in some cases babies and things it was frightening. I mean we found it frightening'. This is also tied into locality. Moving away from the area signifies leaving certain gendered and classed positions behind. In a similar way to Sally, Deborah characterised what she has left behind as narrow and restricted and again emphasised her independence and freedom.

Apart from these suggestions from her school days, Deborah presented few struggles over her gendered, class or raced identity. She had worked in a profession where the majority of her colleagues were women and where there was a good atmosphere as a woman. Nor did her relationship with her partner represent a possible 'turning point' (this is at least partly maintained by keeping a strict separation in her account between the public and the personal or emotional):

> But, yes turning points? I mean, even when I decided, well we decided to get married it was kind of a logical step really, and I didn't change my name I still haven't changed my name, because it wasn't part and parcel of being me. You know, I didn't, I never thought of being married as anything terribly significant as far as the world was concerned, I mean obviously from an emotional point of view yes, as far as I was concerned but it didn't change my status or make me feel any different. I mean maybe if I had changed my name – maybe that's why I didn't change my name because I didn't want it to change my sense of me. Because I got married when I was 33, so maybe if I'd done it earlier when I was in my 20s I would have changed my name or something, but it was never really a big deal.
>
> (Interview 40)

Deborah did not present her subjectivity as racialised. This did not mean that she did not see herself as white, but that she saw her self occupying a normative position that did not need to be described, elaborated or questioned. In the following extract, I was asking about her experience of working in an office. She had explained how the working environment was good for women.

BB: Was it mainly a white environment or . . .?

Deborah: Um, . . . Yes, it was, but then you get all these other factors because everyone knows that its more difficult, . . . because . . . racial inequality is so rife, for people to you know, it starts off with education, home life and all that kind of thing, maybe for say, a black man, to get into that area – that would be difficult, . . . and for a black woman even more difficult. And quite difficult for anyone, I suppose, to end up working on a magazine, not that many people do it, when you think of the population as whole, when you think about people who work in shops or banks, you know just sheer numbers and it probably all goes back to education. So it's not surprising when you work your way back, to realise that, no it was a mainly white environment . . .'

BB: Do you think you were conscious of that at the time or . . .?

Deborah: I don't think I was conscious of it, . . . I mean was *conscious* of it, I don't think I thought it remarkable, because there weren't that many, as I said before. We had a lot of contact with other people you know, when I worked on teenage magazines, with musicians and models and people like that, and actors and everything and yeah and those walks of life. They've all got their own kind of issues about race and everything. So there was a lot of contact with a lot of people but as far as the day-to-day office was concerned . . . I am just trying to think of people . . . it was mainly white.

(Interview 40, emphasis Deborah's)

While Deborah appeared a little defensive about the whiteness of her former workplace, she was clear that discrimination was located at other points in the system – for example in education, and possibly in the 'home life' of those who suffer inequality. There were not 'issues' of 'race' for her at work because it was a white environment. However, again, we get a sense of gradation within the normative. Deborah explained that she also had 'contact' with 'other people' from more marginal or bohemian 'walks of life', such as musicians, models and actors. For Deborah, racial identity and, in particular, whiteness was something that one only really becomes conscious of in the presence of non-white others. This did not mean that Deborah is never conscious of being white. The following extract shows that whiteness was something that she sometimes feels guilty about. But there was also the suggestion that she feels threatened by the resentment of others:

I'm conscious that I am in a privileged position. You know, that I've got advantages before I even do anything. Just from the colour of my skin and the way I speak. Um, I start off at an advantage, so I'm conscious of that. And it does make me uncomfortable sometimes. Very uncomfortable. Because I wonder if it's resented and I'm sure it must be. I'm sure I would resent it if I were in a different position. Very much.

(Interview 17)

For Deborah, normative discourses offered her a subject position which she inhabited with comparative ease. Her experiences of being positioned as a white middle-class woman had confirmed her sense of her self as a normal and coherent person with agency. Her sense of self was heightened by the sense that she was in a privileged position, in that she worked in a professional and specialised field and had an uncomplicated sense of being white and belonging in England (this will be discussed further in Chapter 7). Some of this privilege was lost on becoming a mother. Deborah found that she was unable to continue to work in exactly the same field because of her responsibility for her son: 'it was quite difficult to let go because I built up quite a lot of contacts and lot of work'. Yet she was able to continue working in a different field, and it did not seem to affect her sense of herself as a subject with agency.

Rosemary: 'going with the flow'

In contrast to Deborah, Rosemary, a white working-class woman with four children who lived in Camberwell, presented herself as someone with very little agency. She had lived in the same area all her life and the same block of council flats since she was a young child. Rosemary had an extremely close relationship with her mother who lived in the same block of flats and who provided childcare for Rosemary every day. It is striking how, over the course of two interviews, Rosemary did not provide any narrative of her self.[8]

BB: So I was wondering if I could ask you a bit about, we talked a bit about being a parent, and I was wondering if I could ask you a bit about life before being a parent, your life?
Rosemary: It was years ago! What before I had the children?
BB: Yes, like one thing I ask is what would you say were the key turning points or crucial events in your life?
Rosemary: My children [laugh]. They're my life. But I didn't go out to having four. And I didn't really think: 'oh I want children now', before having children. It weren't like, 'oh I'm 24, or 23, I want a child now'. It just sort of happened.

(Interview 32)

Other questions met a similar response and there was a continual pull to the present:

BB: And like being a mother, does it make you look back at your childhood and remember it more clearly or in different ways?
Rosemary: It don't really make me remember it. It might, like if we're doing something and I think 'oh I done that when I was a child'. It might remind me of things that I do with them that I did as a child. Or like we might be walking somewhere and I go 'oh, I

used to come down here when I was a kid'. But it's only through
them that I'm remembering.

BB: Because they're doing it?

Rosemary: Yeah, and I think, 'oh I done that'. And I suppose more so that
you've got children that you do remember that. Because if you
didn't, then you probably wouldn't remember back to when you
was a kid, and that's you know.

BB: And you try and do things the same or different according to
how you?

Rosemary: Um, mind you, I had a nice childhood. Like I say, my mum tried
to do everything, I mean I was an only one.

BB: Oh were you?

Rosemary: Yes. And she tried to do [interrupted by children] what was I
saying?

BB: Your childhood, you were saying you enjoyed it?

Rosemary: Yeah, my mum tried to do everything for me and I try and do
everything for them. If they want something, you know I'll try
and get it for them. I'll work for it, or I might say: 'well, that's
how it goes, you can't get'. But it's all for them that I do everything. And I don't think they understand that sometimes. I mean
I see them happy, well-dressed and that and it makes me happy.
(Interview 14)

It is difficult to get a sense of Rosemary's subjectivity. She presented it as
totally subsumed within being a mother and she stressed how she was the
same as her mother – 'my mum tried to do everything for me and I try and
do everything for them' (although, as we shall see later in this chapter, she
also presents them as having very different styles of mothering). Children
were her 'life' and her only happiness was seeing them happy. Rosemary
seemed unable to make her life the subject of a narrative. Rosemary did not
lack the art of telling a good story. She told stories about her children and
was interested in exploring their different personalities. But it is interesting
that she does not suggest *why* they might behave in the ways they do, or why
they are as they are. Rather, the characteristics she described were essential
to each of them.

But, our Michele, is like so quiet and, well, not indoors, but at school.
At first I had a real problem with her – crying every day and not wanting
to go, used to be in class saying 'what time is it, what's the time, what
time is it', you know, to the teachers. And throwing up outside the class.
When we went to school the other morning we walked out and as we
walked out she burst out crying. So, I'm, we've got to find a school that
she feels comfortable with
[. . .]
This one [referring to another daughter who sat in on the interview]

she pleases everyone – loves adults and loves children. Will look after a little baby, except her own sisters, and loves adults. Or anyone younger than her, she'll mummy them, or smaller. Put her arm round them. And very nosy! [directed to daughter, jokingly].

(Interview 14)

Rosemary also had recourse to other narratives – such as the way in which her local area had changed (for the worse) over her lifetime.

How it's getting lately I'd like to move out . . .. It's just there's a load more crime and that going on round here. You just can't walk out. It's frightening to walk down the streets at night. So many people hanging about.

(Interview 14)

Rosemary was also interested in presenting a particular portrayal of herself, that of the good mother who has her children at the centre of her life – she stressed that she worked only to be able to buy her children more things, that she never left them with anyone other than her mother, she kept them with her at all times – and joked that she would probably carry on doing so until they were forty. The following extract shows how part of this representation of the good mother included the need 'to be friendly to everybody':

BB: So you basically said that things like class and race, they don't come up as issues, you don't talk about them with the kids much?

Rosemary: No we don't, we just go from day to day really. And if they come across anything, they might mention something, but not really. No we don't talk about that. I mean class, personally, we're the same as everyone, you know. You either like us or you don't. But we get on with everyone, there's not any people that we say 'oh no, we don't get on with them, no they're too posh, no they're this colour, that colour'. I don't say to them, 'oh no, you mustn't . . .'. It's them, they're growing up, they need to be friendly with everybody. That's what I like to see from them. I don't like them bullying.

(Interview 14)

Despite this, one gets the sense that Rosemary had a relatively strong attachment to differences of 'race' and class, but simply believed that her children should not bully. Her account of the changes in the area she lived in was certainly racialised. Rosemary told me (off tape) not only that she felt the area had changed with the influx over her life of black people, but that she did not like 'Africans', who she found to be rude.[9]

Despite having a clear sense of her self as white and English, Rosemary did not (cannot?) produce a narrative of her life in which she gave herself the role of the central subject. In contrast to Deborah, Rosemary presented herself as largely without agency – she is someone who simply 'goes with the flow'. This discourse has an echo of Sally's account of her former self as 'one of those little wish things that just blows through life'. She did not present herself as making active decisions. Just as the children 'just sort of happened', so leaving school was not a particularly significant event in her life and she found herself in a particular job by accident:

BB: So, like, getting a job, was that a big event?

Rosemary: No, not really, it was sort of I was at school and I didn't know what I wanted to do. I used to be into cameras, like I wanted to probably do photography [interrupted by baby].

BB: You were talking about how it wasn't a big . . .?

Rosemary: Yeah, so I was looking for a job. And I wanted to do photography, but I weren't really bothered. It was just like go with the flow sort of thing. And a few of them went into the insurance company. And they said 'why don't you try for the company?'.

BB: These were friends at school?

Rosemary: Yeah, and I said 'all right then'. But I loved it. I applied for it, went for an interview and they sent back and said I'd got in. But they was all young at the company. It was just like going to school again, doing your work, they was all the same age, they was all 16, except the managers of course, but we was all the same age – must have been about 18 of us – all the starting at the same age, well, roughly, over a couple of months, starting at the same time.

(Interview 32)

Rosemary also described herself as taking a passive role in finding a partner. A friend organised a blind date for Rosemary and she went along with it, eventually going out with and then marrying the man selected for her:

Rosemary: And then one year he said 'do you want to get engaged'. And I wasn't really, I was really like going along with the flow, and I said 'well', and I was still young. He was 6 years older than me. So I think he must have thought time was getting on [laugh].

BB: How old were you when you got married?

Rosemary: I was 21 I think, 21 and he was 6 years older than me, 26, 27. It was about a year or so after that. I just went with the flow, 'oh all right then, we'll get married after that'. But I could've easily just left it as it was, you know, I weren't into rushing into getting married.

(Interview 32)

Not only did Rosemary lack agency in this narrative, but other agents were left undefined. The major force in some of her accounts was unspecified and represented only by 'they'. This imparts a sense of powerlessness. In the following extract, Rosemary vividly presented a life that was not in control, which provided a contrast with those of Deborah and also Sally. Rosemary did not just lack the freedom to do what she wanted, she lacked the material means to control her physical environment:

> But there does seem more crime round here. I mean what they're doing round here, I mean they're putting cameras up round. I mean it's a good thing but why are they having to put cameras in?
> [. . .]
> And they moved quite a few of them in here. And the last place I was living, they moved a child molester in. You know, and like the tenants found out about this and ended up burning him out and burning his car out. And that's only just across the road from here. I mean, I was nothing to do with it. It weren't till they had like the car going up in flames and the fire engines arrive, but I didn't know anything about it. But it's frightening, you don't know what's going on out there.
>
> (Interview 14)

Rosemary's life had not been uneventful. She had grown up, left school, found a partner, married him, had children, left work (she was made redundant 'but I didn't blame them'), established her children in schools, taken up part-time work, etc. But these events did not provide the hooks for Rosemary to produce a narrative of her life. Rosemary did not feel that she had much power and agency over her life, nor had she changed – except in the way she has mothered. The events in her life had followed a pattern of inevitability that, she felt, left little to tell. There were few highs and lows. In the account of her life in the interview, only one event was described in terms of her feelings, but here too it was one over which she had little control: Rosemary described her first pregnancy:

> But I had a lot of problems with the pregnancy, [. . .] So, I went through a lot with her, it was really emotional. But that was from about 20 weeks of pregnancy. That was an emotional time. When she was born, that was emotional, because she had to have an operation done. But it's all gone well, touch wood, since then.
>
> (Interview 32)

Here, we get a sense of emotional trauma, but little sense of how it affected Rosemary's sense of herself, except perhaps an understanding of the worry and vulnerability of being a mother: 'it's all gone well, touch wood, since then'. Indeed, in the earlier interview, Rosemary had said that the way in which she had changed on becoming a mother was to become 'more of a worrier. I was never a worrier before I had them [laugh]' (Interview 14). When Rosemary compared herself with her own mother, there was, for the first and practically only time, a sense of the past and of Rosemary as an active subject. She presented a picture of herself as a child as a strong person, independent and even feisty and fearless. This is, in many senses, the impression that Rosemary continued to give me when I interviewed her, although it is not the way she spoke about herself.

Rosemary: Yeah, I mean at the age of eight, I was on the bus to the shopping centre, I was. I was so, do you know what I mean, I was really street road worthy. I mean from the age of four, I don't know if I told you that on the last one, I walked from the park on me own. Because my mum thought I was mucking about. I said 'I'm going down Tracey's'. She said 'all right then'. Because me cousin, we was all up the park. She just thought I was mucking about. And I'm trolling down the park and these street markets. And that was what, I weren't even five then, I was crossing major roads and everything. I remember doing it.

BB: But you wouldn't let yours do it?

Rosemary: No!

BB: Are there other kind of differences about the lives that they lead and the life that you led as a kid?

Rosemary: Yeah, really I suppose. More that I was more outgoing, I was, my mum was forever standing outside crying her eyeballs out [laugh] 'cos I was always out with my friends. She was out crying. But there wasn't that fear that there is now, you know, of being abducted and letting your kids out. But it's not only . . . it's the roads and that. I mean even with me crossing the road. I'm out crossing in front of one car and there's another one taking over. And with kids, if a car stops, they'll run. You know, but there's another car behind it taking over. And if they'd run, when I walked, they'd be up in the air. When I think of that . . . But they're as good as gold really. It's not *them*, it's the people out there. I mean I'd let them play outside downstairs. It's the people out there.

(Interview 32, emphasis Rosemary's)

The interviews with Rosemary left me with a sense of a gap or an untold story. It was difficult to get a sense of her subjectivity. Here was a cheerful, friendly and active woman who gave no sense of who she was or how she had come to be in the course of these conversations. This is not to suggest that Rosemary lacked a sense of self. But it may be that, through her strong identifications with others, particularly her mother and children, the interview and narrative form did not offer her the means to account for her self. She simply was as she did and there was little more for her to tell. Rosemary did not account for her subjectivity through a reflexive narrative. Rather, she felt and understood her self through her actions and particularly her mothering. In some sense, her interviews do provide the sense of a narrative. It is contained in the transformation from (the particularly evocative) 'street road worthy' 4-year-old child 'trolling' around the streets to the mother who is concerned above all to protect her children and keep them away from 'people outside'.

Conclusion

This chapter has been concerned with how the interviewees did, or did not, tell the story of their lives. I have argued that the process of producing a narrative of the self can involve a route into understanding processes of subjection. Telling a narrative about one's life involves making oneself the subject of the story, claiming both intelligibility and agency for oneself. It often involved taking a particular approach to the self, as experiencing transformation and change. Through examining these accounts of subjection, it is also possible to analyse how subjects are constructed through raced, gendered and classed discourses.

The first interviewee discussed in this chapter, Sally, demonstrated how narratives can enact processes of subjection. Sally produced her self as the subject of a coherent narrative. Gender, 'race' and class were clearly important in this account. Sally presented herself in processes of being 'girled' and/or 'womaned'. Through this account, we saw her struggling to change her class position and subjectivity. This transformation was framed within a story of how she naturally did not fit within that position. Within this narrative, Sally was not only 'raced', but also 'race' came to signify her difference from others. Through her friend, who was not white, and who had introduced her to new ways of thinking about 'race' and herself, Sally said that her life had been transformed. As a result, she said that she had found a new way of being.

While Sally's account provides a dramatic example of how narratives can illustrate processes of subject construction and subjection, the other three narratives show in different ways how this is not always the case. Some selves are not readily reproduced through narrative. The idea of 'turning points' within a life does not always prompt a narrative account of a life. Madeleine had significant events in her life, but she was not able to use them to construct a coherent story of the self. This was partially because she occupied too many (classed, raced and gendered) positions to give a sense of wholeness and coherence to her self. The event provided points of disruption to her narrative rather than giving direction and meaning to an unfolding story. 'Race' proved to be one of these disruptions. In the face of challenges to her whiteness – from a boyfriend – she was forced to look back on her former selves in a different light and recognise their limited perspectives and how they were framed by both 'race' and class. Both Madeleine's and Sally's accounts reveal the importance of others in the construction of a sense of self, the influence of contrasting or alternative discourses and perspectives in forming your subjectivity.

In contrast to Madeleine, Deborah did not have a story of her developing self because she constructed her experience as so normative that there was not really a story to tell. Her sense of self was built on suppressing notions of change or difference within her own life. Deborah presented herself as a subject with agency and subjectivity, but was not willing to explore ruptures or contradictions within this. Therefore, the narrative form had little to offer her as a genre for communicating her subjectivity. Finally, Rosemary lacked the sense of agency required to see any interest in telling a story of her self. Her subjectivity was framed by doing, not telling. Therefore, she was not interested in looking to the past or exploring her sense of self.

These different accounts and their different use or non-use of the narrative form have illustrated some of the complexities involved in understanding and analysing subjectivities and the self. While the renditions of self can only ever be partial, I would argue that the analysis has shown how even the personal and individual processes of understanding the self are formed within racialised, classed and gendered discourses. The next chapter turns more directly to examination of racialised discourses by exploring the question of how race was talked about by the interviewees.

5   Seeing, talking, living 'race'

Introduction

'Race' is a sensitive issue for white people to talk about. It is a modern taboo. When I started the pilot interviews for this research, I soon discovered the urgent need for a good external microphone. The microphone on the tape recorder would pick up much of what was said in the interviews, but often the introduction of the subject of 'race' would cause a sudden drop in volume and what the interviewee said would be lost. This was not something that I noticed at the time, but it became frustratingly clear when I played back the tape afterwards. Dropping one's voice when speaking suggests that the conversation has touched on a sensitive topic, a subject that has to be dealt with carefully and where one would not want to be misunderstood or overheard. It also creates a conspiratorial atmosphere and suggests a relationship of trust in which confidences can be shared. Dropping one's voice when talking about 'race' indicates the sensitivity of the subject. White people (apart from those espousing extreme racist positions) are generally anxious not to be seen as racist – hence the clichéd coupling of a prejudicial or racialised statement with 'I'm not a racist but . . .'. However, the simplest way not to appear racist is to avoid talking about 'race' altogether. This was a strong instinct for many interviewees. They did not refuse to talk about 'race', but appeared to prefer not to do so. Because of my reluctance to introduce too directly what I knew was a sensitive topic, I would often introduce questions about 'race' in a way in which they were coupled with either class or gender, or even both. For instance, 'do issues of race or class ever come up with your children?'. This 'weak' form of questioning provided an exit route for those who wanted to avoid talking about 'race', and it was very rare for someone to choose to respond to the 'race' element of the question first. The following extract shows how it can be difficult to maintain 'race' as a topic of conversation. Helen attempted to answer the question but was constantly diverted to other subjects:

BB: So it must, I mean the kind of racial mix that you grew up with must be very different from here?

Helen: Totally, absolutely, completely different, yeah. Where I live, I actually went to a school which was 20 miles away from where I lived. Which is another thing I don't want my children to have. I want them to go to a school that's round the corner and to be able to see their friends after school. For me that just wasn't an option. I used to catch three buses to get to school, every morning. I used to leave home at 20 past 7 to get to school at quarter to 9, from the age of 11. It's just too much, I wouldn't want my children . . ., and all my friends lived miles away, so as I said it was just staying over, it was a bigger deal than just going for tea, I missed out on that completely. And in the summer, a lot of the time I was just on my own. My brother and sister are a lot older than me, so in a way I was an only child. And the racial mix was completely . . . my parents I would say had become middle class, but say for example, both my grandfathers were miners. One was a lead miner and one was a coal miner and very much working class. They decided that they didn't want their own children from fairly enormous families to become miners. And so they moved from, down to the valley, if you like and the whole family clubbed together and bought a farm.

(Helen, Interview 12)

Helen initially appeared to answer the question about 'race' directly and even emphatically. But she found it difficult to sustain a discussion on 'race' and went on to explain other features of her childhood environment and geography. Nonetheless, 'race' is implicated in her account of her family's history and class position. She was describing a social geography which *is* raced, in that it is almost completely, but not entirely, white. However, Helen could not quite find the words to say this directly; she approached the question 'And the race mix was completely . . .' but lost courage at the final hurdle and diverted away from it. It appears here, and in other interviews, that 'white' is even more of a taboo word, more difficult to say, than 'black' or 'Asian'. The most interesting feature of her childhood for Helen was its classed nature. Class, geography and family were all of more immediate relevance and interest to her than 'race'. They are also easier to talk about. This extract illustrates both the seeming irrelevance of 'race' to white lives and some of the reluctance on the part of some white people to talk about 'race'. Toni Morrison has also written about this delicacy, although in her case she is referring to white American literary critics:

The habit of ignoring race is understood to be a graceful, even generous liberal gesture. To notice is to recognise an already discredited difference. To enforce its invisibility through silence is to allow the black body a shadowless participation in the dominant cultural body. According to this logic, every well bred instinct argues *against* noticing and forecloses adult discourse.

(Morrison 1992: 9–10)

I have argued that 'race' needs to be understood as performative and, more specifically, as a product of perceptual practices. It is through such perceptual practices that externally evident physical differences are seen and categorised as racialised differences, and that various inferences are drawn from these differences. This chapter will explore further the perceptual practices involved in the performativity of 'race', particularly in the context of talking to white women interviewees who generally wished to avoid appearing racist. I would argue that the women I interviewed generally worked within a discourse in which racism, although rarely discussed, was accepted to be a 'bad thing'. Yet at the same time, I would argue that they were living in a time and space that was and is highly racialised and which conditioned their perceptual practices. Their thoughts and actions were structured by their whiteness as much as by their class and gender.

In order to explore the ways in which racialised performativity was present in their lives, this chapter will examine three aspects of the interviews. First, the discussion with mothers on their children's attitudes to 'race' will provide a window on the ways in which seeing or not seeing lies at the heart of racialised perception. Then, I will examine some of the ways in which 'race' was raised explicitly by the interviewees and argue that the image of a masculinised threatening/desired black man retains a dominant position in the white imaginary. Finally, the chapter will explore another level at which 'race' is perceived and experienced by the interviewees – in terms of the ways they organise their lives spatially and relate to different localities.

'Race' in the eye of the beholder (or seeing is believing)

As Paul Gilroy points out 'when it comes to the visualisation of "race", a great deal of fine tuning has been required' (Gilroy 2000: 42). Acts of seeing and being seen as racially different are far from simple or inevitable. The visualisation of 'race' needs to be understood as discursively constructed. Perceptual practices, particularly those centred on visible difference, performatively construct 'race'. Racial theories are based on physical, visually determined characteristics that are then related to internal characteristics. Yet the boundaries between physical characteristics shift and have to be understood in their social and political context. Who is visibly 'black' or 'white' changes over time and in different contexts. Thus, questions of visibility and invisibility are mediated by power. The consequences of either depend upon the subject's position within normative regimes.

Visibility and invisibility are both dependent on the acts of seeing and looking as well as the experience of being seen, unseen or ignored. Patricia Williams (1997) writes of the tensions around 'race', the 'forbidden gaze' of 'race' and what one is 'cultured to see or not see'. To see or not to see 'race' or difference is a politicised act. It is an act which, as the interview material shows, is riven with doubts and confusion for the white women. In the interviews I carried out for the research, the issue of 'seeing' 'race' or colour came up when I asked the mothers whether they thought their children (both preschool and primary school age) had any understanding of 'race'. This question was designed to prompt the women to talk in a way that would illuminate their own thinking on 'race'. At the same time, I also asked similar questions about class and gender. In the rest of this section, I will focus on the question of seeing 'race' and, more specifically, on how the white respondents talked about seeing, or not seeing, those who were not white, and what they thought their children saw. Children are an interesting place to start in this discussion. In general, it is assumed that children are 'innocent' of racism. However, there may be different positions on the 'naturalness' of attraction towards one's own and suspicion of others. How one's 'own' is defined and who is the other are of course critical. In addition, children are also discovering the world around them and rapidly developing and being interpellated into wider discursive practices. They are engaged in the process of working out frameworks through which to view the world. Mothers play an active role in shaping this process.

There was little consensus between the mothers on the development of their children's understandings of the concept of 'race' or their own racialised identities. This contrasted strongly with what the mothers said about gender. Many of the interviewees gave lengthy responses to questions about their children's gender development and their understanding of gender differences. In the vast majority of cases, the interviewees stated that they wanted to bring up their children 'equally' or without reference to gender stereotypes and that, to this end, they endeavoured to buy a wide range of books and toys for their children to play with. Almost all the mothers also stated that these attempts were futile and, in the face of girls' desire to wear pink or boys' desires to play with sticks, cars and trains, were eventually abandoned. This is illustrated in the following anecdote told by Deborah, a middle-class woman living in Clapham:

> A friend of mine took part in this sort of survey that a friend of hers was doing to find out how you could influence boys and girls, and she had to give her son girls' toys to play with, dolls. A doll's house, and she said it was ridiculous. The doll was used as a soldier, and the doll's house was used as a fort, and he just got behind the doll's house and started shooting people through the windows and things. You know, she said, 'well, yeah, what can I do?'.
>
> (Interview 17)

Traditional gender categories were usually accepted and used totally unproblematically by the interviewees, with sexuality not mentioned at all, apart from the occasional reference to cross-dressing and how it was 'really nothing to worry about'.

But there was less consensus on the subject of 'race'. 'Race' was something that the mothers were less used to talking about and had widely varying views on the perceptual practices of their babies, toddlers and young children. Different interviewees felt that quite old children had no sense of visible racialised differences whereas, as we shall see, others ascribed a sense of difference to very young children. While this could be the result of the different ways in which the children are brought up and their different development, I would argue that the question is less about what children actually see and more about what their mothers think they see, or want them to see. Seeing and talking about 'race' was a difficult and awkward practice for many of these women. Part of the explanation for this was that, for those mothers whose children are positioned as white (in contrast to those who described their children as 'mixed race'), 'race' was always about others, those who were black, Asian or otherwise non-white. There was no discussion of their children's own racial identities. This meant that seeing racialised difference and remarking on it became a practice of power, of labelling others (while of course unconsciously labelling oneself). For some of the women I interviewed, both the act of seeing and the notion of colour lay at the heart of their attitude to 'race' and whiteness. The safest action was to do nothing, or risk being seen as racist. For these women, colour blindness[1] functioned literally as a claim to be blind to – unseeing of – colour, where colour means blackness or non-whiteness.[2] This also meant that, unlike gender, where they might consciously choose appropriate books and toys for their children to guide their development, they did not consciously play a role in directing their children's vision and understanding. It would seem that there was nothing for a parent to do but to step back and keep quiet. Seeing racialised differences is clearly much more contentious and complicated than seeing gender differences.

Heather was the only interviewee who was prepared to suggest that her baby had a strong reaction to the visual impact of racialised physical differences and skin tone in particular:

Heather: I've just got one, and she's 10 months – although you do get an interesting reaction that she definitely . . . we have a couple of black friends but not a lot of . . . so she tends to stare at black people.

BB: Really . . .

Heather: Because they're different, so she's aware there's something different. We had a guy come round to do a survey – we seem to be on everyone's survey list, and he was, I think he was probably Nigerian 'cos he was very, very dark, you know, with that almost navy blue, it's so black, and she was absolutely transfixed. Completely fascinated because it was different, it was something new, which was what babies absolutely love, so it was interesting to see that they are aware, that people look different [. . .] You know, it's very obvious, it's like she'd stare at somebody with glasses or at somebody that had very, very bleached blonde hair or something. They'd all be things that would be eye-catching to her, so that she would, you know, comment on it in her way.

(Interview 15)

Heather did feel the need to assert her baby's innocence – the attention she gives to black people is no different from that she would give to someone blonde or wearing glasses. The fact that she said this suggests that she had some anxiety about it – as if I might suspect that her 10-month-old daughter was harbouring racial ideologies. Although, at the same time, she suggested a possible social explanation, in that part of her daughter's interest was due to the infrequency of her daughter meeting people who have darker skin than herself. Certain differences are more 'eye-catching' than others. Other interviewees, whose children also commented on racialised physical differences, were also at pains to point out the lack of racism behind these comments. Asking about the colour of a person was the same as asking about the colour of a toy only 'probably even more interesting' (Interview 17), or commenting on someone's skin colour 'that's just the same as them saying they've got blonde hair' (Interview 20). It is interesting how, in these two examples, what comes to mind as a contrast to blackness is blonde hair. This could be argued to be an iconic formulation of white femininity.[3]

In contrast, Claudia, who described herself and her daughter as 'half black',[4] discussed her daughter's fascination for blondeness:

She had a fixation for a long time about dyeing her hair blonde. [. . .] It's beyond us, it's kind of beyond us. Because she's always, she's got more black dollies than she's got white dollies, but she adores Barbie. I just don't know where . . . she just from a very early age got into her head that blonde is good. I mean her best friend who she's played with since she was about one and a half is blonde and she's always adored him. But then she's made friends, you know, . . . I don't know where she's got it from, we just *don't know*. And now she's got it as a bit of a joke, to say 'oh I'm going to dye my hair blonde like Barbie'.

(Interview 6)

Another interviewee, whose daughter had a 'half-Asian' father, also said that her daughter had a fascination with blonde hair. These examples are not presented here to support the problematic literature on the 'problem' of black and mixed-race identity (for a discussion of this, see Tizard and Phoenix 1993), but rather to suggest the dominance of certain forms of whiteness in ideals of femininity and beauty. Nonetheless, I would also argue that the act of seeing 'race' depends on how the individual is interpellated into racialised discourse. I would suggest that the avoidance or evasion of 'race' and particularly its visual 'markers', which I will discuss in this section, is more available to white people than to black people. Certainly (although this is by no means a statistically significant survey), none of the mothers of mixed-race children suggested that their children had such empty responses to colour differences, as the following extract demonstrates:

BB: Do you think that she, does she ever talk about race? Does she know that it's a kind of . . .

Madeleine: Well, her dad is, um, half Asian, um so, but she doesn't look, she looks like me basically. Although she tans quicker in the sun and that kind of stuff. So she has been aware from quite an early age that her dad is a different colour to her. And funnily enough, I don't know if this is to do with her relationship with her dad, but when she was very little she made a *very* big point of saying she was white she wasn't brown, she was white.

BB: That was when she was what kind of age?

Madeleine: Um, God, probably at nursery, probably three, four something like that.

BB: Because her dad's not around?

Madeleine: Well, he is, he sees her once a week. But they had, it took quite a long time for that to become something she would look forward to, rather than just 'who is this man?' [laugh]. So she has, she also has cousins, who are her dad's brother's kids, who are *also* at the same school and one of them is white and one of them is brown. So you know, that's always been a kind of talking point, the fact that Rose is . . . because Rose is brown skinned, Rose does get called names, do you know what I mean when why doesn't Emily and why doesn't Yasmin?

(Madeleine, Interview 9)

Whereas, for Madeleine, 'race' and difference were a common family 'talking point', the white mothers of white children tended to downplay those times when their children noticed racialised physical differences or made comments on 'race'. They were not sure how to respond to these incidents, worried perhaps that they were taking the wrong 'line'. Underlying this was a fear that to see 'race' was to be racist. If one could not avoid seeing difference, one might perhaps avoid talking about it too much with children.

In the following extract, Jan was responding to a question where I had asked whether her children noticed differences of 'race', class or gender. Jan responded by addressing the question of gender:

BB: I was going to ask also about, how you think the children, do they have any understanding or notice differences along the lines of race, class and gender?

Jan:	Um, yes, very depressingly they do, depressing in some senses. Hugo is, well four, he's in the nursery year, he's full of things about what's girls' things and what's boys things. I must admit, I was standing in the queue at our local department store this Christmas with my Action Man and my pink secret diary thinking 'where did it all go wrong, all those ideas that I had!'. Never letting Zoe have a doll and playing Duplo for hours and hours and making 'constructive' things. And now there's a pile of Barbies, I don't know, seems like a lot of . . . I don't know. I still have some principles that I hold to heart, no guns and that sort of thing.

(Interview 30)

This marked the beginning of quite a long discussion in which Jan described the work she had put into developing her children's gender identities: 'I feel I've failed in that respect [. . .] Having said that, I don't think I've done that badly when I look at some kids'. She discussed training her son away from 'overtly aggressive behaviour' and trying to teach her daughter to be more competitive. She also mentioned her ambivalent feelings about her daughter's fascination with the Spice Girls (there is further discussion of this in the next chapter). After this long exchange, from which it was clear that Jan had thought considerably about gender and worked to achieve certain gendered identities for her children, I again tried to explore 'race' and class. This introduced a discussion of class. Jan was one of the few interviewees who felt that her child noticed differences that could be regarded as classed, such as accent:

BB:	So, do you find that they do, you know, notice any differences in race or class, other than the gender one? Do they remark on it?
Jan:	Zoe remarks on accents a bit. Just occasionally, one lad had come in the school and it was November, and they always wear, I don't know why it happens really sometimes, but they weren't allowed to wear jogging bottoms outside, they had to just wear their shorts. And this woman had come in, Peter is the name of the son. Zoe had come home one day and she does this fantastic mimic of people's voices. And it is very tempting, you don't know whether you can laugh or not really. [mimicking 'cockney' accent] 'Come over here, I've told you, they're freezing to death out there, I'm not having my Peter . . .'. I just burst out laughing because I *knew* Peter's mum and I just knew that it was just a dead rip-off of her accent. So certainly that she would be aware. But I wouldn't, I would say she's very unaware of people's class, social status. Doesn't really make comments about people educating privately or state or anything. I really don't think she's very . . . , or the size of someone's house , you know, that's where people live. She thinks that living in a flat with a balcony

would be very glamorous for example, so you know she's a bit unaware on that front. Race is an interesting one, I think because . . . , I don't know . . .. I mean, you know, she's very . . . , the school that she goes to, they do have a problem with kids leaving, going to this other school basically. It's been more in the last couple of years because they haven't had a head.

(Interview 30)

There was some hesitation in what Jan is saying. She was skirting round the issue of knowledge in relation to difference. On two occasions, she was about to classify her daughter in relation to her awareness of difference, first as regards class 'I really don't think she's very . . .' and then 'race' 'I mean, you know, she's very . . .'. In both instances, Jan diverted the course of her own account. What she seems to be avoiding saying was how aware or not her daughter was about class or 'race'. The implication is that to have an awareness of these differences would be to be prejudiced. In the latter part of her quotation, it appears at first that she is adopting a strategy of veering off the subject of 'race' again as she shifted from 'race' to the administrative problems of her children's primary school and the class differences between schools. However, it is clear that 'race' was central to some of her preoccupations about the school, and that this was mediated through class. What became apparent in the interview is that the problem with children leaving is that it is the middle-class (and white) children who tend to leave the school, making the upper reaches of the school progressively 'blacker', as Jan explained:

Um, and so, having kind of gone from a situation where you've probably got, I'd say . . . 30 per cent black kids in the school, by the time you get to year six, you're looking at about 75 per cent black kids in the school.

(Interview 30)

The question of mothers' racialised attitudes to their children's schooling and the question of 'mix' will be explored more fully in the next chapter. In the interview, Jan went on to stress that her 8-year-old daughter (and younger son) are less interested in 'race' than she is herself:

I don't think either of them really comment on it really. I suppose I'm more interested in it than they are really. Um, very occasionally, Phoebe will be describing someone and she'll say, it's never the first factor in the description, but she'll say 'oh she's got black skin'. But she'll usually say, 'oh she's that big girl with really frizzy hair', or 'she's that big girl with the silver coat' or something. . . . um . . . and at some point she might say that she's got black skin or whatever. But there aren't really any obvious differences as to what the kids do and the way they perform at school. And they have got some black teachers at school, which is good. And she has one or two black friends that come home for tea. But in the main, her friends are a group of white girls. And I suppose that kind of bothers me a bit. But then those white girls have got white mums that are my friends, that's the way it is, I mean.

(Interview 30)

Despite feeling happy to express her own interest in 'race', there was still an unease in her daughter's seeing, expressed through the insistence that her daughter only ever refers to the skin colour of fellow classmates as secondary descriptors. However, it is ironic that the other descriptors that she mentions – particularly the 'frizzy hair' – are racialised. It seems likely that Jan was summoning up a black child in her imagination as she produced these examples. Jan then shifted back to her own preoccupation about whether there are obvious racialised differences in what children do, how they perform at school and her anxieties about her children not achieving a desirable social 'mix'. It is interesting that Jan did have higher aspiration for her children's racialised mixing than her own social life, although she ultimately recognised that the two were intertwined.

Given multicultural discourses[5] and, I would argue, the racialisation of culture, it was easier for parents to suggest that their children might notice cultural difference than visual markers of 'race'. The women mentioned the 'different cultural outlooks', 'different names', 'different diets' and 'saris' that their children might notice as well as, inevitably, the different religious festivals.[6] The following extract introduces the discourse of *exposure*, which was alluded to in Jan's concern about her children's friends and appeared in several other interviews. Stephanie was talking about her 3-year-old son:

He makes absolutely no comment about the . . . sort of apparent physical differences between him and the other children and the other teachers there. And I think that's because he went there at 18 months. He's been exposed from that age on a daily basis to children who *look* quite different and teachers who *look* quite different. . . . um . . . and have very different names and different cultural outlooks and you know different diets and all those sorts of things. And he passes absolutely no comment on it at all.

(Interview 11, emphasis Stephanie's)

It is difficult to know what to make of this statement. It seems possible that Stephanie assumed that, although it is a good thing for her son to have 'exposure' to difference, he would also maintain his own sense of whiteness. Rather than emphasising sameness – suggesting that he will grow up thinking that other names or 'outlooks' are as normal as his – the emphasis on difference remained. While he was used to being surrounded by 'different' people with various names, diets, ways of dressing, there is a suggestion that he will understand that these names and 'cultural outlooks' are *different* from his, something other than the norm. He is to learn his own whiteness and normality while recognising those who are not the same, who are different and not necessarily to be copied. If this is what Stephanie intended, this requires quite a complex operation.

When differences are seen and talked about by children, this raises the question for mothers of how they should be spoken about. Deborah expressed some anxiety on how to respond to her nearly 4-year old son's mentioning people's colour. This, in the two examples she gave, was because he coupled a negative response to a particular person with a reference to his skin colour ('I don't like that black face'). She did not say whether her son ever made reference to anyone's 'white face'. Deborah had discussed these incidents with her husband, and he helped to reassure her that the statements were innocent. The anxiety appears to revolve around what is 'acceptable'. In the interview, Deborah also reassured herself (albeit still a little unconvinced) that her son 'goes to a nursery where there are kids from all sorts of different backgrounds, so I really don't know. But, I've just got to make sure that I don't get too sensitive about it, I think'. Deborah also felt the issue of how to label her son's own skin colour required some delicacy:

> For example, he said, maybe younger than three, 'what colour am I?'. And I'd say, well, you're um sort of – and I did it on purpose just in case there was sort of anything about race involved in it – um, I don't say oh you're white. I said, oh, you're a lovely sort of pinkie colour, you know, and you've got your nails which are a sort of a whitey colour, and you know, this kind of thing. And later on, he started saying what colour's, um, baby Roy, a little baby he knows, and what colour's so and so, and what colour's so and so, and I just . . . he doesn't do it very often, it would just happen every so often. And I'd say, oh they're brown, you know, um, but he would do the same thing about his toys.
>
> (Interview 17)

This is a clear attempt to ensure that the perceptual practices of the child are directed in a non-racialised way. It shows a good understanding that 'race' is an ideology or perceptual practice, rather than merely a description. So skin was not white, but 'a lovely sort of pinkie colour', while nails were 'sort of a whitey colour'. However, this seems a relatively contorted approach, whereas the skin of others was simply 'brown'. Some of the problem here lies in the ambiguous status of white as a colour (see Dyer 1997) and inaccuracy as a description of skin tone. It is also connected to the idea of white as a 'pure' colour. While 'pinkie' skin is not white, brown can encompass a multitude of tones.

Karon was another interviewee who told an anecdote about her daughter's questioning of her own and other children's colour:

There was a video that I was watching, an exercise video, and she [3-year old daughter] said 'look Mummy, there's a black man in it' and that's the first time she's ever said anything like that. But Joe [4-year-old son] obviously, it was quite a few months ago now, he said 'Mummy I'm white' and I said 'oh yes you are'. He said Kwesi, who was a friend of his who's now gone up to the big school, 'is black'. And they were doing a topic at nursery where they had to do self-portraits and they were sitting down basically drawing themselves as they see themselves, the teacher was obviously saying what colour you are, and crayons, no I think they were doing chalk, and they had to sort of use the hand to rub it there, the paper with the chalk different colours. And one of the, actually I overheard it, because we were just dropping Joe off. And one of the teachers was saying to his black friend who was sitting down 'I'm black' and she said 'but are you black? Look at your hand, what colour would you say? I've got a black chalk here – is that black? And your hand's brown' so sort of trying to get them to see what colour they were, which I thought was quite good in some respects. But in the end of the day, whatever their culture is, they're going to end up saying whatever their parents are saying, 'I'm black' because that's more acceptable thing to say now. But no, as far as race, that's been all he's come out with, it's never been a problem.

(Interview 38)

The story is somewhat contradictory. On the one hand, Karon was confirming her daughter's descriptors of 'white' and 'black', yet at the same time seemed to be approving a teacher's attempt to destabilise them. Karon finally laid the blame for their persistence on black parents and 'politically correct' notions of what was 'acceptable'. There was a suggestion that 'they' have taken a stance on the question while Karon, as white, was more neutral and open-minded. In this extract, the uneasy relationship between a description of colour and a racial category is revealed and goes to the heart of the fragility of colour blindness. It also shows how 'race' is dependent on discursive reiteration and the negotiation between different subjects as to what colours are and which colours matter. There was an ongoing slippage between 'colour', 'culture' and 'race'. For Karon, 'race' was something that was to be negotiated as a potential problem. This was a discourse shared by some other interviewees. The problem here is the risk of being, or being seen as, racist – rather than the risk of experiencing racism, or having to rethink one's own positioning. Colour blindness was often the response to fear of being seen as racist. In this sense, it was a negative move, out of self-protection rather than a positive statement. There was little space for the possibility of changing one's own positioning. The following example is a good example of an instinctive reluctance to talk about 'race' ('of what, sorry') coupled with an approach to the 'problem' of 'race':

BB: And so, does, I guess particularly with Kevin, do issues of race or class come up with him?
Beverley: Of what, sorry?
BB: Does he ask about or talk about people being different race or?
Beverley: No, not really. The thing is he's been brought up with it, with where we used to live and the same here. No, he sort of, he fits in quite well really. He's not really got a preference, he sort of like wouldn't put one or the other down. He's quite good like that really. He's quite like me, you know, if you get on with someone then you get on type of thing really. No he never mentions anything like black people, or Asians or anything.

(Interview 42)

Here 'race' is presented only as a problem. Talking about 'race' immediately becomes a question of being racist, of 'putting' someone 'down'. The risk is that Beverley's son may not always be 'good' about 'race'. Indeed, Beverley went on to talk about her husband, her son's stepfather who she described as 'patriotic' (for example, he would not leave Britain even on a holiday) and presumably not so 'good'. This also explains the significance of Beverley's description of her son as 'he's quite like me'. The solution to the problem is to ignore the issue as much as possible. Her son being 'good' about race was attributed to having 'been brought up with it' as a result of living in particular areas of London. Here again is another version of the 'exposure' discourse, with 'it' presumably being 'racially different others'. Nonetheless, at the same time, there was the idea that it was good for her son to 'fit in' with this difference.

Others had more complicated approaches and recognised that there had been a shift in discourses around 'race' in their lifetimes. Madeleine, for example, explained to me how she felt caught between her mother's approach to 'race' and her daughters' and she herself was unsure of the right position to take:

So, but you know, my mum was always, she talked to me about race so it was always: 'we will be terribly *nice* when we *meet* people of different colours' [laugh]. Whereas Yasmin has just grown up with people of *all* different colours. So she goes: 'they're brown and black and white' and you know and she'll go 'ohh I don't like that black person' and I'll be like 'ohhh [mock horror] God you can't say that', you know, 'oh you can't do that at all' and it's not um I don't know, I think it's just so different for her. It's so much part of her life that she maybe doesn't have the same hang-ups about it as I do. And she is aware, now, that . . . I don't know I think when kids are little they point and say: 'that person is different from me' and you kind of teach them over time that because somebody looks different from you or because someone's in a wheelchair that you have to kind of *not* see that. You have to educate yourself not to see those things. So she's kind of aware now of not pointing out that people are different. And I don't know, I think it's difficult. I don't necessarily know whether that's the best way to go about it. Because I mean when I grew up it was very much about . . . you know you pretend that nothing's different and just accept people for what they are, whereas now children grow up and it's much more about *celebrating* the differences. So I think I'm probably quite out of touch in that way [laugh].

(Interview 9)

Madeleine was caught between 'pretending' to see nothing, to 'not see that', in order not to be rude or racist and celebrating difference, which leads to an overstatement of difference: her daughter has grown up with people of '*all* different colours'. She suggested that this is a generational shift, but was also suggesting that she feels she lacks the discursive resources to respond to this shift. Is racial difference like an impairment that should be overlooked, or how might all differences be celebrated? Madeleine was aware that the idea of celebration of differences is complex and that there appears to be no innocent rendering of the term 'black'. She also recognises that her mother's approach may be hypocritical, that she wants to be 'nice' to others while remaining distanced. But, lacking alternative discourses and perceptual practices, she was unable to move away from a particular moment of subjection – she retains some 'hang-ups' on the issue. This extract is also interesting because Madeleine was explicitly talking about inculcating perceptual regimes: 'you have to educate yourself not to see those things'. It also perhaps reflects an awareness that she and her daughter do not share exactly the same racial positioning. Not only is there a generational difference, but her daughter is also 'mixed race'. This depth of reflection was rare, and there was in general little consideration of racism in the interviews. Those who did talk about racism directly put it down to ignorance and often placed it in the past and in the minds of others, discussing the racism of their parents or grandparents and explaining how these were people 'of their time'.

By focusing on what the mothers said about their children, I have tried to demonstrate the sensitivity of the subject of 'race' for white people. This material shows how even seeing is a politicised and sensitive act, and parents are in the process of negotiating these difficulties when they talk to me. It also raises methodological problems as to what to make of the material. I am not here raising the question of what the children actually thought – that would be the subject of an entirely different research project – but how to interpret what people say is equally difficult when it is governed by a fear not to appear racist. The attempt not to see 'race' has implications for the way whiteness was being imagined – or not. It was taken as given, as the norm, the state of not being 'different'. But, at the same time, whiteness was not brought into focus or considered directly. While 'race' was avoided at various points in the interviews, whiteness as a concept was rarely mentioned. Indeed, I rarely brought it up myself and could therefore be argued to be complicit in the silence around the subject. I will now go on to consider what the interviewees saw when they did allow themselves to think of, and talk about, 'race'.

Blackness in the white imaginary

The interviewees often appeared to adopt and approve of a 'colour-blind' approach to 'race' and racialised difference. However, this did not mean that it was their only way of seeing, or not seeing. Through the course of the interviews, various representations of blackness emerged, which suggested the enduring power of certain images and meanings of blackness in the white imaginary. Toni Morrison has argued that, for white American writers:

> Black slavery enriched the country's creative possibilities. For in that construction of blackness *and* enslavement could be found not only the not-free but also, with the dramatic polarity created by skin colour, the projection of the not-me. The result was a playground for the imagination.
>
> (Morrison 1992: 38)

Through exploring the way blackness features in the white imaginary, it is also possible to begin to gain a picture of whiteness and white subjectivity. In this section, I suggest that the black other or blackness plays a role in the white imaginary of delineating the field of intelligibility. In this formulation, blackness can represent the constitutive outside and thereby draw the boundaries to, and content of, whiteness. This outside is both desired, in the search for fullness, but also feared for its unstable boundary-marking role.[7]

Big black man

A recurring image alluded to in several accounts was that of 'the black man'. This was a stereotyped and racialised image where the blackness suggested was male and both threatening and attractive (not necessarily to the same people). It is not difficult to see how these images drew on representations of black men that have been both historically enduring but also adapted to particular political and discursive moments. Vron Ware (Ware 1992) and Catherine Hall (Hall 1992) both discuss colonial constructions of black men and the need to protect white women, for example in the Morant Bay uprising in Jamaica and the Indian 'Mutiny' of 1857. The idea that white women need protection also features in New Right and neo-racist ideologies, as well as recurring in popular discourse, for instance in recent discussions around immigration and asylum seekers. In the interviews, I did not ask directly what the white interviewees thought of black people or whether they thought that they themselves were racist. However, I would argue that taking part in the interview and my questions prompted these questions internally for the women and shaped what they said to me. When the white women interviewees asked themselves 'what do I think of black people?' or 'am I racist?', the image of a threatening black man, or 'gang' of black men, was the first to suggest itself in several cases.

Jennifer, who lived in Clapham, gives an example of the readily available image of black gangs in the white imaginary. Immediately after asserting her own (partial?) 'blindness' to colour and difference, an image occurs to her that directly contradicts this:

> I've never been frightened or wary . . . they've always been . . . I suppose at that age I was probably quite inquisitive to know, but maybe that was because my parents were quite . . . had made them out as being people . . . people of different race being no different. Or they are different, but what's different about them is, you know, nothing to be frightened of, or . . . I mean, if I see a gang of black kids now I still get anxious. If I'm out walking. But if I see a gang of anybody, I would still be anxious. I wouldn't be any more anxious because they were black. I would be more anxious because it's a gang, I think. Um, I don't know.
> (Interview 25)

Jennifer began her consideration of her attitude to people who are different with the question of whether she is frightened or wary of black people (this extract is part of a longer account in which Jennifer provided a history of her encounters with people who were different from her). This indicates the place that difference or blackness has in her mind. Also significant is the way black people were readily homogenised into 'them' and 'they'. Jennifer appeared unable to say 'white' – instead producing an opposition between a 'gang of black kids' and 'a gang of anybody'. She herself did not seem to know how to deal with the contradiction of her fear of a 'gang of black kids' and her assertion that she was brought up in a way in which people 'of different race' were seen as 'no different', or at least not frighteningly different. In another example, Heather also conjured up a law-breaking black man. This image appeared in the middle of an empathetic account that is intended to show how, through being on a Kuwaiti Airlines flight where she was the only white person, Heather realised what it is like to be a visual minority. While Heather might innocently bump into someone on a crowded plane, the imagined black person was not a woman but a man, and was committing a crime:

> Just about the fact that you stick out like a sore thumb. Everybody could see . . . there was no kind of melting into the background. You know, if I brushed past somebody and then walked past the other way they would have said, oh, that was the girl who brushed past me a minute ago, and they would not have thought, oh, was it her or was it . . .? Because it was so easy to recognise me out of everybody else. And that suddenly

meant, you know, I suppose if you magnify it up you know it is so easy if somebody says who lives in a predominantly white area and they see a black guy break into someone's car, then they would be very keen to identify that black guy, you know, it becomes a very easy way, and I felt that if I bumped into somebody there would have been no question that it would have been me.

(Interview 15)

While these examples appear to come directly from an imagined image, unmediated by direct experience, Emily produced a more complex example in which her experience has confirmed racialised representations. Emily was unusual in that she admitted that 'in one sense' she was 'racist'. Her racialised and negative response to 'black youths' on the streets was justified by referring to her own negative experiences – rather than simply being the product of prejudice.

Well, I think racism is very bad round here. In one sense I'm racist in the fact that if I saw five black youths together on the street, I would not walk through them. Purely because I've been mugged once by a black chap, I've had three black men trying to get in my car on different occasions – it's always been a black person, be it by just chance but again, it's my experience. So, I would be concerned. I mean, if I saw five white youths, I probably wouldn't walk through them. Put it like that. But as a personal thing, a black chap tried to knock my front door down. I can only say what's happened to me. Yeah, so I was wary. [. . .] we've seen black people do it, and so I do get worried. Which is a horrible thing to have to say. Like I said, my best friend at school was black, and she was wonderful, and her family were lovely people. Actually, she ended up marrying a white man.

(Interview 21)

Emily was able to recount the incidents that have led her to be so suspicious of black men. Yet at the same time, her language reflected the racialised treatment of crime and black men in the media. The imagined group were not young people or boys (for they surely were male) but instead 'youths' on 'the street'. Emily's experience was mediated through particular discourses. She was unable to respond to the events without seeing them as evidence of racialised difference and antagonism. She was perhaps aware at some level that her use of language may be interpreted problematically as, in contrast to the 'youths', she referred to being mugged by a 'black chap' – a characterisation that rings slightly oddly. She also opposed 'black youths' to 'white youths'. Emily suggested that she would have the same response to white 'youths', but even she was unconvinced as she returned to the question of black male aggressors. Perhaps she was even unsure that white young men hang around in the same way as they do not register in the same way on her racialised visual schema.

Emily had admitted her own prejudice, describing it as 'horrible' (although perhaps inevitable and justified). But she also stressed how she had had black friends. Black women do not fit so neatly into this schema of the violent black man and, indeed, were hardly mentioned by any interviewees. But Emily had a narrative of the loss of a friendship with a 'wonderful' black friend. However, her status as truly black appeared to be undermined in Emily's mind because 'actually, she ended up marrying a white man'.

Madeleine was someone who, as we saw above, had thought extensively about issues around 'race' and had a fairly racially mixed social life, including long-term relationships with black and Asian men. However, she explained in the following extract how the idea of blackness as male and threatening persists and can be summoned up by particular incidents. Unless she was in a 'stage' of her life where she has friendships with black people, this black 'other' became dominant in her imagination and responses to events:

Madeleine: I don't know if this happens for other people. Kind of the way I think about issues kind of goes up and down through my life. Do you know what I mean? It depends about the people that I'm in contact with. And, you know, if I have . . . black women friends that I get on really well with, then I will tend to feel more open towards black women. And if I am in that stage of my life where I don't have any black friends, then I will tend to feel, you know they're different, they're. And I had a, in January, this January, it was just the most awful month. There was an armed robbery round the corner [laugh] which was a *huge* black guy and there was a bloke outside who was just *kicking* his kids so badly, he was a huge black guy. And I didn't feel like I could intervene, do you know what I mean? But I came home and phoned the police, and thought [in barely audible fearful voice] 'don't let him know it's me'. You know, and when you have kind of things like that happen to you in a row, then you start thinking 'I can't bear to live in this area, because it's just, I need to go and live where there's more white people'. And I actually went to live with my mum for a bit. I packed everything up and went to stay with my mum.

BB: after this incident?

Madeleine: after this incident. [. . .] and just couldn't stand it [laugh]. They're all so *old* and *white* and *middle class* and it was just hideous. You know so it does, that's what you were saying about it's about how people feel at the time, isn't it. And if you've had bad experiences then. And at the end of the day, it's about people isn't it? The quality of your contacts with people that kind of informs your views about race and class.

(Interview 44)

As Madeleine's account shows vividly, this image of blackness did inform an image of whiteness. Blackness was frightening and something to run away from, even to the extent of uprooting herself and her daughter. Yet whiteness was also something to be avoided for its 'dullness', 'stiffness', for being 'old and white and middle class' and representing the establishment.

In other interviews as well, another side to the threatening image of blackness, and black men in particular, was presented – that of exciting, vibrant, exotic and masculinised blackness, which may potentially provide an escape from the dullness of whiteness. The sexualisation of blackness also has a long history and was first discussed by Franz Fanon (1967). R.C. Young describes colonialism as the 'desiring machine' and traces how racial theories have always had at their heart anxieties and theories about sex and inter-racial sex in particular (Young 1995). Researching identity in contemporary Britain, Les Back has described how young white people aspire to 'blackness' and adopt black dress style and language. He has traced the importance of sexuality in these cultural translations and how black men are constructed in terms of fear and desire. He writes that 'for white young men, the imagining of black masculinity in heterosexual codes of "hardness" and "hypersexuality" is one of the core elements which attract them to black masculine style' (Back 1994: 178).

While Back is referring to working-class young people, and particularly young white men, some of the middle-class women that I interviewed had similarly eroticised views of black men. Emma was someone who had ro-manticised views of whiteness and particularly Englishness (examined in depth in Chapter 7). At times, she also used a discourse that saw whiteness as dull and moribund (for discussions of whiteness and death, see both hooks 1992 and Dyer 1997). At different points in the interview, Emma described an area and a school as 'too white middle class' and as 'kind of frigid'. In contrast, she presented the 'one black person in her childhood' (a common motif – see below) in very sensual terms:

> Well there were no black people where I grew up, except for one who was married to a white woman. And he was gorgeous and everybody fancied him. So he was always considered to be 'ah look there, let's go to his dance class!' and all that kind of stuff. And my mother would always say, (going back to my mother), 'oh they have such wonderful rhythm' um, and she was being really kind and generous. Because now when I think about it, it's probably, 'cos they probably do have good rhythm, but it's quite labelling really.
>
> (Emma, Interview 16)

These two discourses, of whiteness as being 'frigid' and black men being sexually attractive, are of course complementary and mutually reinforcing. Emma was trying to question her mother's approach to 'race', this was part of a process of questioning her parents' outlook on many issues ('I get on very well with them [her parents] and we're very close, but I do feel different from them now. I do feel, I don't know. I mean it's partly age, obviously, but I just feel, I have kind of shifted a bit to what I'm most happy with'). Despite this questioning of her mother's position, Emma could not deny the seeming truth that 'they' have 'good rhythm'. She also went on to explain the differences between an African Caribbean friend from college and the white middle-class background that she came from. Despite the fact that she attributed these differences more to class than to 'race', they still managed to fall into a racialised rubric and one that accords with sensual blackness:

> Because I think there's something about middle-class people who expect people of about 20 going on 25, I think from my experience they expect them to be very go-getty and 'oh I'm going to go off around the world for a year, and then I'm going to go to college and then I'm going to' you know that kind of thing and to be very kind of go-getty and wanting to make a fortune. Whereas, my friend. I mean, he was incredibly laid back actually. He was much more laid back than practically anyone I'd ever met. And that was a cultural thing I think.
>
> (Interview 16)

At a later point in the interview, Emma declared (without prompting) that: 'if Lucy [her daughter] married someone who was black it wouldn't bother me at all. I wouldn't even think twice about it, it's who that person is'. This was a statement made (similarly unprompted) by other interviewees and suggests a particular anxiety around blackness, whiteness and sexuality. As Young has emphasised, racial theories are critically about the possibilities of inter-racial sex:

> Racial theory, which ostensibly seeks to keep races forever apart, trans-mutes into expressions of the clandestine, furtive forms of what can be called 'colonial desire': a covert but insistent obsession with transgres-sive, inter-racial sex, hybridity and miscegenation.
>
> (Young 1995: xii)

One's reaction to the idea of one's son or daughter marrying a black person has become a popularised 'test' of anti-racist sentiment, as repre-sented in the film *Guess Who's Coming to Dinner*. Mixed-race relationships are far from uncommon in Britain, and the interviewees were asserting that they were comfortable with the idea. Nonetheless, the fact that they feel the need to say this indicated ambivalence around the issue. Emma said that she wouldn't 'think twice' about the 'race' of the person her daughter married but would only consider who he is – in effect that she would look at him and block out, or look beyond, his colour.

For Heather also, the most notable difference (or the first that springs to mind) between whiteness (and Asianness) and blackness was a sexualised difference, which was also addressed in terms of culture:

Heather: I became more aware of the way different communities work [. . .] In the way that you will get a group of young black adolescents, the way they will talk to each other. The way they flirt with each other. When they hang around a bus-stop. That kind of social interaction can be quite noticeably different from a group of Asian adolescents or a group of white adolescents. Their body language is very different, their choice of vocabulary is often quite different. I think flirting is one of the main things, the way people are physically with each other. I was aware that that was very different. I mean most of the black guys I came across were very touchy-feely.

BB: Towards you?

Heather: Yes, and not in an aggressive way at all. In a friendly way. But a lot more physically open than a lot of white guys.

(Interview 15)

This dual image – of threat and excitement – fits into a theme that is dealt with in more detail in the next chapters, which discuss mothers' desire to achieve the 'right' social and racial 'mix' for their children in schooling and socialising. As the chapter will show, this 'mix' requires just enough, but not too much, of the 'other'. The discourse of the excitingly different 'cultural other' appeared in many interviews. For Barbara, this difference was presented in terms of an escape from whiteness. She had had children outside marriage and with an African Caribbean man 'that was my rebellion' and explained that this was also in response to her perception of the dullness of her white family:

Well, because I hated myself, I hated myself, I didn't like myself. And I always wanted something romantic. I felt that my lineage was *exceptionally* boring. They were these sort of in-bred people [. . .] [laugh]. And that really even they were quite similar, they had come a little way away from each other, but in *many* ways they were sort of very very similar. Even the towns which they came from were very similar. And I always *hated* that feeling of dullness really. So I didn't like myself, I didn't like myself at all. So I always had an inkling.

(Interview 13)

Otherness was exciting and represented by 'foreignness' – cultural as well as racial difference. Barbara went on to describe a carefree and exciting life free of responsibilities that she had lived with her black partner, until the relationship broke down:

There was a lot of fun, and there was a lot of difference, I liked the difference, I *loved* it being different. And I thought it was, oh, a different way of speaking, different thoughts, it was just very exciting. And it was, it was sort of newness and exciting. It was quite fun. And it got away completely from what I'd grown up with, a lot of happiness and so on.

(Interview 13)

Difference for Barbara centred around its difference *from* whiteness, which she described in the interview as judgemental and unforgiving, as representing the establishment, as 'non-touching', 'non-emotional' and 'strict'. Barbara shows clearly how blackness and whiteness revolve around each other and are mutually defining. Whiteness is harsh and cold but also represents the comfort and security of conforming – Barbara felt that she had paid a high social price for her transgressions. Blackness, or difference from the conformity of whiteness, was exciting and dangerous. She also described how she hated her own complexion and hair and was hoping that, by finding them a black father, her children could avoid this. Here, blackness was almost treated as a commodity with a clear biological materiality. But the exciting difference provided by the 'other' also required that black people were 'different' enough to be able to serve the role of enlivening whiteness. In the following extract, Jennifer expressed regret that those non-white people who come into her house were not different enough.

BB: And how about equally . . . are you . . . is there a similar extent to which you are conscious of being white, or are there times when you're . . .?

Jennifer: No, not really. No. I think . . . no, not really. I don't think so. 'Cos we get quite a lot of mix in the house, I think I don't. It's very difficult, 'cos you don't want to be false with them, do you? You don't want to . . .

BB: False with . . .?

Jennifer: Children. You know, you don't want to go over the top at showing them lots of different people. You know, 'cos they'll just wonder what's she doing, why . . . I don't know. I mean, in some ways, I wish I was . . . I knew more.

BB: . . . because of differences, or literally you wish you knew more people who weren't white?

Jennifer: No, I wish I knew more differences, 'cos I suppose the people that I know that are of different ethnic backgrounds are quite white in their backgrounds, maybe.

BB: Because . . .?

Jennifer: Maybe they've been over here from . . . maybe they're second generation, maybe they're . . . well, Mark's [a black friend] not . . . and maybe when you're with each other, you don't portray that side of things. You know, maybe you're a bit false

> with each other, I don't know. But I think the children will be
> much more accepting of different races, just the fact of being in
> London, than I was. And I don't think I was particularly bad.
>
> (Jennifer, Interview 25)

This passage was a complex expression of an apparent desire as well as regret, which is somewhat difficult to interpret. On the one hand, it was desirable that visitors and friends were from racially different backgrounds 'we get quite a lot of mix in the house'. Another interviewee used very similar language to describe positively the experience of having 'different races that come into the house'. Teresa spoke of always having 'every nationality in the house' (Interview 18). The underlying assumption was that 'difference' was good and even something to be proud of. Nonetheless, the image was uneasy, with an underlying sense of black intrusion into the otherwise white space of the home or house. But then, on the other hand, the differences should not be too extreme or that would constitute being 'false' with one's children, and the friends: 'you know, you don't want to go over the top at showing them lots of different people'. I suspect that class was operating here in making Jennifer's friends not so different from herself. In addition, those friendships that Jennifer did make seemed to operate on the avoidance of conflict and utterances about difference 'maybe when you're with each other, you don't portray that side of things. You know, maybe you're a bit false with each other'. It is difficult to know what to make of this regret of Jennifer's. I suspect that her friends who came from different ethnic backgrounds were 'white' through their class position. They acted and thought as Jennifer did – or at least they appeared to: 'maybe you're a bit false with each other, I don't know'. This latter uncertainty hinted at some doubt in the reality of 'colour blindness'. Jennifer's final comment about the impact on her children of growing up in London suggested the racialisation of space and location in the white imaginary, which is dealt with in the following section.

Geographies of 'race' (small white girl comes to big bright lights)

Malcolm Cross and Michael Keith write that 'race is a privileged metaphor through which the confused text of the city is rendered comprehensible' (Cross and Keith 1993: 9). It could also be said that geography and space provide a map to living and understanding 'race'.[8] One common way of talking about 'race' and cultural difference in the interviews was in terms of geographical area. As Les Back writes: 'Racism produces a particular kind of urban imagination' (Back 1998: 59). The previous section dealt with the position of the black man in the white imaginary. This blackness is not free-floating and always present but, as the last two examples suggest, located within and prompted by particular contexts and juxtapositions. This section will deal with the question of spatiality and location and its import for the white imaginary. The racialisation of the imagining of space is quite far advanced in many areas of London, as Phil Cohen has explored (see Cohen 1993, 1996). Areas may be considered to be 'white', 'black' or 'Asian' in different 'urban imaginings' (Cohen 1996: 171). New settlement and/or 'white flight' may also involve a shift in the identity of an area and those who live in it (for an in-depth study of one area and notions of culture and community, see Bauman 1996). Susan J. Smith emphasises the political processes behind discursive shifts behind immigration being racialised and then conflated with residential segregation. She argues that neo-conservative ideologies have drawn territorial links between black residence and urban violence. This has occurred in the context of the racialisation of culture: 'whether because they are potentially disruptive or simply "culturally" alien, the "black" inner cities have been successfully depicted as a threat to the fragile cohesion of the nation' (Smith 1993: 140). The racial imagining of space of course intersects with the way in which areas are also 'classed'. Tim Butler, for example, examines the 're-occupation' of Hackney by white middle-class graduates (Cohen 1996). Just as geographical areas may be racialised, so individuals or groups may be characterised by the areas in which they live. Pnina Werbner has spoken about the way Asians in Britain are represented (by both academics and the media) as spatialised communities with, for instance, Asians in Bradford and the East End being represented as poor, fundamentalist and dangerous, whereas those in Southall are appreciated in some mainstream discourses for the flowering of Asian youth culture, and Leicester or Brent are seen as areas for rich and successful East African Asians (Werbner 1999).

Many respondents clearly had a racialised imaginary of space and locality. Most respondents had grown up in areas that they remembered as white. However, they were often not entirely white.[9] A common motif in the interviews emerged as that of the 'one black person in childhood'. Sometimes, there were references to several classmates who were Asian or black. For example, Sally described her rural village: 'everyone in the village was white anyway, I think without exception. I know occasionally there would be a black child that came to my secondary school, for a short amount of time and then they seemed to move on again' (Interview 7). Similarly, Helen described her school: 'From the age of 11 onwards, I went to a private school and there were, it was a girls' school and there were Indian girls there. And they were *all* doctors' daughters' (Interview 12). But for other interviewees, a particular and isolated child was remembered, by name. Naming this child, perhaps remembered by an exotic or unusual name, summoned them up from the past:

> When I was 15, we had a Chinese boy come to school, a Japanese, Kohji Furuhata, I still remember his name! And that was the first time really that I'd ever come across a child that was of a different race. [. . .] he was a novelty, a total novelty. And, you know, it was almost to see if he worked in the same way as me, it got to the point where you'd prod

him . . . it was very strange, I mean, he wasn't really that different in physical appearance. I mean, he was a whiz at origami-type things, we used to get him to make us bookmarks and things like that. But that was quite odd.

(Jennifer, Interview 25)

You have to remember that when I first got there [university] I'd come from a small village [. . .] I didn't know any black people [. . .] oh, there *was* one, I can remember him, called Marcus Thomas, but it was . . . so that was a whole new world.

(Rosalind, Interview 36)

As well as emphasising change and generational difference – in terms of providing a contrast to how their children were growing up – I would argue that this particular way of spotlighting an individual child also served to highlight the whiteness of all that surrounded them in childhood. The narrative of the white childhood – highlighted by the few exceptions – contributed to a common narrative that was told about the respondents' move to London (few of the interviewees had grown up in London). This was a narrative of a loss of innocence telling of: the first encounters with non-white people; the need to alter one's way of being and behaving; the need to understand new codes and politics; the process of adopting a new identity; and, in particular, the need to understand the nature of different areas of London. In the following extract, Helen, who grew up in a small village in the north of England, describes her first impressions of London. When Helen referred to the different areas, they needed no introduction or explanation. She was working on the assumption that I would 'know' that Brixton is an 'Afro-Caribbean' area, associated as it was not only with African Caribbean residence but also black political activism. There is no doubt in the way she characterised these areas, nor doubt that I would understand what she was referring to.

Yes. Size first of all. The obvious thing. Just so enormous. I remember getting to grips with getting around the Tube system, everything was just, you know, a bit difficult at first. But exciting because it was . . . I quite like cities 'cos you can be anonymous in them if you want to be. It's quite nice. Yes, it can be so claustrophobic in a small place. What else? I remember going to Streatham so I was close to Brixton, and I'd really never come across Afro-Caribbean people before, and of course, it's got to be one of the biggest concentrations in the country, and with Peckham just along the way as well, I remember that being sort of, not a huge shock 'cos I'd been to university by then and I had come across people of different races, but not really Afro-Caribbeans at all. And I remember remarking on it, mentally if you like, but, 'God, it . . . this does feel like I'm in the minority', you know. Almost like the tables had been turned. But by the time you get down to Streatham it becomes white again, it's ever so odd, it's like you sort of go through waves of colours in London, concentrations of people.

(Interview 26)

Despite these big changes in her environment, London had now become home for Helen. It was a place where she had roots and felt that she belonged. However, areas within London were clearly racialised and marked for Helen, so she would not necessarily have felt so comfortable everywhere. Helen went on to explain her understanding of the subtle gradations between different areas:

Helen: Yes, I've never felt, you know, like I stood out. I think, well, because there's every variety of person coming from every background here, I think . . . unless you ended up in the middle of a sort of enclave, which you could say you . . . I don't know, say you lived in [. . .] you know, in a massively sort of Hindu area or something, you probably could feel quite strange, but generally speaking I think most people can be accepted in any big city, without problems. [. . .] I expect that comes from people wanting to feel comfortable where they live, so people gravitate towards their 'own'.

BB: And do you feel yourself doing . . . I mean, how would you characterise Camberwell within that kind of scheme?

Helen: Camberwell's a mixture. I mean, I see Brixton as predominantly black, and Peckham predominantly black, and Camberwell sort of a little bit of a mixture, quite a nice mixture really, in the middle. Lots of black people, lots of white people, see some Indian women around . . . and I find that . . . I'm not sure I would feel comfortable living right in the middle of Brixton, to be honest with you, any more than a black person would feel comfortable living in my village in the north-east. I'm sure they would feel very uncomfortable. So . . . but I think people can live very happily side-by-side, but just as the house share that I ended up in Streatham, the people . . . we got on because we were all really from very similar backgrounds, wildly varying experiences, but the backgrounds were virtually the same. And so people do gravitate towards their own, don't they, because familiarity makes you feel comfortable.

(Helen, Interview 26)

Again, the visual becomes important. In Helen's description of the area in which she lived, with its mixture of colour, black and white and 'a few Indian women', she seemed to be describing the mental image she had of a street scene, rather than demographic statistics she may (or may not) have come across. Presumably, Indian men also live in the area. Heather, who like Helen lived in Camberwell having come from outside London (the south-west of England), also had a narrative of wide-eyed learning on coming to London. The way in which space is racialised has an impact on where she wanted to live. She stated that she preferred living in Camberwell to Hampstead (an area of London associated with the prosperous, liberal middle classes), because of the stimulation and excitement that difference brings. In her account, however, there remained the concern that the difference should not be too different, what she wanted is a 'nice mix' – in terms of both 'race' and class:

Heather: Camberwell is very mixed culturally, but it is still predominantly white. It's not like going to Brixton or Hearn Hill or something like that, where the balance is quite different. [. . .] But Camberwell is a very weird mix because there are areas up Crescent Road and stuff which are incredibly professional middle classes. You know, I mean the people that we back onto . . .

BB: That way . . .?

Heather: That way and that hill . . . people that we back onto, he's a QC, and then you can go down to the high street and it's estates and most of the people are on benefit. And they're living within 100 yards of each other. You know, it's very kind of, it's very mixed here. And that's one of the reasons why I like it so much [. . .]

BB: What is it that you like about Camberwell, what is it about the mix that attracts you?

Heather: Just because there's nothing more boring than being with everybody that's the same. You know, it's deathly dull. The thought of living in Hampstead, yes, it's beautiful and there's great shops and stuff, but everybody's the same. You know, they're all media-based, they all earn seven-figure salaries, they all have a house in France . . . it's actually bloody boring after a while. I get to meet lots of different people being here. Um, it's just much more varied. Life is more varied. It means that your choice is more varied. You know, there's a strong Greek Cypriot community here as well, so there are great Greek delis. You know, the choice of veg in the Greek greengrocers is very different from what I would get in a greengrocers in my home town. Because they're Greeks so they specifically pick stuff that they know their Greek clients know what to do with and enjoy eating. So that opens up your mind to things. You know, most days I walk past there and look at something, and think I have no idea what that is, which is great, that's very good for you. It makes life enjoyable. But then there's also in this area people that come from a very similar background to me. So there are also people that make me feel kind of cosy and comfortable and know where I am, which is just a really nice mix. And it means that I have you know, friends from lots of different backgrounds around here. Which is great and it means that you know conversation becomes lively, that one's attitudes are constantly being challenged and changed and that you have to be really open-minded about things.

(Heather, Interview 15)

Heather discussed difference as a lifestyle or consumption issue – in areas that were marked by difference (there were exciting, unknown things available in the shops). But she also suggested that contact with different people – from 'different backgrounds' – had an effect on her own subjectivity and identity: 'one's attitudes are constantly being challenged and changed'. There was a tension in Heather's feelings towards difference, between pleasure – it 'makes life enjoyable' – and 'worthy' education or tolerance – 'that's very good for you'. Heather's experiences of being challenged had not always been pleasant or productive as the following extract demonstrates.

Heather: When I went to college I was perceived as being very, very middle class.

BB: Right, this is in London?

Heather: Yeah, and that was when I started to get a real . . . feel very different about it. And that people treated me in a certain way because of the way I spoke, very much, and they were very, very prejudicial about me because of the way I spoke. They made all sorts of judgements about my background that had no basis, other than my voice, and were completely incorrect. [. . .] Very quickly I learned that there was no point in arguing with these people. That I had utter contempt for them for the fact that they were prepared to judge me that quickly. The fact that they were prepared to be, you know . . . if you went in with a working-class accent or if you were black, or if you were gay, they would be completely open. But what they hated was white, British, middle class. That's what they absolutely hated. And they made all sorts of value judgements about that, and I absolutely despised them 'cos I thought how can you say here we are being totally open-minded without any sort of bigotry, and yet you are, you are picking . . . you are being absolutely racist about a certain group of people. They happen to be the group of people who have been most privileged in the past, and yes, I can understand the pendulum swing against it, but you're still being just as racist, just as classist, just as sexist, as anybody else. You're just choosing to do it to a different group.

(Interview 15)

Heather had experienced the discomfort of being categorised by others. She had found this a deep affront to her sense of self, and used extremely strong language to counter it. She spoke of 'despising' and having 'utter contempt' for those who labelled her. This section stands out in her interview, which otherwise did not contain such strong emotions or language, and it is possible that she was referring to a particular disturbing event. Other interviewees also identified college as being a time when their identity was brought into question in a way that was new to them. Melanie (Interview 39), for instance, described feeling 'like a bumpkin up from the country' who was not 'streetwise' and became aware of her own 'naiveté'. Emma also described feeling naive, but also having to reposition herself in terms of accepted assumptions.

> When I first went to college, I found it very hard because I was naive in, I don't know, I think people didn't want to accept me because of the way I spoke. I had a hard time with that, I wasn't very streetwise. I came out with some great clichés all the time. You know, my heart was in the right place, I'd say some of the most crass comments. And I'd talk about politics only from what my father and mother said. I'd just state their views.
>
> (Interview 16)

Emma said that one of the main reasons she wanted her daughters to go to state schools was that they might avoid being so naive. This would also be helped by the fact that they would not grow up in the countryside. This sense of living in London as producing different subjectivities or identity was felt by other interviewees, including those who had grown up in London. Deborah felt that growing up in London had given her a particular perspective on cultural difference:

> I think I take for granted living with a lot of people who don't come from, say, London because I've always lived in London, apart from when I was abroad, and I got very . . . I mean, I just take for granted that this is a very, very sort of cosmopolitan kind of area.
>
> (Interview 17)

Beverly, in the following extract, was describing the difference she had noticed in her step-children who had moved from London to the countryside:

> They talk different, they *are* different, you know, everything, their mannerisms. They're not so aggressive as they used to be in London. Although it did them good because it taught them, you know, to be streetwise and everything else.
>
> (Interview 42)

Beverley returned to the issue of confidence and being streetwise when I pointed out that one of the differences between London and the countryside was that it was 'more multicultural'. Her response showed that part of what being 'streetwise' entails was being able to 'cope' with racialised difference. The need for confidence in being on the streets again recalled a fear of racialised aggression:

Yes, it is definitely. And it's good that they've known that as well. It's as if they've started off there first and just like put bang into it, you know. I think they've got a lot of confidence now, more than they would if they started off there. Because when they come here, they do go round to the shop on their own, which is literally round the corner. I think if they hadn't lived here first, they'd never have the confidence to do that. Because my youngest step-son's like that, he's not got the confidence. Funny really, because different areas, how it affects the children. I think my youngest will be much tougher than Kevin [older son] really.

(Interview 42)

This sense of fear and the need to behave in different ways in differently racialised areas comes out clearly in the following extract from Emily, who was one of the few women I interviewed who had grown up in London, in fact in Camberwell:

Emily: When I go to Brixton, I'm conscious of being white. Very much so. I don't very often go there for . . . simply, I don't need to go there. I go to Bromley if I want to go shopping. But yes, I am conscious because I . . . yeah, I can be walking in the street, and be the only white person in the street. I do feel conscious. I've never been hurt there or anything, but I do feel conscious.

BB: But do you think that makes you act differently than when you're . . .?

Emily: I am very quick in walking and things like that, yeah. And I walk very assertively I think. But the word . . . I've been told that if you walk like this, they won't mug you! Do you know what I mean? Um, I don't know. I don't know really. Yeah, I suppose I am. I mean, my kids have been up there with me, and I wouldn't jeopardise their safety, so I can't feel that much threatened up there. They've been up there with me.

(Interview 21)

The question of whether an area is regarded as 'black' or 'white' or a 'nice mix' or an 'extreme mix' is largely subjective. Whereas, for both Helen and Heather, Camberwell was a racially 'mixed' area, for Joan, who lived on a council estate, it was 'black':

BB:	Where would you put Camberwell on a map?
Joan:	A black area. Definitely. There are a lot of African people moving in around this area as well.
	[. . .]
BB:	You definitely feel like, you feel like it's a black area?
Joan:	Oh definitely. Only I don't feel like it, it is [laugh].

(Interview 8)

This raises the question of how many black people are required to make a black area and how many white people a white area. One might assume that at least 50 per cent of a given population would need to be black in order for it to be designated as such. However, the identity of areas and the perceptions of people do not work in such a way. There is no space here to do an in-depth analysis of the relationship between the ways in which an area was characterised by the interviewees and its actual population. However, one indication of this relationship would be the fact that Brixton, which was taken by all the interviewees who mentioned the area to be an accepted 'black' area, has at least over 50 per cent white people living in each of its electoral wards (according to the 1991 population census). In a racialised perceptual schema, numbers and dominance can easily be overestimated, as the following extract illustrates. I had asked Liz, who was a school governor, what the racial mix of the school was:

> So I don't know, quite a big mix I think. Actually, it's so difficult, I was just thinking, there was one photograph of Rachel's in her first year in fact. And when I looked at it I was quite surprised I think she was only one of three Caucasian children in her class [taking the photograph out] I think that's, so I don't know if that's [looking at photo]. No there are more, aren't there. Girls I think I was looking at the girls or something, so I don't know if that's any indication, I mean obviously it depends from class to class. But that looks like it's sort of half and half, doesn't it? You know, there's a good mix, children of all . . . [laugh] sorts!

(Liz, Interview 43)

In her mind, the black children had been much more visible (to the point of obliterating) than the white children. Here, we perhaps partly return to the visual nature of racial differences. Black people may have a bigger visual impact than their numbers justify. But they may also be perceived to have a bigger social or cultural impact than is suggested by numbers alone.

Conclusion

I began this chapter with a discussion of the taboo nature of 'race' for those who are positioned as white in Britain. This is not to say that the interviewees were not prepared to talk about 'race' at all, but that 'race' was a topic that required delicacy and negotiation of difficult issues to talk about. There were certain silences and absences, but also the presence of different narratives and motifs. 'Race' was present in the interviewees' lives in terms of their interactions with others; it was not something that they were conscious of intimately affecting their own sense of themselves. Thus, while they took care to talk about and act on gender in various ways with the children, 'race' was something that they avoided, lest they might make their children view people and behave differently. To see difference was to risk being racist. Therefore, the most 'healthy' or risk-free response was not to notice anything. When children did remark on racialised physical differences, mothers largely sought to reassure themselves that this did not 'mean anything'. Some, however, also suggested that perhaps perceptual practices were undergoing change and that what children saw, and in particular how they responded to what they saw, may be different from their parents.

Other aspects of the interviews shed some light on the ways in which the perceptual practices of the white interviewees were racialised. The examples of the image of the threatening/exciting black man and the vividly remembered 'one black person in childhood' both suggest ways in which there is a constitutive outside to the norm of whiteness. This was both threatening and desirable, reflecting the ambivalence entailed in occupying the position of the norm. 'Race' was also imagined in conjunction with the urban, and thus living in London was understood as a racialised experience. Living in London was understood not only as offering a certain 'exposure' to difference, but as productive of subjectivity. In particular, the metropolitan subject was contrasted with those living in rural, or even suburban, areas. It should be noted that this was particularly the case for those who lived in the more 'racially mixed' Camberwell than for those living in Clapham. Here, again, as with accounts of childhood, whiteness was figured as an absence of 'race'.

This chapter has opened up and explored some of the ways in which 'race' and blackness were understood and imagined by the interviewees. In particular, it has examined the ways in which the concept of 'race' as a perceptual schema can enable the analysis of qualitative material. This has highlighted some of the difficulties facing research in this area. In analysing interview material with individuals, one is involved both in tracing the discourses they use, but also in attempting to surmise how they are influenced by discourses that tell them what not to see and say. This is of necessity a tentative process.

The chapter has also raised several themes that will be taken up in different ways in the rest of the thesis. The next chapter will explore further interactional aspects of the interviewees' lives in a way that also relates directly to the questions raised here of spatiality and location. A further way of imagining location will be explored in the chapter on national identity.

6 In search of a 'good mix'
'Race', class and gender and practices of mothering

Introduction

> I remember sitting outside a winebar in the summer down in Chancery Road which is just up the High Street, a couple of roads away, just at the time when people were collecting their children from school, and you see mothers in enormous cars with children in school uniform, who are obviously going to private schools. And you see women pushing buggies with children and having collected other people's children going to the estates just round the corner. Um, there is . . ., considering in such a *small* area, there are so many *different* kinds of backgrounds, it never ceases to amaze me how little people socialise.
>
> (Deborah, Interview 17)

Deborah provided an evocative account of a particular street scene. There she was, sitting outside a winebar, which in itself suggests a certain classed nature of the area and of herself as a subject. And as she watched people go by, she was able to see just by looking at them how they too were classed. Class is embodied and marked. She 'knows' by their 'enormous cars', or their wearing of uniforms from private schools, or the ways in which they are dressed, the buggies they push and the collection of children with them, which told her that they are bound for 'the estate'. 'Race' was silent in this account, but no doubt she would also have remarked racialised differences as she sat watching the world go by. What struck Deborah most in recollecting or reconstructing this scene was not so much the existence of these differences, or her own ability to read these differences, but 'how little people socialise'. In the interview, Deborah went on to suggest possible reasons why people fail to socialise across these differences. She blamed the lack of 'facilities', including the way schools were unable to create a sense of 'cohesion, make the community stay as a sort of community'. She discussed the rise in house prices in the area and the effect this had on patterns of residence. Deborah conjured up the fantasy of a time in the past when things were better, although there was also some uncertainty that this ever existed 'I just think people of different backgrounds and different "races" have just sort of drifted. I mean, if they were ever together in the first place, I don't know. There's no chance really for people getting together'.

Deborah produced a narrative around social differences that not only had a time dynamic – suggesting that things were different once – but also suggested some of the ways in which differences are constructed and marked. Differences are classed and conditioned by material resources. They involve how people look and behave on the street, how they move through the streets, where they go and what they do. They also influence who interacts with whom, and how people interact with each other. This chapter explores one specific intersection of 'race', class and gender by looking at what some of the women I interviewed said about being mothers. The previous chapter discussed how perceptual practices, ways of seeing and being seen, as well as the imaginary are formed within discursive frameworks. This chapter will broaden the scope of analysis to a range of other practices. It will look at the social lives of the interviewees and their children; how they characterised their roles as mothers; what they looked for when choosing a school for their children; how they organised their children's after-school activities. I argue that the activities involved in being mothers and bringing up children can be understood as performative of 'race', class and gender. That is, that practices of mothering are implicated in repeating and re-inscribing classed and raced discourses. The women, as mothers, are also engaged in gendered – and gendering – work.

Class, as a discursive construction, maps onto material inequalities and forms of social exclusion and exploitation. Like 'race' and gender, it is also embodied:

> Bodies are the physical sites where the relations of class, gender, race and sexuality and age come together and are embodied and practised. A respectable body is white, desexualised, hetero-feminine and usually middle-class. Class is always coded through bodily dispositions – the body is the most ubiquitous signifier of class.
>
> (Skeggs 1997: 83)

Class and 'race' cannot always be easily disentangled from each other. Historically, the working classes, perceived as 'other' by the normative middle classes, have been ascribed racialised characteristics (see Cohen 1988). Sander L. Gilman traces how, in representation, working-class and black women were ascribed similar positions in relation to deviant sexualities (Gilman 1985). 'Race' and class are not only inter-related, but can be subject to a similar analysis. Perceptual practices of seeing (and hearing) difference are as important in constructing class as they are with 'race'. Class is inscribed in bodies, functioning at the level of the visible, both because classed bodies are different shapes and sizes (see Lawler 1999: 83) and through the functioning of classed 'dispositions' (Bourdieu 1994) or tastes. Through class, differently adorned and managed bodies are produced. In addition, as with 'race' and gender, class is embedded in processes of subjection and in subjectivities. Class is one of the ways in which subjects come into being, one of the modalities through which subjectivities are constructed:

> Class is not just about the way you talk, or dress, or furnish your home; it is not just about the job you do or how much money you make doing it; nor is it merely about whether or not you went to university, nor which university you went to. Class is something beneath your clothes, under your skin, in your psyche, at the very core of your being.
>
> (Kuhn 1995: 98)

Beverley Skeggs highlights the intersections between class and gender, noting 'the category "woman" is always produced through processes which include class, and classifying produced very real effects which are lived on a daily basis' (Skeggs 1997: 2). In particular, she traces the way femininity is always classed, representing middle-class respectability, and how this involves ambivalent identifications or dis-identifications in femininity for working-class women.

Valerie Walkerdine and Helen Lucey highlight the ways in which motherhood and mothering are classed concepts and practices. They argue that working-class motherhood has been judged negatively against the model of the middle-class 'sensitive mother' (Walkerdine and Lucey 1989). But motherhood is also raced, with black mothers often cast by public and state agencies into a model of deviance (see Phoenix 1991). Thus, at the core of practices of motherhood lie the intersections of 'race', class and gender. The experience of and practices involved in mothering are inescapably and irreducibly gendered. It is a 'women's' activity and requires individuals to reorientate their identities, their sense of being as women and their relationship to other women, particularly perhaps their own mothers:

> Motherhood is not only about having children. It is about having a mother; that is, about being mothered too [. . .] the position of the mother is mediated by desire and longing, and much more complicated than a biological event or than a role which can be learned.
>
> (Woodward 1997: 243–4)

Motherhood is also classed and raced. In addition, as the material in this chapter makes clear, much of the work of mothering involves negotiating, repeating and reciting gendered, classed and raced norms. The everyday practices of mothers are the performative re-inscriptions of norms. They are, at least in part, the product of classed, gendered and raced imaginings of how children are and should be positioned, as well as what mothering and parenting should be.

The women were interviewed at a particular moment in their lives when they were concerned with the activities involved in bringing up young children. Their practices, and what they said, involved negotiating with, sometimes competing, discourses derived from their own situation, their upbringing and parenting, the norms presented by their peers and others around them, the resources available to them, and the actions of wider public institutions and state agencies, in particular the education system. The question of being a mother, bringing up and overseeing the education of children, involves the encounter between the intimate psychic level of the individual with wider public discourses. This encounter takes place is and is shaped by the material, in the form of both the resources available and the nature of placed and localised interactions.

This chapter focuses on the accounts of a particular group of women and examines a range of practices connected with motherhood. This enables the exploration of raced and classed practices of inclusion and exclusion,[1] as well as the ways in which mothering involves work to produce raced, classed and gendered subjects. The first section, 'Sensitive mothers', explores some of the ways in which motherhood has changed the interviewees' sense of who they were and how they described their work as mothers. The next section explores how the women talked about the friendships that they had made as mothers. Friendships were focused on the local area and clearly involved classed and raced practices of inclusion and exclusion. The women discussed the different practices of 'filtering' that were involved in finding friends in the local area. Friendships with people who fell into similar classed and raced positions were easily made, whereas encounters with others were limited, and sometimes a little fraught. In the next section, 'Choosing schools', the question of primary education for their children is explored. This was a much more contentious area. In the interviews, there were many discussions of the different state schools locally and their relative merits. It emerged that mothers were looking for schools that had a particular classed and raced composition. The 'right' school was one that had the right social and racial 'mix' of students. This, it emerged, was a school that was not seen as being too black or working class. Raced and classed 'others' appeared to risk disrupting or threatening their children's ability to gain the right racialised and classed social capital from school. As the final section, *Guess who's coming for tea Mummy?*, shows, this desire for the 'right mix' influenced not only the choice of school but also the ways in which mothers organised their children's social lives and viewed some of their interests.

Sensitive mothers

The majority of the women whose accounts are examined in this chapter belonged to two groups of white middle-class friends or acquaintances who were living within a one and a half mile radius of each other in Clapham. They worked, or had worked, in largely professional occupations, as teachers, journalists or in private sector management. They were living in an area where housing was expensive and which was largely white and middle class. However, this area lay in close proximity to areas that were more socially and racially mixed. None of these women was born in the area, and it is likely that many of them will move on, further out of London, in the search for bigger houses or gardens and a different choice of schools. Several of the women mentioned the same towns, for example Twickenham in Surrey, as desirable locations. Therefore, these women did not have deep roots in the local community in terms of residency over generations or even their own lives. Social mobility was linked to this geographic mobility. With the changing of geographic place since childhood, their social space had also often shifted. As a result of social mobility and changing social structures, these women did not necessarily have models of parenting that could be adopted unaltered from their parents.[2] Thus, their mothering involved new negotiations of place and social space.

At the time when the interviews were being conducted (September 1997 to April 1998), several different high-profile political and cultural events and discourses impacted on the ways in which motherhood was perceived. These, along with the social and economic context, form part of the social space in which the interviews were conducted and the accounts produced. The new Labour government was putting into legislation its position on the long-running political debate on single mothers. The idea of single mothers as an unnecessary burden on the state was underlined through the removal of single-parent benefit. Single mothers were also defined as a particular social 'problem' because they did not work and thus failed to set a sufficiently industrious example to their children. The government claimed that it was enabling single parents to do what they wished – that is work. But this was not a discourse of increasing choice, rather one of delegitimising one choice, that of staying at home and caring full time for children. High-profile women such as Cherie Blair and Hillary Clinton could be said to represent an ideal of successful working motherhood. At the same time as the validity of poorer single women staying at home was called into question, several high-profile, high-earning women left work in order to be full-time mothers. In addition, the Louise Woodward case in the United States, in which a British nanny was accused of killing a child, provoked anxious debates around issues of childcare, leading to criticism of ambitious working women who could not care for their children (the mother of the child, a working doctor, was given fairly unfavourable press). Several 'celebrities' (Madonna, Pamela Anderson) became mothers in this period, giving rise to discussions of babies as 'fashion accessories'. The role of fathers did not receive the same level of debate or attention as that of mothers, and there was no serious challenge to the idea that children are the primary responsibility of women. For instance, the Labour government made no suggestion that it wished to overturn Britain's exemption from European legislation on paternity leave obtained by the previous government.

All the interviewees agreed that motherhood was a major transformation, involving great personal and practical adjustment in their lives. At a practical level, having children had changed the pattern of their lives. All the women in the Clapham group had worked full time before having children. None was working full time at the time of the interviews, but several were working part time, often from home. Others had worked when their children were first born, but subsequently left work. Clearly, becoming mothers produced a major change in the ways they lived their lives and the activities they were involved in. Many, such as Rosalind, remarked on the way in which this changed their interaction with their local areas:

> I think you suddenly start to talk to people, so I think until we had Anna, we probably didn't even look up when we went out to work and see the neighbours, but once we had her, we started to meet all the neighbours. And I know the people in the shops and all sorts of things. [. . .] I think perhaps you want to be part of it.
>
> (Interview 20)

More significantly, however, it changed their sense of self. Having children involved taking on a new identity as a mother. This in turn involved negotiating various different models and discourses of motherhood – shaped by their own mothers, those around them and wider public discourses.

Jennifer explained how her mothering self was different from her self at other moments in her life:

> And I think it's with a lot of things . . . like when you know people from school and when you know them from university, you are almost a different person to all those people, aren't you. And it's the same I think when you've had a child. You're then somebody's mother. Initially, I think. And I think it's very easy to become . . . to allow yourself to become somebody's mother, and forget that you're actually, you know, a thinking, talking human underneath.
>
> (Interview 25)

Teresa also described how she felt that motherhood had changed her sense of self and her relationship to others:

Teresa: You start to question whether you have an identity outside of it after a while. But yes, absolutely, everything, your whole perspective, everything you see, your whole attitude to things is entirely as a parent. Like it is quite different – it's much more sensitive.

BB: Sensitive to . . .?

Teresa: Whatever's around you. I mean, social issues, environmental issues, anything really. I mean, anything that comes nearer to home, you know. Dinner party conversations, National Health

BB: Service and education, suddenly become far more relevant to you, once you're a parent.

BB: And how about your kind of sense of who you are? Does it have an impact on that?

Teresa: I think on a personal level, I'm absolutely certain it's my greatest achievement to date, and I don't imagine I'll surpass it. I mean, I'm not suggesting it's a wonderful bed of roses, or anything like that, but I know that I always felt that before I had children that I'd like children. One always assumes that. In another way, you sort of think 'oh, one day, this will happen', but it was never sort of a burning urge, or anything like that. [. . .] I know now that if I was unable to have children I would feel this huge gaping hole.

(Interview 18)

This account of change in perspective and priorities was common to many of the respondents. Priorities were generally changed in favour of what might conventionally be understood as the feminine. We see this in Teresa's description of how she has become more 'sensitive'. Others stressed how the world of work no longer seemed so significant to them, often after years spent developing a career. However, as Teresa's reference to questions around the National Health Service and education suggest, it would be wrong to characterise this simply as a shift to the private world of mothering, even though, as the following quote suggests, it might feel like that:

I was privileged to enjoy a very good job and doing things that men are doing easily. And when I got married and had children, I was suddenly relegated to a different model [. . .] One is invisible because one is doing it quietly behind closed doors and you might be in despair and nobody else would know. Or the other people who know are other women on the whole and they're all doing the same thing.

(Philippa, Interview 24)

While the experience might be isolating, mothering involves not only negotiating many public discourses, but also interaction with public fora and institutions, as will be explored later in this chapter in the case of schools.

The women saw their practices as mothers as providing a supportive environment for their children. Part of their perception of what motherhood entailed was formed in response to the mothering they had received as children from their own mothers. This was sometimes expressed as a reaction against their mother's approach . Teresa described her own mother as: 'a wonderful mother and there was a very strong sense of security through our childhood, and I guess I would want to replicate that' (Interview 18). Philippa described what she saw as her role as a mother in similar language:

Well, I currently feel, and of course one is learning, that it's most important to help them to grow up as balanced and as wide-ranging in their outlook as possible. One obviously wants one's children to be very happy, to be safe, to be well, these things aren't really in our control, but we contribute to them. And we, I think, have a large role to play in how they enjoy life at any rate, not just in what we can give them materially, but in what we give them emotionally. I mean, a lot of people suffer because of emotional difficulties or deprivations of various kinds when they're little. So, I feel very responsible, probably too responsible, as a parent to give my children as secure a background as I can.

(Interview 24)

In addition to this provision of emotional support, and in particular security, Jennifer describes a more classic socialising role for herself:

Well, I mean I'm not too bothered about table manners. I mean, I was drilled with them at home, but I mean, I would say don't speak with your mouth full, and if you've got the implements in your hand, I'm not too bothered how you've got them in your hand. But more, I think, to do with interaction with other people. You know, if somebody's talking, you wait till they've finished, or if it's desperate, you say excuse me. You know, when someone's talking to you, you look at them, and tell them that other people are shy or . . . and you must say hello first.

(Interview 25)

As was mentioned in the previous chapter, this role also involved discussing gender differences with children and guiding their development as gendered subjects, as well as monitoring their expressions around racialised differences. For example, in the following extract, Jan described how she tries to counter gendered stereotypes in her children:

I think with boys, it's much more, it's much easier really. I think you know what you're aiming for, or I think I do, really. There's the obvious things I'm trying to combat really, like overly aggressive behaviour, or over competitive behaviour and the things I'm trying to nurture, like nurturing. Which is quite easy at the moment with Hugo because he's got a little brother. But I find it much more difficult with Zoe, when actually, you're not actually encouraging her to be aggressive, but to be a bit more competitive, you know, just to *take* the opportunity or whatever, to go for it.

(Interview 30)

The two issues raised in this section – of the need of children for 'security' and emotional support, as well as for socialisation – will be drawn out in other parts of the chapter. The section on schooling addresses a critical moment when parents hand their children over to schools for a large part of the day. Decisions about schooling involve a reappraisal and reimagining of what mothers (and fathers[3]) want for their children. This will be explored in the section on choosing schools. However, the next section will consider one resource used by all the women in the Clapham group to cope with the transformation in their lives – that of social networking. This will illustrate the role of class and 'race' in shaping daily intimate practices and interactions.

Mothers' friendships and social networking

As mentioned above, for all the women, motherhood meant that they were suddenly spending much more time at home and in their local area. Some responded to this situation, and their new position of being mothers, by actively seeking out other mothers to spend time with and as a form of support. For many, these friendships and social activities affirmed their sense of motherhood. It enabled them to meet people who had a common cause and could, hopefully, confirm their sense of doing motherhood well. This was not the case for all the women I interviewed. Madeleine, for example, explained how she avoided such public enactments of motherhood:

> I *hated* one o'clock clubs and ohh no, I couldn't cope with them at all [. . .] I don't know if I very really saw myself as a mum, really to be honest. I didn't enjoy it very much when she was little. I was quite young, . . . it wasn't something I'd decided I wanted to do . . . um . . . and I found it very hard to identify with other mums [laugh].
>
> (Interview 9)

Discussions of this particular moment of socialising offer an opportunity to see how the women in Clapham negotiated differences within their social worlds. Through their accounts, we are able to see the complex (and sometimes not so complex) processes of mutual appraisal, selection and filtering involved in establishing a friendship group. As Bourdieu writes:

> Individuals do not move about in social space in a random way, partly because they are subject to the forces which structure this space (e.g. through the objective mechanisms of elimination and channelling), and partly because they resist the forces of the field with their specific inertia, that is, their properties, which may exist in embodied form, as dispositions, or in objectified form, in goods, qualifications, etc.
>
> (Bourdieu 1994: 110)

A criticism of Bourdieu is that he tends to focus solely on distinctions of class. Savage *et al.* note how Bourdieu makes little mention of gender and his discussion 'slides between individual and household analyses of cultural practices and habits' (Savage *et al.* 1992: 103). However, it is clear that the 'movements in the social space' discussed in this chapter are not only classed, but also raced and gendered. They are also involved in the affirmation of a particular sense of self, suggesting a more complex interplay between subjectivity and practice than Bourdieu might imply in his discussion of 'dispositions'. This section examines how the women moved in the social space of motherhood and the non-'random' collection of friends that they made in that space.

The women in Clapham met and made friendships with other mothers in various ways. They went to ante- and post-natal classes, both those run by the health authority and those run by non-governmental organisations such as the Natural Childbirth Trust (NCT). These were classed and raced, by virtue of both their geographic location and the nature of the activity. For instance, Jan noted that the NCT 'tends to be very kind of, um, terribly well-heeled and all of a type really' (Interview 30). They also made friends through chance (or not so chance) encounters in baby clinics, in the street and through mutual friends. Playgroups of various forms are also forums for socialising, for both mothers and children. While not all women used them, some made a point of taking their babies and toddlers to activities (including swimming and music classes) almost every day. This was generally presented as a strategy for relieving the intensity of full-time care of young children, allowing both parent and child to have other company.

In my experience of being in one o'clock clubs or playgroups, which I attended in order to contact potential interviewees, there is a great degree of social segregation with middle- and working-class women forming separate groups (childminders and nannies, particularly those from abroad, formed another group). The playgroups I attended were largely white. The social segregation was also noticed by Karon, a working-class woman living in Clapham who was not part of these two friendship groups. She was forthright about the impact of class on the interactions at the one o'clock club that she attended:

Karon: Well, you get the yuppie mums, or so we call them. I call them the yuppy mums and they are all interacting and they stay together and they turn up and have their own little social things. In the summer, they do make you laugh actually. They come over and they've got their picnics and they're sitting under the trees and they really do make it *known*. Then there's, well I'd class myself as a working-class person, you know, we have different . . .. But then saying that, don't get me wrong, I do socialise with the 'upper market' you might call it [laugh]. You know, some of them are very very friendly and some of them make it known that they won't be you know dirtying with you.

BB: Really, how do they do that?

Karon: They just ignore you. They just think they're better than you. Nose up in the air, they don't even acknowledge you. And they're the children that you find are the worst behaved. They have no manners, they have no control over their own children and basically I think it is probably because a lot of them work and they're with the nannies a lot of the time. And when they're with them, they just don't know how to control them. Which I think is quite sad actually, you see that quite a lot. And they do run absolutely wild. Whereas if my children, don't get me wrong, are sort of doing something wrong, I'm there straight away, sort of reminding them and telling them 'look, don't do that'. But some people just sit back and think 'oh they'll sort it out', which is just not the case, because if you don't correct them then they'll never know.

(Interview 38)

Karon showed the painful experience of feeling social exclusion: 'they make it known they won't be dirtying with you'. But she also took care to reverse some class stereotypes – here it is the middle classes who let their children run wild. She consciously labelled herself as 'working class' and referred to both working- and middle-class people as collectivities: 'we' call 'them' yuppy mums, 'they' behave in certain ways. This marks a contrast with the skirting around labels and more vague talk of different 'social groups' that was more common in the interviews with middle-class women. In the following account, Stephanie explained that social geography ensures that there is little social (or racial) mixing in the area she lived in:

I think I mean my experience tends to be around things, in Clapham, tends to be around things you know mother-and-child activities and the one thing I think is very noticeable about them is they are *accessible*, much more accessible to the middle-class women, um . . . [. . .] It's difficult to know whether it is just about, you know financial accessibility and the information being spread widely enough, or whether it's simply because *I* go to groups that are very much in the sort of heartland of what I was talking about. And therefore, you know someone from Battersea *wouldn't* come up to that group, but they would go to a group more in their local area, and they would find in their *own* groups that they don't have . . ., that the number of women from the social classes that I'm talking about go to the groups that *I* go to. So I don't know, but certainly ones that I go to are predominantly white women. . . . I don't know in percentage terms, but a *huge* number with partners in the city. You know, most of the people I know are married to bankers or stockbrokers or people in insurance.

(Interview 31)

In the above extract, Stephanie appears to be awkward in talking about both class and 'race'. She skirted around various possible reasons as to why the groups she went to were so middle class and white. Geographical location was the most obvious, but didn't quite seem to fit the bill (the areas she was discussing are all within a 10- to 15-minute walk of each other). Rather, what she was perhaps unable to say was that there were wider processes of self-selection and inclusion and exclusion going on. While she did talk about 'middle-class' women, she could not name the other 'social classes', instead identifying them by geographical area. She assumed that I would understand the different, classed nature of the other areas she named. 'Race' worked in a similar way; she identified her playgroups as white, but does not name the 'other', other than naming racially marked areas.

In contrast to Stephanie, her friend Teresa who lived in the same area found that involvement in a playgroup did bring her into cross-class interaction. This was not always a comfortable experience.

Teresa:	We had to do so much and raise so much money, which is fine, I mean, I'm pro all of that, um, but it did have its frustrating moments when it was you against the world, and nobody else was helping [laugh]. When you were trying to collect sponsorship money, and everybody would walk out of the room as soon as you walked in [laugh]. You began to feel like a social pariah really.
BB:	So that was a voluntary-run kind of . . .
Teresa:	Yes. It was. Playgroups in essence are like that. Well, they have playgroup workers that are generally a part of the Playgroup Association, but they do have a very limited amount of funding from the local authority . . . but generally you have to have a good parental input for them to survive. That's why many have closed down. Um, Clapham's an interesting area, as you know. I mean, it is quite a mix of people. It's a mix of a lot of privilege and money, all the rest of it, and a lot of deprivation. So . . .
BB:	So how does that . . .?
Teresa:	That exactly reflects the playgroup. Very much so in its composition. Which is *great*, just very frustrating . . . when you couldn't get any help. It was quite ironic actually because . . . it was quite absurd because people although I guess you can understand it . . . mothers who probably had a choice but again probably the more educated mothers were doing all they could to keep it running, and those that had *no* choice whatsoever, but probably had 15 million other things more pressing to worry about, were doing nothing. You know, and not just doing nothing, but . . . fairly sort of 'what good is this?' . . . But I can sort of understand that as well, you know. You see these . . . pushy women, I don't know, get you to do something when you've got other things on our mind.

(Interview 18)

Teresa approved of the 'mix' of 'privilege and money, all the rest of it, and a lot of deprivation', which was 'great', but did not elaborate why. Again, neither class nor 'race' was mentioned explicitly, but implied in the significant 'all the rest of it' and in the 'pushy', 'more educated' mothers who were taking the lead in running the playgroup. Here, for the first time in this chapter, there is the introduction of the concept of 'mix', which was central to the discussion on schooling developed below. Despite her positive attitude to the 'mix', it was not without problems and frustrations. Teresa did put herself into the shoes of these 'others' – she tried to imagine their point of view and the other pressures in their lives. But she still resisted identifying tensions as having a classed or raced element. Questions of material resources and inequalities were hinted at, but not faced directly.

Stephanie and Teresa were referring to broader level raced and classed differences that might potentially cause conflict. However, for much of the discussions around social networking, the differences that most exercised the middle-class women I interviewed in Clapham were more subtle distinctions between different kinds of middle class. This was the level at which they were most aware of making conscious choices about friendships. It is not likely, for instance, that Teresa considered the 'deprived' mothers she met at the playgroup as potential friends to spend time with outside the context of the playgroup. Thus, in the following extract, Jan, who described how 'I sort of threw myself into ante-natal, post-natal networking with great gusto', was describing a very different level of social contact and filtering:

> Certainly I was very aware when I first had Zoe that it was like being a fresher, first term of university when you find yourself joining the rowing club and thinking afterwards *'what* was I thinking of? – oh you must join everything and meet lots of people' and actually realise that I don't *want* to meet all sorts of people, I want to meet people that I like and who have similar, you know similar with differences that are interesting, but not sort of in-your-face kind of, I don't know. It's a bit like that when you have your first child. I remember going round to someone's house for tea who I'd met at a baby clinic and the *only* thing that we had in common was the fact that we had a baby under 6 months, almost nothing really. And we never saw each other again. It was just a mutual realisation that it was, you know . . .
>
> (Interview 30)

The comparison of what Jan was doing as a new mother with being a 'fresher' immediately suggests the classed nature of the activity. This involved certain material resources – meetings are generally held in people's homes, requiring space and home environments to which you want to invite people, as well as mobility and the time to go to the meetings. But, more significantly, this particular, almost aggressive, socialising being referred to assumes certain forms of social and cultural capital. This includes the willingness and ability to 'join everything and meet lots of people'. Jan also made clear how processes of inclusion and exclusion were involved in this 'networking'. She was interested in meeting people who were not too 'similar' but whose differences were not 'in-your-face'. She did not elaborate on this carefully modulated distinction. In the example she gave, it was a lack of 'things in common' that was a problem, rather than objectionable differences. It seems clear that class and 'race' would play into Jan's notion of differences that were 'too in-your-face'. Jan had previously explained an objective that shaped her involvement in pre-natal and mother and toddler activities: 'At each stage, you meet people. You tend to sift out what activities you're not going to find like-minded people in really'. The quest for meeting 'like-minded' mothers was one that was mentioned (using the same words) by several other middle-class interviewees. Middle-class respondents would mention activities that they undertook with other mothers, such as visiting Kew Gardens or art galleries.

These activities are clearly instances where class and 'race' are performatively re-inscribed. Some of the mothers mentioned (sometimes with regret) that most of their friends were, like them, white and middle class. As well as undertaking activities that reinforced and reiterated classed and raced subject positions, inevitably these friendships would involve exchanges of ideas and opinions that also involved the reiteration and negotiation of normative discourses. This was particularly apparent in the context of decisions over schooling. Jan was involved in a particularly close-knit group of friends who had met through an ante-natal group and who continued to meet regularly. She described these women as 'my kind of people'. Nevertheless, the group had experienced tensions around the time their children first went to school:

Jan: But it's quite interesting, this group, when we meet up. Because we've been through this choosing nursery schools and schools and some fairly *uncomfortable* afternoons while people sat there and basically sort of felt that they had to justify endlessly, me included, why they were making the choice that they were, you know. And out of the original people, I think of the eight of us that still meet up (two have gone out of London now), three went privately and three went to the other school, the other state school, and two have gone to Heathcote [the school that her children attended].[4]

BB: And you had to justify it?

Jan: Well, no people sort of sitting there saying, 'well which school are you thinking of' and all that kind of thing. And those people that were going privately felt that they . . . you know were going to get a rough time for the fact that they weren't going for a state school and vice versa, you know. Um, and I was just *really* glad when it was all sorted. Because all the schools have sibling policies, so you wouldn't have to face this discussion every 2 years.

(Interview 30)

Other interviewees stressed how friendships made in this context of local mothering were not of the same calibre as those made in other contexts. Friendships were described as not being of the same 'depth' as those made before children or 'BC'. As Teresa described:

You embark on a friendship with another mother and *generally* it's on a very different level. If you really, really click, then I think that's quite unusual. You know, if you could really close your eyes and imagine there were no children there, would you really make an effort?

(Interview 18)

Teresa put this down partly to the context of building relationships where conversations are disjointed as they are interrupted by young children and also to the potential political differences that parenting can draw attention to. Here, both the social and the moral dimensions of mothering were brought to the fore:

The politics of parenting is quite acute, I think. You know, how you bring up your child, your approach to discipline, your approach to this as against another person's style of parenting, and it's a *minefield*.

(Interview 18)

Again, much here went unsaid. What was involved in developing or identifying a different 'style' of parenting and in the clashes between different styles? How much did class and 'race' play into these concepts? Teresa went on to give the example of someone's child who might be 'a bit of a bruiser, a bit antisocial' and parents who had 'very different discipline styles'. But Teresa also had a discourse of those middle classes who were very different from her and 'never the twain shall meet'. These she characterised as 'the Alice band and Volvo set'. Stephanie, in a similar conversation, described how talking about children can expose differences between herself and other middle-class white people who have a more 'traditional approach and outlook':

If for example, you know, I was explaining what, I mean I had wanted my child to go to a particular nursery and someone was saying you know, they wanted their child to go to a particular nursery because it was completely *different* to that, you know, you might then start straying into more sort of political territory and getting an understanding of where each individual stood in relation to, you know, those sort of beliefs. So it can certainly open things up.

(Interview 11)

In the context of making friends, it was generally taken for granted, and therefore implied rather than stated explicitly, that the friendships were between people who were all middle class and generally white. Here, it was frequently the differences between different 'types' of middle-class people that matter. A key axis of difference that many of the Clapham group mentioned was that of class – of the difference between them and those who were more middle class. The areas where they lived, the activities they undertook, ensured that these were the distinctions that mattered most. However, in a different field of practice, such as negotiating the state school system, questions of class and 'race' were approached in a different way.

Choosing schools

Schooling was something that the women of the Clapham group were very aware of and concerned about at the time of the interviews as several were at the stage of applying to schools for their eldest children. The women in the Clapham group were intending to send their children to state schools. For some, like Jan, this was a clear 'ideological' commitment. For others, it was the favoured option, but they would consider private schooling if they could not find a state school that they were happy with, or accepted that they might send their children to private schooling at a later age. In the area, primary schools had become part of a highly charged debate about schooling and were credited, for instance, with a major impact on local house prices. However, what emerged from the interviews is that issues of 'race' and class lay at the heart of the way parents approached the question of which school to send their children to.

Decisions about what was a good school were made on various bases. Parents had access to Ofsted reports and school league tables. They could also view the schools on open days. But the most important sources of information were other mothers and the school's general reputation in the area. There was a total consensus among middle-class mothers as to which were the best schools (and nearly all the working-class women in the area whom I interviewed agreed). Despite debates at the time about unsatisfactory levels of literacy in primary schools and 'New Labour's' drive to overcome this, the women in Clapham tended not to focus on concerns about their children's acquisition of concrete academic skills. This may well have been seen as too obvious an issue to mention or, alternatively, as middle-class parents they may have been confident of their ability to impart basic reading and writing skills to their children. Rather than standards, the primary focus was often on less tangible questions. Interviewees spoke of schools that were 'nice' or 'felt comfortable' and had the right 'atmosphere and ethos', and it was here that 'race' and class entered the story. Openness to difference and multiculturalism fitted into general liberal desires for freedom, creativity and friendliness, as long as, as we shall see, there was not too much difference. Getting the 'mix' right was key. The schools concerned had very different class and racial make-ups. The racial breakdown of the pupils in the school not only coincided with whether it was seen as a good school or not (white being good, black being bad), but was frequently mentioned as an indicator of a problem school. Thus, these middle-class white women, who espoused multiculturalism and embraced difference, also admitted that they found a school 'too black' or perhaps, rather, not white enough.

In the previous chapter, I mentioned briefly the general influence of multiculturalist discourses on the interviewees' ways of understanding and talking about 'race'. This group of middle-class women from Clapham were among those who espoused multiculturalism most strongly. They wanted their children to have an understanding of many different cultures and to feel comfortable by being surrounded by people of different 'races'. This was often vaguely extended to class, in that it was good that their children should know others from 'diverse backgrounds'. School and education was the site where these questions were really raised for parents. Schools are the location for the majority of public discourses about multiculturalism. They were also the places where many of the women found for the first time that their personal lives intersected with people from different 'races' and classes. Rosalind pointed this out herself: 'I mean, the mix of culture really, the most that I've been exposed to really is at [my children's] school. Which is a great mix really. And you don't really realise how you are stuck in your little world' (Interview 36).

Yet, at the same time, this desire for multiculturalism was combined with, and might be in conflict with, many other desires that the women had for their children's schooling. Issues that the mothers had raised in terms of their own roles – of providing stability and security – were returned to here. However, as we shall see, in this context, they mapped onto discourses of 'race' and class. The presence of too many raced and classed 'others' appeared to threaten the desired stability. It also raised the possibility that children might not acquire the right social and cultural capital and raced and classed subjectivities.

It is interesting to note some of the issues that did not generally emerge as a concern for the parents when discussing schools. For instance, all viewed schooling as a potentially positive experience, suggesting that they themselves had enjoyed their own schooling. None of these parents said or implied that they were intimidated by either the staff at the various schools they visited or the whole process of putting in applications for the school. This was in contrast to some of the working-class interviewees who were worried about how they should present themselves to the school teachers and others representing the educational system. For example, Rosemary, a working-class woman from Camberwell, explained her hesitancy in phoning the local education authority:

It is a night[mare] and it's on my mind all the time. And I rung them up just to see – I didn't want to ring, because I thought they might think [exasperated] 'oh what have we got here', you know 'some . . .'. But I had to ring to see if they'd got my appeal form back. Because I thought what if they haven't and I just leave it and they haven't got it, then I've had it. But I rang up and she said loads have appealed.

(Interview 32)[5]

In contrast, all the Clapham group were confident of their ability to navigate the education system (although not necessarily of their success in achieving what they wanted from it). The women expressed high levels of frustration concerning their children gaining access to the 'right' schools. This may partly be a reflection of the experience of powerlessness in the face of the education system – a powerlessness that was possibly a relatively rare experience for them. In addition, none expressed any concern about their children's ability to achieve educationally.

In the course of the interviews with middle-class mothers, various discourses were used to explain what they expected from primary school. One common discourse was that of 'hothousing'. This phrase was always used in pejorative terms, with women defending their motives as *not* being a desire to 'hothouse' their children. Here, we return to the distinction between the middle classes. The implication was that they were not *those* kind of pushy middle-class mothers.

In private nurseries, I have heard of these places, they are proud of the fact that a one and a half year old can spell squirrel!! I find it alarming . . .. And I think its because people are paying for it, they want to see results [. . .] They just get burnt out, what happens to their imagination?

(Deborah, Interview 40)

There was an uneasy tension running through these interviews between notions of freedom, and creativity and order and control. The interviewees had a clear idea of discourses of middle classness that they do *not* aspire to for their children. Stephanie described why she and her husband had rejected some local schools for their children:

So, you know, there are a lot around here that are like, traditional English public schools for tiny tots, which is not what we wanted. I mean the one up here where it's boys only and they all wear short trousers. And they literally do things like shake the master's hand in the morning and things like that.

(Interview 31)

The desire to be able to walk to school was a common concern. While it has much to do with environmental and health concerns, as well as teaching children road sense, it is also possible that the idea of walking to school conjured up a romantic village-like image (like the old advertisement for Clark's shoes of children walking along a country lane hand-in-hand). This can be seen in Teresa's reference to village schools, and their contrast with inner-city schools, in the following extract:

> It's funny 'cos one of the schools he's down for is a church school but we've got a long church application to it. It's a bit like a village school, it's small, it's . . . and it really appeals to me, you know, it's a small school and at aged four, I just want somewhere that looks warm and friendly, I mean, it's what I'm looking for really. You know, nice feel to it. But Heathcote, which is the other option, which he's got more chance of getting into 'cos it's not a church school, and it's bigger, it's got three reception classes as opposed to one, so it's three times the size, it's your typical inner city *big* school, big Victorian building, and part of me hates it.
>
> (Interview 35)

Alongside this warm, cosy and potentially creative image, there was also a desire for moral order and control as Teresa outlined in the following extract:

> I mean, I'm looking for a strong moral code in a school, a strong sense of community. I mean, I went to . . . Catholic schools but my primary school in particular was wonderful. *Absolutely wonderful.* And there was a **very strong moral code**, a very strong sense of, you know, **respect** for your neighbour – you know, the other children, the teachers, the wider community, and I want that. [. . .] [On a visit to a prospective school] I would just look for, I'd look for work on the walls, the quality of that which should be a indicator of standards, I guess, developmental standards. Look for interest in the class, that they're happy. That it's **controlled**.
>
> (Interview 18, italics Teresa's emphasis, bold mine)

The desire for control and a moral code might also have been part of the attraction of Church of England schools for some of the women in this group, despite their own non-practice of religion. Grant-maintained schools, with their different source of funding and relative independence from local authority control, often have the reputation for better academic standards. But with their religious basis, Church of England schools are also reputed to offer a different atmosphere, which may be part of the attraction. Deborah explained why she would like her son to go to a Church of England school:

> I would like him to go to the church school across the common but I am not a churchgoer – which is one of the problems. There are 21

places for churchgoers and nine for non-churchgoers [. . .] it was one of anti-slavers, it's got a perfect tradition really and I would like him to go to a church school, and I certainly didn't [go to one] when I was abroad, but there is a lot of emphasis based on religious education which I think is really important because some of the culture is tied up with art and history to do with religion. There is a big gap if you miss out on that, and I think that it's really good to have some kind of *moral code*. Parents who aren't necessarily religious at home but they support the *values*, important from that, I think they need so many *boundaries*, kids, it makes them feel *secure*, and it gives them something to rebel against and I think its very healthy. I like their *rules*. Like learn to *control your temper*! That's a good rule! And they are very conscious of other people's... religions, needs and beliefs, and I would really like him to go there I think it's a good school. I would be very happy, and they are very good on music too, which is very unusual for a primary school. Unless it's a private school which is completely different. They don't just do recorder, they have got an orchestra, which is very telling. They do a lot of sport.

(Interview 17, emphasis mine)

There are various reasons that Deborah gave for her preference, including the desire, like Teresa, for a 'moral code' and 'boundaries'. This resonated with discourses against 'liberal' or 'trendy' schools that had lost a sense of these values and thus contributed to the degeneration of society. But, as Deborah expanded on why she liked the school, this extended beyond its religious nature to broader issues of cultural capital – art, history, sport and, in particular, music. Deborah's idea of culture was racialised and classed; it was explicitly western and Christian and associated with 'high' culture. The desire for children to learn classical music was mentioned several times in the middle-class interviews. Frequently, these parents felt that their children were musically 'gifted' and, therefore, they wanted schools that could support this. For instance, Stephanie explained that:

Um, there are quite specific things we look for, like we have a particular interest in music, and my little boy seems to be gifted musically so we want to know that there are good facilities for supporting that, enabling that.

(Interview 11)

What is interesting here is the way in which the desire was expressed more as a special *need* – for a 'gifted' child – rather than as a desire on the part of the parents. Bourdieu, studying class and taste in France in the 1960s, found that 'nothing more clearly affirms one's "class", nothing more infallibly classifies, than tastes in music. This is of course because, by virtue of the rarity of the conditions for acquiring the corresponding dispositions, there is no more "classificatory" practice than concert-going or playing a "noble" instrument' (Bourdieu 1994: 18). I would argue that the same was still true of Britain in the 1990s. The desire for children to grow up with an appreciation for music allows for the expression of both the potentially contradictory desires that I have identified within this middle classness. Music is able to represent both free-flowing creativity and expression of self as well as order and a particular type of middle-class habitus that values 'high' culture and particular modes of appreciating it.

The women were keen to establish their difference from conservative, over pushy and aspirational middle classness. Sometimes, these middle classes were condemned for the way they did not support the state school system. The argument was that they distorted the intake of local schools by their absence. In contrast to the conservative positions they ascribed to others, the interviewees emphasised their desire to give their children the freedom to develop their imaginations and creativity. Steiner schools were mentioned favourably as an alternative route to state schooling, and there was an anxiety about too much emphasis on reading and writing at an early age. But the key concern that emerged from the interviews with the middle-class women in Clapham was that of the 'right mix' of children in school. In the following extract, Deborah began to explain why she was unhappy with Crooms Hill. Her son was at a preschool nursery at the school, but she wanted to move him before he started primary school. She brought up the issue of the community and her search for a school 'where there was a really good mix'. At first, this appeared to be largely to do with class:

Deborah: And it's just . . . really sad actually, they've just become really underfunded, rundown, everything. [. . .] I was very anxious, still am, for Tom to go to a local school and to walk to school and to socialise with kids from the school, and to go somewhere where there was a really good mix that reflected the community, and um, the schools *don't*, really – as far as I can see, the schools close to us just don't.

BB: Because they're dominated by . . .?

Deborah: Well, . . . I think what's happened is that in this road, I think this road is a good illustration of it probably, people come in, do up the houses, send their children to private school, . . . and a *lot* of new private schools have opened up, they're opening all the time, and so the local schools are, well, I think they've really become sink schools in a lot of ways, and then they're sort of fused between Lambeth and Wandsworth and um . . . all sorts of things I think contribute to it. But basically the mix that I wanted to be there isn't there.

(Interview 17)

Deborah, like others, felt caught between the 'wrong kind of middle class'

– those people who are not interested in community and who 'come in, do up the houses, send their kids to a private school' – and others whose dominance in a school will turn it into a 'rundown' 'sink school'. Teresa, for instance, described it as 'a typically inner-city dilemma'. The reference to 'sink schools' was not only classed, but also raced. Deborah was drawing on a discourse of 'sink schools' where schools in deprived areas fall into a downward spiral of reputation and standards as schools are increasingly unable to recruit 'successful' pupils and are left with those who 'sink' to the bottom. This wider discourse is often coded for 'race'. As Paul Gilroy points out, education has come to play an important role in the discourses of new racism:

> For a long while, the crime question provided the principal means to underscore the *cultural* concerns of this new nationalist racism [. . .] However crime has been displaced recently at the centre of race politics by another issue which points equally effectively to the incompatibility of different cultures supposedly sealed off from one another forever along ethnic lines [. . .] Where once it was the mean streets of the de-caying inner city which hosted the most fearsome encounter between Britons and their most improbably and intimidating other – black youth – now it is the classrooms and staffrooms of the inner-city school which frame the same conflict and provide the most potent terms with which to make sense of racial difference.
>
> (Gilroy 1992b: 54–5)

Deborah appeared to be drawing on this discourse. She went on to explain in the following extract that, when she said 'sink schools' or 'rundown', what she meant was too black, or not white enough, and a threat was posed by the presence of 'too many' black pupils:

> I went to an assembly recently – I go to quite a lot of the assemblies, they have assemblies on Fridays for parents . . . [. . .] and . . . I'd say it was *probably* maybe 80/85 per cent Afro-Caribbean, and . . . I'd say probably . . . maybe 5–10 per cent, 10 per cent maybe, Asian and a few other minority groups. And I just don't think that's a good *mix* because it doesn't reflect the community. I mean if I went into an assembly and saw sort of 95 per cent white children, I'd be worried. I'd think well that doesn't reflect the community, and I just don't . . . you know, that sort of idea that I wanted Tom to have a *mixture* of friends, from *lots* of different backgrounds.
>
> (Interview 17)

From this account, it is clear that, for Deborah, considerations around schooling were highly racialised. In fact, 'race' emerged as the central reason for her not wanting her son to continue in the school he already attended at nursery level and where he was very happy. It does not appear to be a problem for her son, who she said was so keen to start 'big' school that he had been known to take himself off and try and tag onto a class queuing up and about to enter the school. Deborah's hesitancy about the school did not rest on unsatisfactory standards or equipment or even the behaviour of teachers or pupils.

> I mean, I haven't actually got that many worries about the, really, the teaching or the standards there . . . so much. It's not a great standard, but I don't know how much that matters when children are younger, and when you teach them at home . . . and it's no worse than a lot of schools that have got more of a mix of kids in them.
>
> (Interview 17).

Nor was it solely the lack of other middle-class pupils. It was also that it had 'too few' white faces. Thus, her account of how the people in her area did not send their children to the local state school became at least as much about white flight as middle-class flight:

> It's very difficult to separate class and race a lot of the time, but I suppose they do go hand-in-hand just through necessity, and that's the way things work out [. . .] And that's what really worries me about this school, and I think it's *sad* because what happens is that I think a lot of people see this, and they don't send their children there after . . . reception, or nursery, and the children get moved and the mix *never ever* gets any stronger. The mix doesn't become more like a mix, as it were. You know. And it's really sad.
>
> (Interview 17)

The way in which white middle classness functioned as a norm is clear in this account. Deborah had a clear idea of a very specific group of white middle-class people who constitute her norm: 'But you know that's why I wouldn't want him to go to a private school. One of the reasons. In fact, I can't afford it, but you know, I would be very worried about him just mixing with people from his own background, or similar background to his'. There is a powerful sense that the white middle class constitutes an everyday or common sense norm – a group with predictable and reasonable responses to situations. This norm was measured against those who did not make such choices – who could not move into the street because it was too expensive or who did not react against a school having less than 50 per cent white pupils.

Deborah was careful to try to avoid the appearance of racism in what she was saying about the school. She had developed a concept of the appropriate racial 'mix' that properly reflected the 'community'. Both these notions of mix and community merit some examination. Deborah used mix in various ways: it could be 'good' (or presumably bad); 'strong' (or presumably weak); 'more' or less of a mix, or no mix at all. It could be too black, too white or mixed enough. She emphasised that it was this 'mix' that she was striving for rather than total white dominance: 'I mean if I went into an assembly and saw sort of 95 per cent white children, I'd be worried'. However, a school that did not have 'enough' white children was defined as being excluded from 'good mainstream education' (despite the fact that it is meeting national standards in all subjects; Ofsted 1995). To some extent, her use of the concept of mix seemed to draw on an (unlabelled) discourse of multiculturalism where she wanted her son 'to have a mixture of friends, from lots of different backgrounds'. Thus, the right mix was a positive thing. However, exactly why it was positive was not clearly elaborated. Deborah did not explore what her son would be seen to gain from this 'mixture'. But it was clear that accompanying the desire for 'mixture', which was expressed by others as 'exposure' to difference, was also a fear of what one might call 'overexposure' to non-whites. You could certainly have too much of a good thing. The threat of a wrong 'mix' was enough for her to want to take her son out of his school. Thus, Deborah's discussion drew on, albeit perhaps unconsciously, racist discourses of the threats to white people from being outnumbered or swamped by racial others. Deborah's anxiety surrounding the concept of 'mix', while not directly concerned with the reproductive mixing of 'races', did echo some of the anxieties about hybridity and mixing that have periodically appeared in racial theories (see Young 1995). The wrong 'mix' was not just a threat to the academic standards, but also to her sense of security and stability and the social development of her child.

It is interesting that Deborah appeared to drastically overestimate the proportion of pupils from ethnic minorities in the school. She was right about white pupils being in the minority, but it was a much larger minority than she estimated. The 1995 Ofsted report (Ofsted 1995: 3) found that just under 60 per cent of the pupils came from ethnic minority groups, as opposed to the possible 95 per cent that Deborah saw in school assembly. In this case, blackness was not only visible, but had invisibilised the white children, who made up 40 per cent of the school population. It would seem that Deborah's perception of 'race' was fuelled by fear.[6] There may also have been a conflation of 'race' and class in that her estimation of 95 per cent would have been more accurate in terms of class. The Ofsted report states that 'most of the pupils come from local authority housing with a very small percentage from owner occupier housing' (Ofsted 1995: 3). It also adds that unemployment in the catchment area of the school is well above the national average and that the number of pupils eligible for free school meals (56 per cent) is well above both national and London averages. Another possible hint of a sense of being 'swamped' by racial others was the bewilderment Deborah expresses about the dominance of black pupils in the school. 'And it's quite a big school as well. I'm not sure how many children there are. I could understand it more if it were a small school'. In the interview, I assumed that she was saying that smaller schools might have more potential to become 'unbalanced' in their representation of the community. But it was also possible that she was expressing more a sense of 'where have they all come from?'. If this is the case, it would seem to spring from an invisibilisation of the black communities who lived in the borough, but not in her particular, closely circumscribed area. She was either unaware of their existence – or thought that they somehow constituted a different 'community'.

At first, it was not entirely clear what Deborah was afraid of in the 'mix' she saw at the school. Later in that interview, she was a bit more specific: 'It's terribly important, you know, at this age, and I think really because of the socialising aspect, to me. That's why I think it's important that he goes somewhere that has a good mix of children'. Deborah did not explain exactly the nature of this socialising aspect that meant that the racial make-up of her child's school was important, and I did not specifically press her on this point. However, there was clearly an underlying fear of racialised social behaviour that she was alluding to. Children who were non-white, and perhaps poor, were clearly an 'other' that she would like her son to be able to cope with but not to be totally influenced by. If he were to go to a school where there was, according to Deborah, only 5 per cent white pupils, he would not learn how to be white and middle class in the right way. This learning process was less important at pre-nursery level, so Deborah was happy to send her son for a limited period to a local playgroup where 'all that reflected was background because people couldn't afford to send their children to private nurseries'. However, 'I just don't think it works when they get older and start going to primary school'. Thus, the context of education itself was highly racialised. Deborah's son must learn social rules in the right racial and class context. In mixing (like miscegenation), there is a risk that something is lost.

Teresa had similar worries to Deborah and, by the time of the second interview, she was beginning to prepare to move out of Clapham if her son was not accepted into the school of her choice. She compared the situation in Clapham less favourably with other areas in London that had reputations for being more liberal middle class: 'I don't know if left of centre is the right word? I think there's a lot more going to the state schools' (Interview 18). Teresa was more explicit than Deborah in describing the 'mix' that she was looking for. After saying that she was interested in a 'happy' atmosphere, the following extract explores what she said she looked for when visiting prospective schools:

Teresa: I'm keen on a good social mix, and ethnic mix. But I don't, I think I would feel . . . I certainly 50 per cent representation of a . . . white influence, I think. Do I mean white, or do I mean Christian? I don't know. You see, I went to see a school yesterday, and I really liked it, and they have about 15 different languages there. And I really liked it. But I would definitely want to feel that there was a reasonable representation, . . . I think. Interesting what you confront . . . I don't think that's unreasonable.

BB: So, but can I ask why, I'm not suggesting it's unreasonable, but why that's important. What kind of?

Teresa: Um, I think it . . . starts to become a hurdle . . .

BB: To?

Teresa: To academic achievement purely and simply. That is a large part of the schooling. I think if there is a real . . . I think if there's a real problem with English as a second language, it could hold back the general development within the class, frankly. Simple as that. [. . .]

BB: Are there other beyond the kind of language impact . . . are there other cultural or . . .?

Teresa: Yes, and I think that's a very positive thing. . . . Very much . . . cultural awareness of different societies. And I think that's *wonderful*. Absolutely brilliant.

BB: But is there . . . when you said you wanted 50 per cent representation of white . . .

Teresa: [interrupting] Yeah, I don't know whether I meant white. I meant, I guess, Christian influence within the school, I think. . . . I think I would want that. . . . Again, for an identity. Yes, I think so. . . . I don't think that's unreasonable. Yeah, I think I would want that.

(Interview 18)

It is clear, in the extract above, that there were two competing discourses that collided in Teresa's attitude to primary schools. She was strongly endorsing multiculturalist discourses in that she wanted her son to gain 'cultural awareness of different societies. And I think that's *wonderful*. Absolutely brilliant'. Yet, at the same time, she was very clear that the right 'social' and 'ethnic' 'mix' would entail having the appropriate (by which she means majority) 'white influence'. When these two discourses were brought into direct contact, through my questioning, Teresa sought to reframe what she said. What she had, somewhat nervously, asserted as a 'reasonable' concern for 'representation', a vocabulary drawn from liberal democracy, suddenly seemed less acceptable.[7] Was it Christian, rather than white, influence that she was concerned about, or English as a mother tongue perhaps? These three, whiteness, Christianity and English speaking, had very different implications. While talking about whiteness directly raised the question of 'race' (and possibly class), Christianity suggested considerations of culture and, in Teresa's eyes, appeared to be more acceptable than talking of 'race'. She ignored the potential racialised interpretation of this position. In fact, there were relatively few religious minorities in the Lambeth educational system.[8] Equally, concerns about English as a mother tongue seemed to have an unequivocal status of 'reasonableness' to Teresa. They could be stated 'simple as that'. Nonetheless, they all coalesced in Teresa's mind to represent what she was worried about. While Teresa, like the others discussed in this chapter, was not keen to have her son pressurised academically at school, she was also looking for a sense of moral order and control in the school, as we saw in an earlier quote where she emphasised the 'very strong moral code' that existed in her own primary school. This order may be threatened by the visible presence, or too great visible presence, of cultural and racial others.

Thus, while Teresa espoused multiculturalism, she also feared the over-dominance of racial and cultural others. It would seem that the presence of cultural or racial others undermined her desire for a 'strong moral' upbring-ing for her children. Thus, for Teresa, multiculturalism had its limits. She wanted her children to be exposed to other cultures – for instance in learn-ing about other religious holidays – just as long as (white) Christian influence remained dominant. A fear of the unknown was suggested in the following anecdote told about a friend. Neither 'race' nor class was mentioned explic-itly, but could be interpreted as providing the underlying framework for the story:

> I had a friend over yesterday, and she works full-time and her 4 year old . . . she had no idea who's met, who she plays with at school, a state school at Waterloo, and it was her birthday and so she said, you know, tell me, write down the names and I'll send them invitations, and you know, she had this party in the park, and *she had no idea who's going to turn up* [laugh]. But she said they were great.
>
> (Interview 18, emphasis mine)

Guess who's coming for tea, Mummy

One issue that played a greater role in other interviews, but was less rel-evant to the Clapham group as their children were younger, was that of after-school activities. During the fieldwork, I occasionally arranged to meet interviewees or be introduced to other mothers at the school gate. This was a good time to be introduced to mothers, as women would chat while wait-ing for their children and make the sometimes complex arrangements for what I ended up calling the 'going home for tea scene'. This social practice is structured by material factors such as availability of resources that makes having other children over to play easy – such as space, transport, provision of the 'tea'. These issues play an important role because reciprocity is a key reason for entering into the arrangement. The practice is also structured by questions of cultural capital – in terms of children knowing how to 'behave themselves' appropriately, play in the desired manner and eat appropriately, all of which are also classed and may also be raced. The arrangements also tend to be made between parents who are friends or at least already know each other. It became clear that this was a highly classed and raced activity.

It seemed to be confined largely to white middle-class mothers and involved the recitation of classed and raced norms.

Teresa mentioned several times in her interviews that none of her son's friends will go to the school that he was most likely to get into, and this appeared to be a central concern. The fear was about who would her son be socialising with, or whether there would be enough appropriate children for him to socialise with. Teresa cited the experience of a friend in contributing to her decision not to send her son to the nearest school:

> It is interesting because Harry goes to a private nursery now, . . . and this friend of mine, talking to her, it's only gradually dawned on both of us sort of the differences, and it wasn't a *conscious* thing, it was just because it was a 5-minute walk and we got a place, . . . but . . . my friend's son is the same age, similar age, there are no party invitations, there's no . . . the social infrastructure is very different, there is no sort of play dates at people's houses, you can go back to a house after lunch, and it never even occurred to either of us that would or would not happen, it just hadn't entered our sight. It was first-time mothers experiencing our children going to nursery. And that's pretty depressing really. I mean, very nice for Harry, but it hadn't even dawned on me or her that that might be absent.
>
> (Interview 18)

Not only did the children miss out on particular kinds of social activities, but so too did the mothers, as their home-based social life was interconnected with their children's. Deborah pointed out that much of her future, mother-based, social life would depend on the people she met at her son's primary school. This concern with socialising meshed with that of cultural identity. There was a concern, I believe, that, without sufficient white middle-class peers, the children would miss out on the learning process involved in activities such as going to friends' houses for tea, being taken out. Thus, learning 'race' and class were central to being a 'normal' child at a 'normal' school.

Liz, a middle-class woman who lived in Camberwell and therefore was not part of the Clapham group, had older children (aged between 7 and 10) and, particularly as she worked part time, she was heavily involved in the 'going home for tea scene'. In the following extracts, she made clear its raced and classed nature:

Liz: I mean obviously there is quite a big social class difference between a family like ours and families that live very close by. And there are certain differences, it *is* more difficult to have the level of social contact that I imagine one *might* have in an area where all the families came from a similar background. I mean one of the things that happens is that we have children here and they come to tea and the invitation is *not* reciprocated, for perhaps a number of reasons. You know, perhaps they live in small flats and they don't *want* other children to come round, which is perfectly reasonable. But there are enough of us with sort of 'middle-class' families, for want of a better word, that they can spend time with out of school hours and do things with that both families might enjoy doing. So, it's not been a problem.

BB: So their, kind of, out-of-school friends, as opposed to their in-school friends are more middle class?

Liz: Yes, I think that's true.

BB: And how does that relate to the children they play with or spend time with in school?

Liz: . . . Funnily enough, they're not the same group of children. Yeah, they don't necessarily spend . . . [. . .] Susanna, I suppose she's got three girls who she would consider best friends. One is a neighbour whose family are very like ours – and we see each other socially and da de da de da. The other is a little girl who I don't even know where she lives and she's come recently to the school and I haven't actually met her mother. So she never comes here because that seems to be very difficult to arrange and I've often said to Susanna 'Oh why don't you invite Ruby?' and she says 'Oh no mum, it's not, that isn't going to work, you know, Ruby doesn't *do* that sort of thing'. And the other little girl fortunately lives just across the road and her family of course are very different from ours. In that her mother's a single parent and . . . the child's father hasn't lived with them for some time, it's quite a complicated situation. But she's fine because she lives across the road. And there was a bit of difficulty sorting things out to begin with. But that's been quite [questioning] well reciprocated. Susanna's actually spent the weekend there and stayed the night. But I think it's much more difficult for her mother to have Susanna to stay than it is for us to have Chloe to stay. So I think it's not entirely quid pro quo. Which is *absolutely* fine anyway. You know, things sort of work themselves out.

(Interview 43)

It is interesting that Liz's children also understood that there were some families that take part in the practice of after-school play and others, such as her friend's, that did not. Children may be more aware than parents realise of the way in which social differences structure people's behaviour and socialising. Liz clearly marked this form of socialising as classed. The particular child in question whom Liz's daughter thought would not want to come and play was black. Liz did consider that 'race' might be connected, but did not know if it was significant (and it is also impossible for us to judge):

So I'm not sure really, what. I mean this child is a black child and wheth-er that's got anything to do with it or not I don't know. And funnily enough, none of her immediate friends who come to the house are black children. Yes, although she's very friendly, particularly with Ruby. So whether that's got anything to do with it I *really* don't know.

(Interview 43)

The practice was not determined by who her daughters spend time with in school. What was important was to find families to spend time with that 'do things that both families might enjoy doing'. Thus, out-of-school socialising was not just a matter of passing time or childcare, but involved the whole family. This demanded that the families were similar enough and had enough in common to want to spend time together. 'Race' and class were important factors in this, as Liz explained:

But I mean it's very clear that, you know, one is culturally very different from another group of people. Racially, culturally very different. But obviously we mix, but we don't understand each other *at all* well. You know, so I think we, you know, I'm very well aware of the fact that black families here and, sadly not many of them [are friends], *because* they have a very different cultural life to mine. You know, and black families that one does have anything much to do with are *middle-class* black families, you know and at the moment there aren't that many of them. I mean, hopefully there will be *more* . . . you know in the near future. But you know, one does mix with people who are socially . . . much, and I think that's more of a binding factor than race, actually.

(Interview 43)

Children's socialising mattered not just in terms of quantity, but also qual-ity, as Liz explained in the following extract, again showing how music can be a sensitive barometer of class:

I suppose *sometimes* I think . . . that it would be nice if the girls per-haps had the opportunity to mix more with children who perhaps had a slightly broader experience. You know, I'm not saying that what the children offer at the school they go to isn't very valuable, but it's quite limited often. [. . .] In terms of what they've done or what they've expe-rienced or . . .. But maybe that's foolish as well. I mean one of the things that Susanna does is music. She's quite a talented pianist. I don't think any of her friends play the piano or are involved in music or ever go to concerts or anything with their families. Mind you, I don't expect 8 year olds sit down and discuss what theatre they saw with their parents last night or which, which piece they're doing, . . . but . . . you know, some-times that crosses my mind. And I think well, maybe they are mixing with fairly limited, with children with reasonably limited experience.

But I don't know how important that is at this stage, I don't get too excited about it.

(Interview 43)

One aspect of children's play and interests that arose several times in the course of interviews with mothers reveals another way in which mothers were having to deal with issues of class and gender. The interviews took place at the peak of the impact of the Spice Girls on British popular culture. The Spice Girls were particularly popular among young children, particularly young girls, and therefore were almost unavoidable for parents (except parents of preschool children where the Teletubbies held sway). What is particularly interesting about the Spice Girls is how they brought up classed concerns (especially around sexuality) for the interviewees. The Spice Girls were a classed phenomenon. They were working-class women who had found a powerful route to success, without recourse to the more accepted routes, such as education or even their own entrepreneurship (this is akin to more classically working-class male routes to success through sports such as boxing and football). The Spice Girls played with highly sexualised images, often dressing in a sexually provocative way and delivering a particular message of 'girl power' and control of one's own destiny and desire.

For mothers, or at least those with daughters of the relevant ages (6 or 7 years old and above), the phenomenon of the Spice Girls could not be ignored. Their daughters wanted to decorate their rooms with posters of the group, listen to their music and imitate their dress (or the dress of their favourite Spice Girl) and their style of dancing. The subject of the Spice Girls often arose in the context of considering gender differences between children. Among middle-class mothers, there was an almost universal discourse that it was desirable to try to bring up children in a 'gender-neutral' way, but that this was impossible. They argued that girls will be girls and boys will be boys. But this left the question of whether girls had to be Spice Girls. In the following extract, Madeleine moved swiftly from discussing her daughter's gendered dress to the Spice Girls and their ambiguous relation to her aspirations for her daughter:

I mean I was just *horrified* when Yasmin was old enough to start saying what she wanted and she wanted to wear pink dresses and high heels and have blonde hair and you know, I was just '*how* did that happen to me, how did I produce a child like this' [laugh] and then you just realise that everybody's little girl is like that it's so rare . . ., they just all go through that stage and they want to wear bows and frills and pink, you know have pink bedrooms [laugh] and she's actually now grown out of that and she likes dark colours and she wants to wear black and dark blue, terribly serious. [. . .] I think that the Spice Girls brought up a lot of issues for parents of girls [big laugh] because you then had to start – they wanted to know about girl power – and you then had to start talking about all sorts of complicated issues with them . . . and I think has actually been quite interesting.

[. . .]

I kind of get really hot on the collar about Posh Spice being an unacceptable role model for small girls. Teetering around in high heels and tiny clothes and never moving her face [imitates]. She doesn't seem very natural to me. She doesn't express herself very well. She doesn't seem very at ease with her body [laugh]. Yes, so the Spice Girls has brought up the whole gender thing for us. And I'm really shocked sometimes with Yasmin how, I mean I know kids don't, but when people ask her sometimes what do you want to be when you grow up and she'll say 'I want to be a shop assistant' and it's 'oh [horror] no, you have to want to be a doctor' [laugh]. . . . So I think . . . I mean obviously she's had that message drummed into her about 'you can be anything you want to be, do anything you want to do, go anywhere you want to go' you know, and it's just whatever you want to do and there are no restrictions. And if you come across them you have to challenge them. But having said that she's still very much, she's still quite girlie, do you know what I mean?

(Interview 9)

There are different levels of 'girlie' behaviour being discussed – they range from the sexually 'innocent' (wanting to wear pink) to the more sexualised (wanting to wear high heels or behaving like 'Posh Spice'). Particularly the latter, more sexualised or feminised behaviour, is classed, and it is suggested that they are incompatible with middle-class aspirations such as wanting to be a doctor. The ambiguous position of the Spice Girls in this was highlighted by the fact that Madeleine's aspirational message, which she 'drums' into her child, was very similar, at face value, to the Spice Girl's 'girl power' message. Jan also expressed ambivalence about her daughter's fascination with the Spice Girls. She did not know how to respond to her daughter adopting Spice Girls style dress – was her daughter showing courage or being a 'tacky tart'?

She wants to go around wearing plastic patent shoes with two inch heels on being a Spice Girl fan and part of me thinks she looks kind of tacky. On the other hand she looks fantastic and not many kids her age would have the nerve to go out of the door wearing that kind of stuff, do you know what I mean? And so you have to try and get that balance between applauding her making her mark and being different and . . . looking like a tacky tart basically [laugh] I mean fashion at the moment I just think is so tacky! I don't know.

(Interview 30)

In the case of the Spice Girls, class and gender are acting upon each other to produce ambiguities in the mothers' responses. She admired the audacity, but wished that it was not expressed in such a 'tacky' (working-class) way. She appreciated confidence and a willingness to stand out, but not the ways in which it was directed.

Conclusion

This chapter has examined a range of mothering practices that were of particular concern to the women I interviewed. They fit into a whole set of everyday activities that mothers undertake with their children and involve the reiteration of classed, raced and gendered norms. Motherhood is a unique combination of mundane, repetitive tasks (or 'drudgery' according to one interviewee); the performance of a particular gendered, racialised and classed self; and the construction of a context for the development of one's child's or children's selves. It is a place where the everyday and the imaginary are intertwined.

The women I interviewed entered a new life on becoming mothers, and they reflected in the interviews on some of the aspects of this change, of changes in perspective and priority, and on the development of different personality characteristics (such as 'patience'). They also discussed how they wanted to create a 'secure' and 'stable' environment that would enable their children to develop freely. These concerns constructed a particular model of motherhood and of childhood. The constructions were classed, raced and gendered. The 'sensitive' mother was caring and protective, but also open to her child's sensibilities and keen to develop any 'gifts' that she displayed. The mothers were not, however, advocating an unstructured or uncontrolled environment for their children. They wanted them to grow in certain ways, with certain values, abilities and attitudes. They wanted them to develop normative gendered, raced and classed positions, and it was these concerns that contributed to their anxieties about schooling for their children.

While discussions about their own friendship groups had focused largely on microlevel differences between themselves and other middle-class women who were, for various reasons, not 'like minded', macrolevel questions of 'race' and class came to the fore in considering local schools. The 'right' friends for the mothers were ensured by going to the right places and through minute processes of sizing each other up, and encounters where the possibility of friendship could be tentatively explored. Mistakes might be made. After an initial meeting, one might decide one had 'nothing in common' with the other person, or discover that they were too conservative or narrow-minded for one's liking. But little was lost in this process.

The stakes are much higher with respect to children's schooling. The choice of school could play a large part in determining a child's future and, perhaps for the first time, a mother was giving up control of a large part of her child's day. A child's social, moral and academic framework, their stability and security as well as their attainment of certain raced and classed positions depended on the nature of the school. For several of the mothers, the key issue was to ensure that their child's school had the right 'mix'. Racialised and classed 'others' posed potential threats to the children that were largely unspecified.

Difference was on the one hand desired, but it also needed to be re-strained. The 'mix' must be 'good' and not 'too much' or 'not enough'. The suggestion here was that, while some cultural difference offered enlivenment and enrichment to children's lives, there still needed to be 'enough' (or a majority) of the classed and racialised norm to ensure its reproduction in children. It would seem that the women were conscious that the security and stability of the white middle-class norm requires constant repetition and recitation in order for it to be ensured for their children.

7 How English am I?[1]

Introduction

> I see myself as British, um because, even though I was born here, society has shown me, has led me to believe that I'm British. Not that I'm *English*, that I'm British. The way that I look at it, just because of what I've seen, just through working, going to school and working in, you know, in England, you *are* British, you're not English. English people are white, that's how we see English people, they're white.
>
> (Dawn, Interview 5, emphasis Dawn's)

> . . . if I said English, I think I'd feel very pedantic about it. I would be saying, you know, I live in this country, but in this bit of the country. [. . .] I mean, my mother-in-law gets so sort of, I mean, I can understand her wanting to keep her identity, especially in a place like Scotland which gets swamped by central power and the government and everything, or has done in the past. I can see that one can become very sensitive about it. But it does irritate me slightly because a part of me thinks, well, yes, okay, I can see that you've got to have your identity like any kind of minority, this is really important, that you're heard and you're understood and you're not trampled over and taxed too much and all this kind of thing. But you know, come on. Can't we just all be British, and do we even have to be that? You know, really. Isn't it all just a waste of time really?
>
> (Deborah, Interview 17)

These two extracts from the interviews show different experiences of national identity. For Deborah, a white middle-class woman born in London, national identity was an issue of minor importance and occasional irritation caused particularly by the minority and secessionist claims of those in the Celtic fringe. 'Race' was not an issue for Deborah, perhaps because there was an underlying assumption that all concerned were white. However, for

Dawn, a black woman born in England whose parents came from the Caribbean, national identity and 'race' were inextricable. To be English meant you were white, at least in Dawn's experience, and to be black in England meant that how you defined yourself was at least partially dictated by others, by 'society'. Both Deborah and Dawn used the collective 'we' but in different senses. For Dawn, it was 'we' the black British who see English as a white category. Deborah was asking why 'we' can't all be British, but it was a call to other white British people, such as her mother-in-law. These two accounts clearly illustrate the ways in which the content of identity, such as national identity, is determined by the position of the individuals engaged in constructing the identity. Dawn's experience is certainly not unique. Her analysis of her ability, as a black woman born in Britain, to claim an English identity was shared by respondents in Ann Phoenix's study: 'It became clear in the study that racialised identities intersected with national identities for many young people, so that some black and some white young people saw Englishness (and sometimes Britishness) as synonymous with whiteness' (Phoenix 1995: 30). Ruby, a woman with a white English mother and Nigerian father, interviewed by Jayne O. Ifekwunigwe, expressed similarly complex relations with Englishness: 'If you're mixed race, if you're not careful, you can fall between two stools. Where you're English, but you're not quite, 'cos you're Black aren't you. Or, you're not really Black are you, because you're English' (Ifekwunigwe 1999: 85).

These experiences show the contested and racialised nature of national identity and belonging to an imagined collectivity. For white people in England, the contestations over national identity also have an impact, but perhaps in a less direct way. Krishnan Kumar argues that the English can no longer be complacent about their own positioning, and the loss of protection he identifies is likely to have particular relevance to white English: 'In whichever direction they look, the English find themselves called upon to reflect upon their identity and to re-think their position in the world. The protective walls that shielded them from these questions are all coming down' (Kumar 2003: 16).

The interviews undertaken for this research took place at a time when debates about nationhood and the meaning of Britishness and Englishness were particularly alive. While the longer historical context was that of the end of empire and changing relations with Europe, current debates about the nature of Britishness and Englishness perhaps first emerged with the attempts by the government of Margaret Thatcher to construct the syllabus for a 'national' history in schools. This prompted an academic debate contesting the notion of a 'national' history and discussing what it might contain (see Samuel 1989; Schwarz 1996: 1). In the 1980s and 1990s, there was a flood of books on the origins of Britain and/or England.[2] In the immediate context of the interviews,[3] the new Blair Labour government had just come into power in an election in which national identity had played a prominent role. The conservatives were riven by debates about Europe. The ascendant voices were those who believed in the need to protect 'British sovereignty' against the threat of Europe. The 'New Labour' government had the devolution of both Scotland and Wales in its manifesto. As it came into power, the government was keen to promote the idea that 'New' Labour was associated with a new view of Britain, as modern and chic. There was an attempt to 'rebrand' Britain as 'Cool Britannia'. The Union Jack was reclaimed from the Far Right as pop stars sported it on their clothes or guitars. 'Brit pop' was born and with it the idea that Britain could be 'hip'. Yet there was also a re-signifying of the St George Cross with the Euro '96 Football Cup based in Britain. This was marked by a resurgence of fans sporting the flag of England – the St George's Cross (rather than simply wearing the Union Jack and ignoring its Scottish and Welsh elements). John Gabriel discusses the media representation of this football championship and 'its significant role in the confirmation and reworking of English national identities' (Gabriel 1998). Gabriel points out how the championship was staged as a battle and took place while the Conservative government was struggling with the European Union over the banning of beef: 'The scene was set for the media to frame both the football championships and the beef war as twin European battle-fronts' (Gabriel 1998: 26). The death of Diana and the popular response to this in ways that were deemed 'unBritish' or 'unEnglish' also prompted discussions of whether Englishness or Britishness was changing. There were challenges to notions of the restraint and reserve of the English as crowds flocked to places of mourning with flowers and candles. Their response was compared with popular Argentinian expressions of grief at the death of Eva Peron. Were the English/British becoming 'Latin'? These debates were accompanied by press coverage that strove to emphasise the multiracial nature of the public mourning, in particular with many close-ups and interviews with Asian and black members of the crowd. Presented as the quintessential English princess at the time of her wedding, Diana was being repackaged as a representative of multiculturalism in Britain as she died. London, as national capital, was often the site for these events. Yet at the same time, London occupies a distinct position in that it is also constructed as a cosmopolitan space which can, at times, stand outside the national space.[4] These events were not necessarily mentioned in the interviews, but they nonetheless provide one backdrop to the discussions.

In the midst of theses different contestations about the meaning of national identity, the contrast between Deborah's and Dawn's responses to the question of national identity point to the different significance of claiming a national identity depending on a subject's position. What for a middle-class white woman is a minor irritation may for a working-class black woman be a highly charged political issue. National identity is one modality through which 'race', class and gender work. To be positioned or to position oneself as English has different implications according to how one is raced, classed or gendered. Englishness can act, like whiteness, as an unacknowledged norm or position of privilege that structures identity and experience. What is interesting is that, in contrast to whiteness, it is something that interviewees were relatively willing and able to talk about. Where there are few public discourses that explicitly focus on whiteness, in contrast, as I have argued, national identity and belonging (and therefore also exclusion) are widely debated in Britain.

But what does it mean to position oneself within a national community? How does one imagine one's self to be part of a larger collectivity? National identity involves much more than the simple possession of a passport or residence in a particular place. It involves ways of being, a sense of place and belonging, myth-making and narrative construction. There are different levels at which the question of national identity and its changing nature and formation can be addressed. National identity is the product of state intervention in terms of politico-legal definitions of borders, citizenship and belonging. But it also exists at the level of what Michael Billig describes as 'banal nationalism' – the language and repetition of nationalism in the everyday (Billig 1995; see also Bhabha 1990a). This national identity, the sense of belonging to an 'imagined community' (Anderson, 1991), is a lived experience involving everyday rituals and practices and acts of identification (and sometimes disidentification). This chapter examines this lived and felt aspect of national identity. The accounts are examined for clues as to how the 'crisis' of identity is being experienced and, in particular, the role played by race, class and gender in these shifting notions of Englishness and Britishness. The material points to the largely unconsidered relationship of the domestic to ideas of Britishness and Englishness as well as suggesting particular ways in which national identity might be gendered. Finally, the chapter explores how locality offers alternative spaces for identity and the possibilities of 'disidentification' from nation.

For Perry Anderson (1991: 4 and 5), nationality or nation-ness and nationalism are 'cultural artefacts of a particular kind', created in the eighteenth century and now universal: 'in the modern world everyone can, should, will "have" a nationality, as he or she "has" a gender'. For those living in the 'English' part of the British Isles, this raises the question of which nationality they have, to what imagined community do they belong? As Bernard Crick (1991: 90) points out: 'I am a citizen of a country with no agreed colloquial name'. This suggests at least some confusions or ambiguities in the imagination and narration of nation (Bhabha 1990b). 'Once upon a time the English knew who they were' begins Jeremy Paxman in his 'portrait of a people' (Paxman 1998: 1) and, after several pages of charting the changes (decline) in England, notes that 'apart from at a few football and cricket matches, England scarcely exists as a nation: nationalism was, and remains a *British* thing'. Krishnan Kumar argues that the English did not work on developing ideas of who they were, as projects of both imperialism without and unification within Britain were best served by emphasising an imperial, or at best British, identity rather than an English one:

> The English did not so much celebrate themselves as identify with the projects – the 'mission' – they were, as it were providentially, called upon to carry out in the world . . .. the English could not see themselves as just another nation in a world of nations.
>
> (Kumar 2003: x; see also Crick 1991: 92)

These projects, and particularly the imperial one, while they may not have been served by emphasising Englishness, did foster notions, not just of superiority, but of racialised superiority in particular, which it could be argued played a central notion in the construction of both Britishness and Englishness (see Cohen 1994; McClintock 1995; Young 1995).

As several feminist texts have explored,[5] the empire was a gendered as well as a classed and raced enterprise. Anne McClintock argues that

> controlling women's sexuality, exalting maternity and breeding a virile race of empire-builders were widely perceived as the paramount means for controlling the health and wealth of the male imperial body politic, so that, by the end of the century, sexual purity emerged as a controlling metaphor for racial, economic and political power.
>
> (McClintock 1995: 47)

Catherine Hall also argues that middle-class white women played a central role in articulating national/imperial identity (Hall 1992: 207). As McClintock shows through examination of advertising, the empire was intimately related to the domestic with imperial 'bric-a-brac' cluttering up domestic spaces in Britain and the domestic playing a key role in the civilising mission of empire. Through the importation and marketing of soap, the imperial powers were spreading a particular version of the domestic to colonial subjects, in a similar way in which it was also promoted to the working classes (McClintock 1995; see also Bonnett 2000a: ch. 3). In this process, Englishness and Britishness involved the imagination of both racialised and classed others, with a particular relationship to notions of 'home' and the domestic. Given the end of colonisation, the expanded immigration of post-colonial subjects ('we're here because you were there') as well as the repositioning of Britain within an expanded and consolidated Europe, the questions remains as to what extent the imagination of Englishness and Britishness has adjusted to this new context.

The enduring racialisation of Englishness in particular can be read from the seeming disconsonance of the phrase black English,[6] as opposed to the politically struggled for identity of black British. In the context of racial exclusions to nationhood in Britain, there have been artists, filmmakers and writers who have staked their claims as black British (see Owusu 2000). Yet others have argued that black British as a political identity has excluded and/or marginalised those non-white identities that are not African Caribbean. Tariq Modood, for example, stresses the need to understand Britain as 'multiracist', particularly in the context of increasing Islamophobia (Modood 1997: 160; see also Parekh 2000). As minority identities within the national space become increasingly complex, but also explicitly narrativised, the question remains as to what happens to 'majority' identities. Anoop Nayak argues that there has been a de-racialisation of the white English, while visible minorities are now correspondingly over-racialised: 'A pressing question for ethnic scholars may now centre on the identities of the hitherto under-researched white Anglo majority – who they are and who they may yet "become"' (Nayak 2003: 139, see also Bonnett 2000a). For Jonathon Rutherford (1997: 6), a key entry into understanding white Englishness is to examine notions of home and motherhood.

This chapter is concerned with how nation-ness is imagined and lived. This is particularly interesting because it gives access to the question of the role of collective identities in subjectivity. How can we understand the ways in which the complexity and collectivity of the national is understood by the interviewees? What processes of subjection are involved in the construction of selfhood, which is tied in with nationality? Through what forms of living is nationhood lived? How is the self imagined in relation to others – both those within the nation and those outside of it? Who is not English, who is more English, who is less English? As mothers, do the interviewees have a sense of 'passing on' Englishness to their children? How English are their children? There is no simple relationship between Englishness and citizenship or holding a passport (particularly as the passport in fact attests that the holder is a 'British subject'). Englishness is not a legal status, but a construction of belonging, an ethnicity. This, however, is sometimes difficult for the English to acknowledge, as Catherine Hall points out: 'In England, the recognition that Englishness is an ethnicity, just like any other, demands a decentring of the English imagination. For ethnicities have been constructed as belonging to 'others', not to the norm which is English' (Hall 1992: 205).

Homi Bhabha argues that nations are based on insecure and ambivalent imaginings that are undergoing continuous transition and mutation (Bhabha 1990a: 1). Individuals who live the idea of nation in their own identifications are also constantly imagining and figuring the collective – what it is and how it relates to them. The rest of this chapter examines different ways in which national identity was constructed by the interviewees. For all of them, although differently, this imagining proved to be an uncertain process.

England's green and pleasant land

Patrick Wright in *On Living in an Old Country* (1985) highlights the importance of nostalgia – as well as 'vagueness' – in certain imaginations of Englishness. In particular, he examines the potency, for some, of England as rural heritage and idyll:

> Deep England can indeed be deeply moving to those whose particu-
> lar experience is most directly in line with its privileged imagination.
> People of an upper middle-class formation can recognize not just their
> own totems and togetherness in these essential experiences, but also the
> philistinism of the urban working class as it stumbles out, blind and
> unknowing, into that countryside at weekends.
>
> (Wright 1985: 86)

For some interviewees, this sense of 'deep England' did indeed have potency and offered a contrast to the 'developing turmoil of the modern world'
(Wright 1985: 86). However, this nostalgia was inevitably combined with a
sense of loss as it failed to be achieved in urban and racially mixed London.
As Wright suggests, it also requires a certain class position to maintain any illusion of deep England, and this national nostalgia may be combined with an
individual trajectory of loss of class position. Some interviewees suggested
that a sense of 'deep England' is not limited to a particular relationship with
the countryside, but also to cultural products and practices, including those
associated with the more traditional wings of the Church of England. It is
also not just defined against the working class, but also racialised others.

I will start with the two women who saw national identity, and in particular Englishness, as a particularly positive identity to hold. This made them
rather unusual among the interviews. For both Emma and Heather, to different extents, Englishness was about myths of history, civility and honour.
Their England was rooted in the past and, in particular, class and gender
relations. Both realised that the place in which they lived, and the ways they
lived, were very different from their imagined England, and they experienced this difference with a sense of loss, although again to differing extents.
This loss was expressed as hostility to those seen as threatening this image of
England. In one case, this was represented by 'Britishness' and in the other
by America. 'Race' clearly played into both these frameworks. Class was
also central to both their accounts of Englishness. To some extent, for both
Heather and Emma, the loss they felt about the perceived changes in Englishness was mirrored by a loss in their own class position. Both women came
from middle- or upper-class provincial families. They were at the younger
end of the spectrum of interviewees, Emma in her late 20s and Heather
in her early 30s. Heather worked in the arts, although at the time of the
interview she was caring full time for her 2-year-old daughter. Heather lived
in Camberwell. Emma lived nearby in Peckham and worked in Camberwell
part time. A change in material and social status had occurred for Heather
at an early age following the death of her father. In contrast, Emma's loss
of social status came with marriage to a man who was perceived as working
class by both herself and her family, despite his professional status, and it
also involved living in what she regarded as an undesirable area. For these
women, to a certain extent, diagnosis of the state of the nation provided a
route for articulating personal experiences and concerns.

Emma

Emma was unusual among the interviewees not only because she said that she describes herself as English when asked for her nationality, but also because this was the result of a strong desire *not* to be 'British'. The following extract demonstrates the ways in which Englishness was associated for Emma with pride. This was immediately followed by the supposed threats posed by 'aliens' or foreigners, who she associated with crime and the unfair burden they placed on English taxpayers. To imagine Englishness seemed almost impossible for Emma without also summoning up the abject – those excluded from the category, who at once threatened Englishness, yet also were crucial to defining what it was. The cost of imprisoning a 'foreign' pickpocket could then be contrasted with that of producing the epitome of upper-class Englishness, the Etonian schoolboy.

BB: So I'm trying to look at what is understood by being English or being British. I mean, if you were asked to put your nationality on forms, what do you put?

Emma: Um, English. Yes, it's about being English rather than being British I think. [. . .] But I'm actually very proud of being English. It's interesting though, because you know this thing about the gypsies.[7] That's been a point of conversation with lots of people really. And, you know that thing of them coming into, it feels like an invasion to some people, and it's mostly to do with money. They're thinking, you know, all this money is being spent when there's not enough, you know they're not giving students enough money, they're not giving the NHS enough money. My purse was stolen from my workplace last week and the woman who stole it was on police bail and she's now in Holloway. And for her to be in Holloway for a year is the same as sending someone to Eton for a year. And she wasn't English, she was Portuguese. But I guess because of this new European thing, you don't just push her back to Portugal. But I don't know really how it works. I was sort of saying to my husband, you know 'what about the money and everything' and he was saying 'yes but they're people and they've been harassed, they've been maltreated'. So it's very difficult, but I think that when you're struggling, when the nation is struggling, it sort of gets annoying when people that you might consider as foreign, when perhaps it's not politically correct to call them foreign.

(Interview 16)

The idea of nationhood and belonging was something that clearly exercised Emma. She used a rhetoric familiar from the tabloid (and other) press and media. Nonetheless, her statement 'I'm actually quite proud of being

English' suggests that she had an awareness of a discourse that might see this as an unusual or even objectionable position to take. Yet, when Emma thought of her pride at being English, a racialised other was immediately called to mind.

At the same time, Emma was aware that what she was saying was contentious. She did not say that she *herself* saw the arrival of the 'gypsies' as an invasion, but that this was what it 'feels like' to 'some people'. She also worried about whether it was 'politically correct' to call people 'foreign' particularly when they might have been harassed and maltreated. Here, the liberal values of justice and sanctuary, ascribed to her husband, are competing with her sense of threat from foreigners. It is possible to see the various discursive technologies at work in producing both a sense of national culture and the feeling of being under threat. As mentioned above, it is possible to trace discourses circulating in the media. Emma also evoked a powerful sense of 'we' the nation struggling financially in the face of external threats. Her personal experience was read through the nation's experience: 'when you're struggling, when the nation is struggling'.

Emma herself made a direct link with cultural production in the form of literature when she tried to describe what Englishness meant to her. For Emma, Englishness was represented by upper-middle-class manners and traditions: 'Well, I sort of consider English and things sort of like *Howard's End* and that kind of thing. And I think there's something, I mean I know it's 200 years ago or whatever, but I think there's something wonderful about all that'. Emma was aware that her idealisation was based on a fictionalised account. She emphasised this by exaggerating how long ago the books were written. Nonetheless, at one time, it had almost had a lived reality for her. For Emma, Englishness was a romantic and nostalgic vision that was in the past in two senses: firstly, because it was based on a representation from a novel, a fictional world rather than a reality. It is, for instance, interesting that this picture of the past that she painted made no mention of imperialism or the basis on which the wealth was built. And secondly because, in terms of her own life, it represented something that was in the past, set in her childhood. Emma described her childhood, particularly at boarding school, as having fitted in with this proposed idyll of manners and civility:

And perhaps I'm being swept away on a story, and perhaps it's because I spent 7 years of my life in a church, all girls' boarding school. And spent my time singing hymns and going to church and it's a very special thing to be patriotic. And you know, going to balls and always being treated very nicely by boys. Who actually on the one hand weren't treating you very nicely, but they'd always hold the door open for you and always pay for your taxi. So it's kind of weird really. But there's something that I'd hate to lose over that, and I think, for me, because where I come from that's about being English.

(Interview 16)

Emma has had something approximating this novelised, fictionalised experience. She described 7 years of processes of subjection, producing classed, gendered and racialised identifications that are wrapped up in a sense of nation. Being patriotic, something that held special value for her, was also associated with particular performances of gender: 'you know, going to balls and always being treated very nicely by boys'. However, Emma immediately complicated this experience. Although it was 'a special thing to be patriotic', in this specifically classed context, there was also the suggestion of disturbing gendered power relations. In fact, the boys were not 'treating you very nicely', but, whatever this unspecified bad treatment involved, Emma suggested that she was compelled to accept it and keep silent as the boys continued to hold open the door and pay for the taxi. The complex interplay of gender, nation and class are encapsulated in this contradiction. Nevertheless, despite the ambiguities, for Emma, there remained 'something that I'd hate to lose over that'.

The only other person in the fieldwork whose positive 'patriotism' could match Emma's did not actually speak to me, but was portrayed by his wife, Beverley. Beverley was a working-class woman living in Clapham and she described her husband Paul's 'patriotism':

> My husband, he's a bit more patriotic [than me], I think. He is, you know, he is English or British. He would *never* go abroad, as in America, *none of that* interests him. He says, you know, there's no point. Whereas I would be a bit adventurous like that. But he's still very, he's very patriotic, Paul is. But then again, it's not drummed into them [their children], they sort of do their own thing. His son's 11 he doesn't sit there preaching saying 'you shouldn't go here, you shouldn't go there because you're British'. He's just – Paul is that way, you know? And because he's been brought up in south London, he thinks south London is the world [laugh], you know! Full stop, type of thing. Yeah, he is very patriotic in that way. Yes I would be a bit more adventurous. I don't think 'oh I'm English, I shouldn't', I don't sort of think like that. I think you should be adventurous, you should dabble kind of thing, you know?
>
> (Interview 42, emphasis Beverley's)

It would seem that Beverley did not entirely approve of her husband's 'patriotism' – she pointed out that he did not drum his views into his children and just had to be accepted as he was: 'He's just – Paul is that way'. But it would also appear that this was a more working-class, explicitly exclusionary nationalism or patriotism than Emma's. Her associations of Englishness, as we shall see below, would probably have little overlap with what Paul values, based as his was in London: 'South London is the world. Full stop'. Paul's 'patriotism' was fuelled by insecurity, which makes him unwilling to take any risks or be open to other experiences. Beverley, in contrast, was prepared to be 'adventurous' and to 'dabble' with difference.

The world that Emma would hate to lose was clearly different from that imagined by Paul. It was, nonetheless, far from the reality of Emma's life in an unfashionable and relatively deprived part of London. Her mother disapproved of her choice of husband and told Emma that, as far as she was concerned, they no longer shared the same class status:

> My mother once said to me: 'Oh Emma, you're working class now' and I know that that's something that she'd look down on, something she'd prefer not to be. And in fact, I know that I'm not working class, I probably don't have class. Or if anything I'm middle class.
>
> (Interview 16)

So, for Emma, Englishness was framed by nostalgia and a sense of loss. Loss because it never actually existed in the first place and because what she had of it was tied to a particular class position and social life that she no longer retained. This loss was expressed in her hostility to things British which represented the opposite of her rural middle-class English idyll, which is constantly described as being under threat. If, following Paul Gilroy (1992b), we read 'culture' as 'race', the threat is also to the whiteness of England:

Emma: Living in London is much more about culture, about different cultures. And it's really, it's very stimulating. I guess, I mean I would like to live in New York and I would like that kind of thing, but I'd never want to destroy England and its grassy plains [laugh]. But where I suppose British means what we are now with all our multicultural mix, with all our, Ireland and Scotland and all of that kind of stuff. And I mean, there's been so many things that have happened to try and destroy England. All the problems with the monarchy and all of that kind of stuff and it's all kind of sour, or it feels sour. I'd put that under the bracket of British [big laugh].
BB: Which under the bracket of British?
Emma: All that nastiness [laugh].
BB: That's your dumping ground!
Emma: The dumping ground.

(Interview 16)

The contrast here was clear. England is a rural place of 'grassy plains' with order, hierarchy and tradition as represented by the monarchy. It was also suggested to be a 'pure' ethnicity that is threatened with destruction by 'all our multicultural mix', which was represented by Britishness. Britishness, according to Emma, had disrupted the order of England and turned things 'nasty' and 'sour'. Emma's frequent laughter at what she was saying revealed a certain nervousness about the subject, or recognition that her particular constructions of Englishness and Britishness may be seen as ridiculous or objectionable. She followed the previous quotation with an uncertain question to me: 'But do you know what I am [saying]?' She also recognised that her own life did not live up to the Englishness of her imagination, or her past, and that this was not something that her daughters would necessarily grow up with. Englishness was almost dead and buried in the following account:

Emma: I guess they'll [her children] grow up British won't they? Probably. Because that's what we live in now. I mean that's not a bad thing really. [. . .] if one of them was to grow up to become an artist, I couldn't ask for more, or a painter, or a politician, I see that as quite interesting. And I'd love them to have the same sense of English culture that I have. But I can't give that to them because I no longer live in those circles really.

BB: So it is quite class bound, that sense of English?

Emma: I think it is, but I'm sure it's just in my mind. . . . yeah . . . .

(Interview 16)

Englishness for Emma was about a way of being, a certain 'form of living' in Bhabha's (1990b: 292) phrase, which she could not reproduce for her daughters. They would inevitably be different from her. Thus, Emma was distressed that the England she was imagining was being 'destroyed' or going 'sour'. The 'nastiness' that was destroying England was represented for Emma by all that was 'British'. This included the demands of the nations within the United Kingdom – Ireland and Scotland and Wales – and the racial or 'multicultural mix'. By associating Britishness with all the things that she was uncomfortable with, Emma was able to preserve Englishness as a 'pure', white and middle-class concept, headed by the unsullied monarchy. In talking about the area in which she lived, which she described as 'probably more black than white', Emma communicated a sense of pollution:

I mean, there are not many parts of Peckham that I'd live in. . . . and we live here because this house was very cheap. And it's a nice road, vaguely . . . lots of light . . . um. But I wouldn't go shopping in some of the shops. Have you walked round here at all? . . . if you go round the back there are some, in the market place you get all this halal meat and all sorts of stuff. I wouldn't touch that with a barge pole. Not because it's different, or because of anything. But just because I think it smells funny. They're not, they're probably not very educated black people. Because otherwise they would have got out. Because everyone's trying to get out really. Everyone's trying to move on. It's not like having a little village shop in the country, it's not as quaint as that. I don't think people want necessarily to be doing it.

(Interview 16)

Emma's version of Englishness and Britishness was stereotyped and lived mostly in her imagination. Englishness was somehow truly what England should be – refined, rural, white and middle class (albeit with problematic gender relations), whereas Britishness was a category that could absorb all that disrupted this notion and disturbed Emma herself. This made it all the more clear for her that the multiracial scenes she witnessed on the streets in which she lived were 'alien' and certainly not 'English'. This contrast, between Englishness and Britishness, was finally represented by the juxta-position of the local halal butcher and 'a little village shop in the country'. The latter was 'quaint' in contrast to the unsettling market shops, which 'smell funny'. The threat that Emma perceived was profound and was ex-pressed here as a threat to the domestic. How could she reproduce English-ness if she had to negotiate these alien shops and foodstuffs?

Emma quoted (somewhat disapprovingly) her mother as remarking after walking around the area in which she lived 'Oh it was just like being in Nairobi or Lagos'. Africa here symbolised the ultimate, racialised other. But Emma's mother was achieving an interesting doubling in this statement. On the one hand, she was accusing her daughter of not only being 'working class' (as we saw above) but, on the other, she was positioning herself as the agent of the colonial gaze.

For Emma, Englishness and Britishness seemed to be mutually incompat-ible. Emma reflected on her daughter's identity 'if she has that [Britishness] and doesn't have Englishness, well then one of the two. Perhaps you can't perhaps – I had both and therefore fall between two stools'. It is ironic that Emma used the same metaphor of 'falling between two stools' that Ruby (a woman interviewed by Jayne Ifekwunigwe quoted in the introduction to this section) used to describe the mutually exclusive identities of Englishness and blackness. While she did not say so explicitly, it would seem clear that, for Emma too, Englishness and blackness were mutually incompatible. Further-more, Englishness (and forms of class and gender relations that are imagined as part of this idea of nation) could not survive in the face of 'multicultural' Britain. Emma's anxieties about national identity appeared to be a means to express anxiety about her own sense of self. The narratives of her self and of Englishness were interwoven.

Heather

Heather did not share with Emma such a clear distinction between British and English. Her rendition of the two identities was perhaps more complex and sophisticated. She would put British on a form asking her nationality, but this did not express exactly how she felt. It remained an empty category, which she used because that was what felt more acceptable:

[I would put 'British' on a form] probably because I am trying to be politically correct. I would say I am absolutely English. You know, I am not Scottish or Irish. They are very different. Very different. There is no point in pretending that I am other than southern English. I am quintessentially English in a lot of those things, but I would be British because I would feel that that was a politically correct thing to do.

(Interview 15)

There was an ambiguity in Heather's feelings towards the category 'British'. While it might have been the 'politically correct' position to take, it nonetheless involved hiding her 'quintessential' Englishness. Britishness was not an identification that Heather felt emotionally. One could not be 'quintessentially' British. This had no meaning for her as an identity. Nonetheless, in the interview, Heather referred to things English and British interchangeably and generally meant 'English'. She had a strong sense of her British/English identity which, like Emma, involved harking back to distant and not-so-distant pasts and was also illustrated by contrasting it to cultural and racial others. Heather was interested in what she called 'earlier British history' of the Middle Ages and the Tudors and Stuarts. She was less interested in 'getting into Victoria and the Empire'. This may have been a means of side-stepping some of the more difficult and contentious aspects of British history. Being British was rooted in the domestic and everyday, for example in drinking tea. Heather joked: 'My mother always says, you know, that she is sure I cannot really be British because I don't like tea'. Britishness was also represented by:

classic British costume drama series, things like that as well as things like stuff like *The Good Life* that when I was young, was on telly and I used to really enjoy, and was quintessentially British and, you know, and *Monty Python* again could never have come from another country. It is very British humour.

(Interview 15)

Heather's reference to *The Good Life* as being 'quintessentially British' is a good example of 'British' used to mean 'English'. This situation comedy was based on the cultural clash produced in the encounters between suburban neighbours living two different forms of middle-class white Englishness. It is hard to think of a more characteristically white, English and middle-class programme. Heather contrasted this British humour with that of black adolescents and Germans, who she said both have very different senses of humour. Thus, 'foreignness' and blackness provided boundaries or points of demarcation to Britishness. When I asked her whether she felt that the black adolescents that she had referred to earlier had secure claims to be British, Heather responded by talking of nationality and sense of belonging in terms of voluntarism. What mattered was simply how people felt themselves, rather than how they were viewed by others. They had to assimilate themselves to the extent that they could 'feel a part' of the nation. It is interesting to contrast this view with that of her sense of her own 'quintessential

Englishness'. This suggests that Englishness was being understood more as an ethnicity than as a nationality:

> You can claim any nationality you want as long as you believe that is your nationality. I think you could, you could move to any country in the world, and if you said this is where I want to stay, you can . . . I think nationality is an attitude of mind, I don't think it's anything more practical than that. It gets bogged down in practicalities because of immigration and because of the way government treats people, but I actually think a sense of nationality is to do with society, and you could live in a country for 40 years and never feel really part of it. You know, you get ex-pats who've been living abroad for years and years and years, but still absolutely see themselves as British. Or never see themselves as part of that culture. And then you get other people who move out and within 6 months have absolutely adopted it, and said, 'yes, this is it, this is the place for me. And I feel part of it'. So, I think fundamentally it's much more to do with an attitude of mind. So, you know, I don't know, I have no idea and I wouldn't wish to say to any racial group or individual that they should or shouldn't feel British. It's up to them. You know, if they're here and they're working, they're paying taxes, they have every right to be here. They're putting money into the system like everybody else is, and if they're here for 2 years or 20 years, you know, that's their own individual choice really.
>
> (Interview 15)

In the section above, Heather promoted a truly voluntaristic notion of national identity. Here, she is not concerned with the cultural identity she brought into her discussions of national history and cultural products. Nevertheless, in the above account, nationality was more than the mere holding of a passport, it involved an intangible 'attitude of mind'. She wanted to avoid 'getting bogged down in practicalities' of immigration – for Heather, nationality was more than a legal status. Nonetheless, while she wished to be open in allowing 'any racial group or individual' to 'feel British', she also set the criteria that they should 'pay taxes' and contribute. This was a complex and perhaps contradictory view of nationality – mixing as it does elements of ethnicity. It is unlikely that Heather would require white people born of British subjects to work and pay taxes before they could consider themselves British. The nature of this belonging was not very clear. What do you have to feel to feel British? When I went on to ask Heather whether the fact that many British people were not white had changed the meaning of the category itself, she appeared to continue to imply that white people remain the gatekeepers of British identity: 'we' are open-minded about 'them':

BB: But do you think . . . I mean, I suppose the notion of what is British, do you think it has changed in response to the fact that there are a lot of non-white British people?

Heather: Yes. Definitely, definitely. I think we are much more open-mind-ed. I think if you asked the average person 50 years ago, could someone who was black be British, most people would have said no. They're obviously from somewhere different, they're not really British. Whereas now, most people would say, yes, if they were . . . I think a lot of people draw the line if they're born in this country, that's what makes you British, if you're born here. I personally . . . that's not the line I would draw. But I think people are a lot more open-minded, there's still a long way to go, but I think people accept that, you know, if you've lived here for some period of time, then you adopt this country and that makes you British.

(Interview 15)

However, in another part of the interview, Heather shows that she was sensitive to claims for cultural difference to be respected and that British culture was characterised by its whiteness which excluded some others.

You know, there are on the surface – you can say: 'yes, everything's fine' and 'yes, it's great. It is not an issue for me', but, to say it is not an issue for me is not fair because it is an issue for a lot of different racial groups because of the way other members of society treat them. So it is not re-ally fair to say if everyone was like me it would be fine because it would not, because they have things they want from society. They want their cultural heritage recognised, they want that reflected in their children and quite rightly so, so you just say: 'okay, that's fine, let's all be white Europeans'. That is not what the people want. I would not want to move to an African country and have everybody ignore what my cultural past was.

(Interview 15)

Yet, at the same time as acknowledging the need for accommodation and change, Heather was suggesting an equivalence between black people in Britain and how she would feel as a white person in 'an African country'. There was little sense of the impact of colonialism, racism and differential power relations in this analogy. Interestingly, she also introduced at this point another form of identification, that of 'white Europeans', which seems to be a strategy for avoiding qualifying English or British with the prefix 'white'. Africa again emerged in this account as the ultimate form of difference or otherness.

Heather and Emma both had an image of Englishness that they were unable to achieve. Their lived experience fell short of their imagining. Eng-lishness was maintained as white and middle class, but as such was unlikely to survive. It was threatened by those outside, by others figured, in the case of Emma, as the pollution of the urban, and, in the case of Heather, as the economic, social and political domination of America.

Empty Englishness

For Heather, much of what she said about Englishness or Britishness was placed in a defensive relationship to the United States. She was worried about England becoming 'just an island state off America if we are not careful' (Interview 15). However, for others, Englishness was defined by its contrast with continental European countries. Thus, Englishness is shown to be a fluid and dynamic concept, the content of which varied according to the boundaries that were drawn around it. Helen, a woman in her early 30s, had a more elaborated view of identity and cultural difference. For Helen, difference was marked more by cultural norms and the domestic than by global power relations. While she had a sense that 'English' cultural practices had more or less disappeared, this was not necessarily associated with a sense of loss. Helen remembered herself as a child being fascinated with cultural differences on school trips to France and Germany. French toilets and different ways of eating marked out the Englishness of some of her family's habits and rituals. But Helen now doubted that there was so much that was distinctively English about the way she lived. What she had to pass on to her children was different from the Englishness that she had experienced as a child. Most importantly, it was an attitude that difference was not something to be alarmed by, as it had been for her:

> One of the first things, was French toilets, it's all changed now but, first of all the ones which were just holes in the ground, which just . . ., you know really freaked you out when you were 11 and you went on a school trip. And I remember the ones in Paris which turned upside down, which we have now. And I remember thinking this is really really odd. And also the way the French ate their meals, one plate that the meat comes on then the vegetables come and just thinking this is so strange. And we were, I suppose, very, just a nuclear family, you know two parents, kids [. . .] We always ate round a table, we always had Sunday lunch. You know I think in the last 20 years since that was the case for me, I think England has changed a lot, but that was very English then, very sort of middle of the road, ordinary, probably no longer is. So I suppose, yes, I think I probably did, and it probably came from things like diet, . . . and just routines, rituals that are very English, like Sunday lunch, the way we ate, um . . . but they only became noticeable to me when I had something to compare them with.
>
> (Interview 12)

The example of the toilets was an ambiguous one. At first, France was portrayed as backward and then as modern and in advance of England (if toilets that turn upside down are taken as signifiers of modernity). This is an interesting play around difference because of the way in which hygiene, sanitation and the scatological[8] has historically been a way of defining whiteness and marking the other. For instance, in *Imperial Leather*, Anne McClintock analyses Victorian adverts for soap and other cleaning products as an illustration of the interconnections between empire, the mission to domesticate and the Victorian cult of domesticity (McClintock 1995).[9]

Helen suggested that her sense of Englishness, or at least the ways in which it shaped her 'form of living', was different from the experience of her parents. For Helen, these changes were connected to class and locational changes as well as altered relationships with Europe. Talking of ways of living identity, of changes in domestic attitudes and arrangement, became, for Helen, a way of marking her separation from her parents. Her parents 'became middle class when their parents were working class'. They stayed in the village in the north of England where they had been born and aspired to regular habits and traditions: 'if we didn't have Sunday lunch at lunch time when I was a child it was *odd*, not having a lunch, you were either having a family crisis, you were on your way to somewhere, you had to have a reason for it'. In contrast, Helen had become 'more' middle class having gone to university and having a career (unlike her mother). She had moved to London and was creating new modes of living for her children in a 'more homogenised Europe-wide' context. It was also in a much more racially mixed context compared with the village in which she grew up:

> It's all about travel isn't it. People have more money, it's easier to go abroad, you pick up different customs and ways of living that you like and then you sort of make a patchwork quilt of what appeals to you, you just sort of make it up as you go along, do your own thing, so. And anyway, how can you be, how can Englishness survive, say in this area where you're surrounded by, people have brought with them all sorts of . . . um customs from, gosh a *huge* variety of places. And we have a lot of mixed marriages around here as well, so you've got the mix of the two.
>
> (Interview 12)

In the face of these new ways of being – what 'English' people have brought from abroad and what has been brought by those who have moved to England bring – Englishness will not survive. This statement shows a sense of Englishness that was closed, fixed and white. It could not include new things and move on to other modes of being, but was faced with extinction. Englishness could not survive in the face of 'mixed marriages'. Here, Englishness was constructed less as a nationality than as an ethnicity or cultural identity that was bound to be disrupted by the influence of cultural influence. In fact, Helen's own children were, as she put it, 'not totally English' because one of their grandfathers was 'Asian'. Here, Englishness was a 'genetic' trait, much like popular constructions of 'race'. Note the shifting back and forth between concepts of 'race', nationality and culture:

Their father's half Asian, his father's Asian, his mother's white English, so . . . you know . . . So from that point of view, you know, they are themselves, not totally English . . . so sort of genetically, if you like, they've got a head start, they've got a foot in a different continent. And the Indian side of the family, if you like, is no longer around, so there's no um, no cultural input and their dad looks quite Indian but he's, like this girl who was at school where I was at school, he's totally English in every sense of the word. But . . . personally I feel that they have an advantage. And I in some way would like to underline that and . . . just remind them that they are in some way not totally English, are part of a wider world, and it's an advantage for them.

(Interview 12)

Helen viewed her children's parentage as a 'head start' in dealing with 'this *huge* world that we live in. With all different sorts of peoples and races and customs and cultures', and she did not hold the loss of Englishness with much concern. Her children did not live with their natural father, but she intended to take them on holidays to India to reinforce the fact that they are 'in some way not totally English'. Helen again reiterated the idea that Englishness was exclusively white. It was also contested between the north and south of England as Helen, who grew up in the north of England, explained: 'for me at the time, we thought we were right and they were wrong and we thought we were English. But I'd say that now, as an adult, an adult that lives in the south, probably Englishness that is perceived by the outside world is embodied by the south of England'. Here, the divisions and exclusions within Englishness became clear. Englishness was internally contested with different regions and classes having stronger or weaker claims to belonging and determining its meaning.

While at some stages in her life, Helen had felt that England clearly informed the ways she saw herself, she had a range of other collective identities to fall back on – such as those of Europe and London. In the following extract, Helen described her sense of belonging in London. This was a constructed identification, built slowly over time, once she had 'wafted' in to London:

BB:	So, do you think you now have quite a kind of London identity? Do you see yourself as a . . . I mean, you say you'll never move.
Helen:	It feels like home, but it's taken a long time for that to happen. But it does feel like home.
BB:	So, why? How . . .
Helen:	I know because when . . . because I love going away, I love going to visit relatives in the country and . . . especially in the summer when it's hot and horrible. But when I get on that motorway to come back, I have that home tug. You can't describe it with

words, but, you know . . . people feel it when they're coming home, don't they?

BB: Which you don't feel when you go near [old home town]?

Helen: No, no, not at all.

BB: And so does it . . . why do you think it takes a long time for that to happen?

Helen: Roots. Putting roots down, feeling comfortable and feeling that you've not just got a shifting base of friends, which is when you first start out, anybody could go anywhere 'cos . . . the wind wafted you down here, you've got no commitments, it could just as easily waft you somewhere else, but after all this time, people are starting to buy places now, and a few have started to have children. Life just becomes more static, and so you know that these people are going to be around, they know you're going to be around, so it all starts to feel more homey. [. . .] It's about friends, it's about feeling comfortable in a place, and I mean, I moan about London, who doesn't? But then I guess you'd moan about wherever you were. If I lived in a small village, I'd moan about it being boring. I live in London, I moan about it being big and dirty and not having enough space, but, you know, that's just human nature. At the end of the day, this is where my root has grown.

(Interview 26)

Here, Helen provided an interesting model of performativity. Identity was created in the 'doing'. She had become a Londoner through the repetition of both actions (settling down) and identifications. Yet the metaphor of putting roots down had both genealogical and organic or natural associations, suggesting an alternative model to construction which she might be understood as elaborating. Helen needed roots to feed her self.

The view that Englishness was empty or contentless, or that it was losing its meaning was shared by several of the interviewees. Like Helen, and unlike Heather and Emma, they did not express much concern about this. Part of the reason for the relative lack of concern about the loss of Englishness was the feeling that it did not contain much in the first place. This is illustrated in the extract below from an interview with Rosalind who discussed the lack of cultural content in Englishness. Faced with celebrations of other cultures, she was left with the question of what she was actually passing on to her children. Earlier in the interview, Rosalind had displayed the complexities of national identity as she explained that she would not call herself 'English' but 'British', as she was Welsh in that her father was Welsh and she was born in Wales. However, having grown up in England, she would only call herself 'Welsh' 'if pushed', adding 'but I'm not, you know'. National identity was thus not something that was simply inherited, but had to be learnt and felt.

Despite this highly ambivalent view of her nationality, it was to Englishness that she looked, unsuccessfully, for a cultural identity. In very similar terms to Helen, Rosalind felt that Englishness was disappearing under the colourful cultural additions coming both from Europe and from other racial groups with different historical trajectories.

Rosalind: It's interesting because I think a lot of people don't think of themselves as English, do they? [. . .] It's interesting, because in a sense school, you know, they learn about lots of different cultures. In a sense, it almost feels we haven't got one. 'Cos they're doing the black history month this year . . . at school . . . and that's kind of . . . I was talking to the parent who's running it and she said it's been kind of really important to her to find out about role models of . . . that come from black history, that have really kind of achieved lots of things 'cos she always felt at school she got no . . . she had nothing to feel proud of. So, in a sense there's . . . you know, the English bit is always a bit lacking. And whether that's . . . because lots of Welsh and Scottish friends I have are quite passionate about their origins.

BB: But is there a sense that because you're able to . . . it's able to be ignored because it's kind of there anyway.

Rosalind: Yes, I'm sure, and it's the thing that's done anyway, isn't it? The kind of English is still the kind of majority way, so I suppose it's something we never have to think about. But I'm not sure what kind of amount of culture we do pass on. 'Cos I don't feel any great tradition to pass on to Anna and James really. I've never really thought about it, but I'm not sure you'd know how much to talk about where you come from, and who you are, because I think living in London, it is sort of quite a European . . . certainly living here, there's a lot of . . . we've got quite a lot of friends who live in mainland Europe now. And in a lot of circumstances, it's always the English who haven't got a kind of interesting cultural thing to do . . .

(Interview 20)

For Rosalind, English was the 'majority way' and was white and could be contrasted with black or other groups who had 'interesting' things to do with their culture and history. Black history month must, by definition, have been about something other than Englishness. In contrast to 'different cultures', Englishness emerged as a boring culture or identity so that 'it almost feels we haven't got one'. Echoing Heather quoted above, who hoped that Scottish, Irish and Welsh culture would give a boost to the culturally staid England, Rosalind also seemed regretful (resentful?) that England was made to appear culturally empty. Public sites such as her children's schools are the location for the construction of culture and identities. Rosalind felt that little work was being done on the construction of Englishness. At the same time, at the level of the everyday and domestic, Rosalind felt that there was little tradition or culture that she had to 'pass on' to her children. What she did with her children was, by the nature of its normality, somehow not about tradition, unlike the routines of her childhood, which she looked back on, for instance in the household around food. The rhythms and priorities of life were different, shaped by different material conditions and gender relations. There was a possible suggestion that now, in this domestic space lacking in tradition, life was somehow less English:

> They eat differently from me at that [. . .] well they eat a much more cosmopolitan, they eat pizza and pasta, they eat Italian food. Yes, and the kind of meat and two veg meals that we, in some form or another, that we had every day is just one choice in ten or twenty to them. So, you tend to do it . . . but that's changed because you're not . . . the focus of the day isn't around me shopping and cooking the meal for the family. And I guess the other thing that's different about family life is in Shropshire, you know, everybody was home at 5 or half past 5, and you had a family meal. I mean, in London, that's impossible, and so it would actually never . . . we would never attempt to have . . . maybe when they're older we will . . . to have supper with children. And all the children round here have tea, you know, they have their tea at 5 o'clock and then adults eat later.
>
> (Interview 20)

It is suggested here that national or cultural identity was constructed through everyday, domestic routines and consumption. It was a lived and felt construction that changed as 'forms of living' change.

Liz, a professional woman living in Camberwell, also said she had little sense of Englishness or Britishness (terms she used interchangeably). It was only when she had spent some time in America that she got a sense of being culturally different 'And I just knew I wasn't part of that culture. I was there for about 2 years and the longer I was there, the more of a foreigner I felt'. But she expressed her cultural difference as feeling 'European more than British'. Nonetheless, she did recognise an albeit nebulous sense of culture 'as far as feeling English, . . . I mean obviously I am, in terms of values and cultural life is deeply rooted here. But it's not something that I really think about that much [laugh] you know' (Liz, Interview 43). Liz also complicated the question of Englishness and culture by referring to her husband's Jewishness. Although he was English, he also had a different set of cultural resources, which came from being brought up in a Jewish family. In Liz's account, this Jewishness was racialised in that it was ascribed to both genes and phenotypic features. The daughter who looked most like her husband was also the one who had inherited his 'racial memory':

It's quite interesting, David for example is *English*, is third-generation Jewish immigrant. But culturally he's got – he's not a practising Jew and neither is his family, but culturally he's quite *Jewish*. You know, he sort of believes in things like racial memory. And certainly I can see in Rachel for example, it's *very peculiar*, because she resembles him most physically in that she's got a dark appearance and an olive skin that are obviously not part of my gene heritage and you know, she's got quite an imaginative melancholic streak in her which is what her *father* has, you know. And that's a *cultural* inheritance if you like, rather than a national one.

(Interview 43, emphasis Liz's)

Jewishness was here about something other than Englishness. Although for Liz, Englishness could also contain Jewishness – her husband could be Jewish and English. This was a reflection of the different trajectories of assimilation and acceptance for Jewish and black people.[10] Liz made a distinction between cultural and national inheritance to distinguish between what was Jewish and what was English, but this construction left Englishness and her identity as something outside of culture. When I asked whether her children were brought up with much Jewish culture, Liz detailed their contact with their grandparents 'who come up once a week and their grandma feeds them chicken soup [laugh]' and occasional participation in religious events and parties. She went on to explain 'but they've never, I mean I think David will at some time, they've *never* really been to a synagogue, simply because *David* doesn't go to a synagogue. That part of his cultural heritage is dying out because his grandparents kept the religious observances [. . .] and his parents don't do it any more and obviously we don't do it'. It is interesting, however, that when I posed a question, echoing her own use of the word 'heritage', it met with incomprehension. White, Protestant, working- or middle-class Englishness did not have a 'culture' or a 'heritage' in the same way.

BB: So do they see your side of the family as well?

Liz: Yeah, yeah.

BB: And is that, kind of, you know, heritage, how important is the kind of family heritage idea to you, do you think . . .

Liz: . . . um, what do you mean by heritage?

BB: Well, I don't know, whether you have any sense of giving them a family . . .

Liz: Um, I don't, it's not a term I've ever given any thought to, quite honestly. I mean if you say to me heritage, I think of national trust properties and things like that.

(Liz, Interview 43)

For Liz, heritage was something that belongs to others, to cultural others who may have Jewish or some other 'exotic' heritage, or to class others.

Again, Englishness was bound up both with whiteness and with middle/upper classness, and heritage could only be represented by stately homes and national trust properties. It was not something to which Liz had a particularly strong identification, beyond remarking, in a similar way to that used by Helen above, that she was 'rooted' in this country.

Evading Englishness

The ambiguity about being English may come not so much from a feeling that it is an empty identity with little heritage or tradition to offer, but from a negative response to what is regarded as Englishness. In this construction of Englishness, there is a rejection, and perhaps an attempt to be something other than what you are. Both Les Back and Ann Phoenix in their separate research found young people who were attempting to vacate Englishness. Les Back found that, in some areas of his research: 'young whites vacate whiteness and Englishness as appropriate identities in favour of an encoded identification with blackness and black people' (Back 1996: 135). This particular form of trying to find identities that are not 'laced with racism' is located within a specific classed and often gendered youth culture and is not necessarily open to all. It may also be difficult to sustain. Ann Phoenix found that '[d]iscomfort on the part of white young people could be warded off by viewing ethnicity and nationality as optional and voluntary. From this perspective, young black people were perceived as having more choice than young white people about opting into or out of Englishness' (Phoenix 1995: 35). I would argue that, for the women I interviewed, options such as 'encoded identification with blackness and black people' were not particularly viable options, rooted as they are in youth cultures. However, some of the interviewees did express negative associations with Englishness and their own reservations about holding such an identity.

Jan, a white middle-class woman who had worked as a teacher, preferred to think of herself as British rather than English (which perhaps involved ignoring the devolutionist demands of the Scots and Welsh). She was also very dubious about the whole endeavour of national identity 'I want to be part of a United Kingdom, I suppose. You know, with Scotland, Wales and things as well, I don't just want to be . . . I do have friends who *insist* that they're *English*, not just British. And it's all to do with things like English beef and I don't know. I don't know really. I don't have a very strong feeling of nationality at all to be honest' (Jan, Interview 30). Despite the fact that Jan 'can't imagine ever wanting to live anywhere else', she was suspicious of the feeling of national belonging and identification. England may not have been something to be particularly proud of, or somewhere that had positive identifications for her, but it was at least familiar in contrast to unknown and potentially more unpleasant places. Yet at the same time, Jan pointed out:

I've no really kind of national identity. I'm quite ashamed of, you know, whenever I see the Union Jack, I don't personally have any feeling of great pride, I have associations of it with, you know, I associate it with football hooligans, British beef and the royal family, really. None of whom I have any particular desire to be associated with [half laugh] really.

(Interview 30)

When I asked Jan whether her preferring to say British rather than English was an indication that there was something in the English identity that she was rejecting, she replied 'I think so, yes. Just a kind of, I think I have, I think I associate English with being a class thing, I think'. Jan was interested enough in the question of identity to ask her elder (8-year-old) daughter whether she thought that she was English or British. Her daughter confidently stated that she was English, to which Jan laughed.

Deborah, who was quoted at the very beginning of this chapter, similarly associated Englishness with a classed sense of superiority. She was explaining why she felt it was 'pedantic' to call herself English rather than British:

Well, I suppose it is only because I'm just thinking of, you know, received pronunciation and BBC and, you know, newsreaders and people like that, who up to a little while ago were all English. They had an English accent. And I'm just thinking of that as a difference between an English accent and a Scottish accent, a Welsh accent, an Irish accent . . . I'm just going back to what we were saying about British and English. Um, but I certainly don't think of it as something . . . well, I don't think of things like, you know, Scotland as being smaller or Wales as being smaller, or anything. I mean, I don't really see – I mean, I just think they're all British, and if people want a national identity, that's really important. They should have it. I mean, I think a lot of connotations of Englishness are really . . . come from other people. And I think that that in turn has been an English fault, um, in being rather snooty about other people's accents and things, and I think, you know, in that case, maybe the English got what they deserved, you know. People do see them as slightly ridiculous maybe abroad, and I'm just thinking immediately of an English person, you know, that's like Americans . . . a lot of Americans still think we have fog, and pea-soupers. And it's really hard to shake that idea off, so I don't think I'd see myself as anything but British really, I guess. And, to be more specific, English.

(Interview 17)

Deborah struggled to decide what she thought Englishness was about and what it meant to her. It was always an identity that she ended up with, when being 'specific' or 'pedantic'. Yet she did this with some reservations because she felt that Englishness may have negative associations. At the same time, she was unclear as to whether these negative associations were 'deserved' or not, and they certainly seemed mostly to come from external representations (or misrepresentations). What was clear, however, was that she herself would prefer to have as little as possible to do with the whole concept of national identity:

> I think on the way, on how deep-rooted your sense of national identity is. I mean, I don't think mine is terribly deep-rooted, and I don't really want it to be either. I think it's a dangerous thing. Um, I mean I don't, really really don't hold with the notion, and I'm absolutely terrified of even the mildest kind of idea that, you know, all these people are visitors, or all these people weren't . . . these people's grandparents weren't born here, or something. I just think that's a terribly sort of vicious road to sort of go along. And maybe I'm just being very hard on people who I hear saying that, I think. Because one shouldn't label people, but I think that's probably got more to do with my shock at . . . because I don't have a terribly strong sense of national identity.
>
> (Interview 17)

Deborah also used the organic metaphor of national identity being 'deep-rooted'. But, in contrast to Helen, who was quoted earlier saying she felt 'rooted' in London, here deep-rooted identities had threatening connotations. It was presented almost as a pathology, something that 'terrifies' Deborah. She saw using national identity to question people's belonging as 'a terribly sort of vicious road to go along', evoking national identity's connections to fascism.

Madeleine, who had spent her earliest years in Hong Kong, but then moved back to Britain with her parents when she was about 9 years old, believed that growing up with Margaret Thatcher in power framed her view of national identity 'um . . . I've never really liked the idea of being British to be honest. It's always been a bit of a "oh, God do I have to be? I'd really rather not"'. Madeleine went on to explain:

> I think that . . . um . . . it's obviously partly to do with having been brought up somewhere else, and having travelled quite a lot – when I was a kid and then again when I left school. And having, you know, been to other places. But I think it's also because I've been interested in other cultures and had close friends from other cultures and been interested in the history of other cultures. And every time you read the history of anybody else, there are the British, do you know what I mean? Enslaving people and shooting people [laugh] and it just gets to the point where you think; 'I can't *bear* it, it's just hideous'. It feels like, sometimes it feels like a weight that you carry around with you. And I know times when I've been travelling. I was in East Africa, when I was about 19 and it was when the Americans bombed Libya and they'd refuelled here. And I'd been having a really nice, I was travelling on my own and everyone had been *really* friendly. And suddenly people would stop you and say

'Are you English?' or 'Are you American?'. And I'd have to go [putting on accent] 'No, Dutch' [laugh]. Yeah because suddenly it was actually quite, I felt quite threatened, you know because people were genuinely very angry about it.

(Interview 9)

Madeleine gave a powerful description of empire, in which the British presence was ubiquitous and an oppressive force: 'every time you read the history of anybody else, there are the British . . . enslaving people and shooting people'. She also had, through her experience of travel, an understanding of what it might mean to occupy thoughtlessly a dominant position.

Madeleine made little distinction between being British or English and used the two interchangeably. She was the only interviewee to put Britishness or Englishness in a truly global frame, rather than one that was restricted to considerations of Britain's relationship with Europe and America, or England's relationship with Scotland, Wales and Ireland. For the first time, links were made between Englishness and empire. Being English meant in some sense having to bear responsibility for the collective actions of its people and politicians. This was a 'weight' to be carried around. Nonetheless, it was something that could not necessarily be avoided, even if Madeleine would 'really rather not' be British. Madeleine was also one of the few to question her *own* sense of belonging – she saw identification with a nation as something that was not inevitable but was influenced by different social and political contexts:

I don't know this feels a bit clichéd, a bit sad. But the first time I thought 'I feel really proud to be British' is when Blair got in on the first of May, [laugh] it was the first time I thought 'right I feel good now, I'm part of the country, I don't feel like an excluded majority who have no voice any more' . . . although I don't know if I still feel that, but I was excited in May [laugh] [. . .] And you can actually read about the things that the government is doing and think 'Yes that's a good idea'. I mean not as many as I'd like, but it is there, which is just *amazing* really. To actually feel like you're part of a community somehow.

(Interview 9)

Madeleine's membership of Englishness was not contested, at least by others, only herself. Nonetheless, she did have a sense of being in a collectivity – she was constructing alternative identities, for instance that of the 'majority' excluded by political processes. She had also had recourse to other locational and cultural identities. Madeleine had a strongly urban identity, which contrasted with the idyll of rural Englishness portrayed by Emma:

Madeleine: um . . . Well, I suppose I've always, I see myself as much more of a *Londoner* than *English* perhaps so I suppose I have that kind of identity.

BB: And that's a more positive one?
Madeleine: Yeah. In lots of ways definitely.
BB: Because?
Madeleine: Because, um, because although, you know London has lots
            of . . . downsides to it, it's also, I don't know, it's lively, it's very
            very multicultural and you can just be part of . . . I went to live
            in Wales for a little while and it was just like [horrified expres-
            sion], it wasn't even *Welsh*, do you know what I mean, there
            wasn't even any *Welsh* culture there at all. Whereas I think in
            London people are very vocal about their cultures and what
            they're doing. And I'm sure people like, even more so in some
            of the northern cities, you know because at heart even us Lon-
            doners are quite repressed and don't like to talk to each other.
            . . . I like, I really like the mix of people here and I like the
            fact that there's different things, there's different colours and
            cultures and, you know, I like the fact that there's different, you
            know you can go and sit in Kensington Gardens and then come
            back to Peckham. You have access to all sorts of different places,
            which is nice.

                                                                    (Interview 9)

For Madeleine, whereas British or English identities were loaded with
negative historical associations (and, interestingly, in contrast to other interviewees, she did not view Wales romantically or positively), London had
more positive associations. Madeleine embraced the 'liveliness' and multicultural aspects of London. However, it is interesting how her description
was racialised and classed. Part of the liveliness of London came from differences, the way in which it offered the experience of spaces that were classed
and raced in different ways. Kensington Gardens and Peckham offer very
different experiences of London life which Madeleine could move between.
Yet at the same time, she was positioned as white and middle class by this
account – it was not one that a black person or a working-class person could
give. The ability to move as easily between Peckham and Kensington Gardens is not available to all equally. Nonetheless, for Madeleine, people living
in London – 'us Londoners' – had a collective identity and shared patterns
of behaviour and attitude much as people might talk about 'the British'.
Unlike Englishness, which in some constructions is threatened by otherness,
for Madeleine, difference was contained within the category of Londoner,
constructed as a positive and constitutive attribute.

Conclusion

I think for black people who live in Britain this question of finding some
way in which the white British can learn to live with us and the rest

of the world is almost as important as discovering our own identity. I think they are in more trouble than we are. So we, in a curious way, have to rescue them from themselves – from their own past. We have to allow them to see that England is a quite interesting place with quite an interesting history that has bossed us around for 300 years [but] that has finished. Who are they now?

(Stuart Hall 1989 cited in Back 1996: 127–8)

Stuart Hall sets out a clear challenge: not only does Englishness or Britishness have to be reimagined (particularly by the white British and white English) in relation to changing social and political contexts, but it must also be acknowledged that 'race' lies at the heart of Englishness. This chapter has shown some of the different ways in which England and Britain are imagined and the way national identities are felt and lived. One result of living the gap between the pedagogical and performative[11] – between the nationalist construction of a continuous and seamless connection with the past and the recursive demands of living nation-ness in everyday life – is an uncertainty about what Englishness contains. A theme that emerged through the interviews was a sense of narrowness and/or emptiness in Englishness. Classic renditions of England as a 'green and pleasant land' populated by historical figures and perhaps even John Major's spinsters cycling to church around village greens are clearly raced and build upon a racialised discourse of national and imperial superiority in which white women play a particular, protected, role. In the interviews, there were clear echoes of this discourse in the juxtapositions between England and others, where Englishness was white, middle class, rural and clean as opposed to the threat posed by dirty others (such as gypsies or Muslims selling halal meat). The interviews also showed the insecure basis of imaginings of Englishness. They were disrupted by urban life, by the presence of differently raced subjects and by the individuals' own sense of loss of a class position. Thus, there is an inflexibility in the formal narration of Englishness, which made it impossible to sustain in the everyday. Some of this tension was expressed in the difference between the image of a nostalgic 'deep England' and multicultural and multiracial Britain.

For other interviewees, the everyday, and in particular the domestic as a space and practice, did not necessarily provide a sense of difference demanded by the nationalist rhetoric. So Englishness and also perhaps Britishness were experienced by some as an empty or unmarked norm that appeared to lack content in the face of what was seen as the cultural richness of other identities and forms of living. Its very whiteness and normality made it invisible. For example, Helen did not feel that she lived Englishness through her consumption of food or in the rituals of life, although it was in the domestic, she suggested, that culture might have real meaning, through which 'roots' are established. Englishness, characterised by an inflexibility towards difference, was likely to disappear in the face of other cultural practices and identities that were more visible and felt to have more meaning.

For yet others, Englishness was to be actively evaded or escaped. There was nothing to be salvaged from an identity associated with class and 'race' prejudice. In this response to collective identity, all national identities were seen as potentially negative, particularly if 'deep-rooted', but Britain's imperial history made it particularly unattractive and sometimes oppressive. What we see emerging in some interviews, and in particular Madeleine's account, is a rejection of pedagogical accounts of nationhood and a turn to more fluid and temporary identifications, for example as 'Londoners'. This enabled difference to be embraced as a positive and integral part of a collective identity, rather than as a threat. Yet there remains some uncertainty as to how this is to be achieved outside the kinds of explicit attachments that characterise certain young people's cultural practices. Madeleine's critique and then evasion of an English or British identity based on whiteness and class exclusion was relatively exceptional within this research. Given the ongoing anxieties about race and national culture, especially those expressed through current debates around immigration, it would seem that her rethinking of national identity remains a minority position.

Through the course of the interviews, it emerged that 'narrating the nation' can be a means of narrating the self. As such, it is equally gendered, raced and classed. When Emma and Heather looked back nostalgically to a 'glorious' English past, they also appeared to be expressing a sense of loss in their own lives. This loss was based on sometimes contradictory classed and gendered experiences. Equally, Helen's narrative of the disruption in Englishness marked a point of rupture from her family. To say that Englishness was changing or fading also marked her difference from her family. The collective was read through the individual and personal. James Donald writes of how the nation is the effect of 'the apparatus of discourses, technologies and institutions (print capitalism, education, mass media, and so forth) which *produces* what is generally recognised as "the national culture"' (Donald 1993: 167). What is interesting in these interviews is how there was relatively little mention of these public discourses and technologies. Rather, the nation was constructed and imagined through forms of living, through personal histories and everyday routines and consumption. As such, it was fluid and multiple.

8 Conclusion

I write this concluding chapter in the last weeks of the 2005 British general election, when 'race' has reared its head in a very explicit manner. The Conservative Party launched its initial election campaign with the slogan: 'Are you thinking what we're thinking?'. This included a poster with the statement, written like graffiti over advertising hoardings: 'It's not racist to impose limits on immigration'. This of course leaves open the question of who the 'you' is. The slogan appears to be directly targeting those white voters who feel hemmed in about what it is permissible to say because of a desire not to appear racist. This opens a Pandora's box of other, now permissible, statements along the line of 'I'm not racist but . . .'. It would seem that, for the Conservative Party at least, the commonsense Everyman of Britain retains a white face.

At the other end of the political spectrum, leading Labour party politicians David Blunkett and Gordon Brown also took time in the election period to intervene in ongoing debates on Britishness. Gordon Brown promoted a move away from racialised conceptions of national identity towards the idea of shared values. While there may be some merit in this attempt to reimagine national identity and belonging, the argument skirted around issues of race, rather than attacking them head on. Brown argued that 'I think the days of Britain having to apologise for our history are over. I think we should move forward. I think we should celebrate much of our past rather than apologise for it and we should talk, rightly so, about British values'.[1] Brown wanted a sense of common identity that is not bound by race, but it is not clear whether he is prepared to do the kind of ground-clearing work that would be involved in reimagining such an embedded notion. Nor is it obvious that the poets he draws on for inspiration (Wordsworth, Shelley and Milton) will communicate to all.

The interest among mainstream politicians on questions of identity during this election did not arise in a vacuum and reflects a political culture in which questions of national identity and particularly immigration have steadily gained increased attention. The debates have also been fuelled by racialised and Islamophobic reactions to what has become known as 9/11, but also have a longer history. In 1998, the Runnymede Trust set up a commission on the 'Future of Multi-Ethnic Britain', which set out to produce a review of the current state of multiethnic Britain. After 2 years of extensive consultation and discussion, the commission produced a report which argued that Britain in the year 2000 is at a turning point or crossroads with different potential roads ahead:

> will it try to turn the clock back, digging in, defending old values and ancient hierarchies, relying on a narrow English-dominated, backward-looking definition of the nation? Or will it seize the opportunity to create a more flexible, inclusive, cosmopolitan image of itself?
>
> (Parekh 2000: 14–15)

The report argued for a 'purposeful process of change' rather than 'multicultural drift' (Parekh 2000: 2). Part of this process was, the report argued, a reimagining of British national identity and its history. An important obstacle to Britain's transformation into an inclusive, pluralist society was that 'Britishness, as much as Englishness, has systematic, largely unspoken, racial connotations' (Parekh 2000: 38). The report further argued that '[u]nless these deep-rooted antagonisms to racial and cultural difference can be defeated in practice, as well as symbolically written out of the national story, the idea of a multicultural post-nation remains an empty promise' (Parekh 2000: 38).

The report got widespread attention, particularly in the print media, and drew an emotional and largely hostile response, which centred on the question of reimagining Britishness. Hugo Young described the response as a 'tirade of anger based on the claim that there are not enough blacks and Asians here to justify any such exercise' (Young 2000). The analysis contained in the report was widely misrepresented[2] with, for instance, the *Guardian* (11 October 2000) editorial claiming that the report had suggested that Britain should be renamed 'community of communities', apparently misunderstanding that this was proposed as a model for society, rather than an actual name. The *Daily Mail* (11 October 2000) argued that to suggest that national stories and identities might be rethought had totalitarian implications: 'Such were the means by which Stalin and Hitler twisted the past to suit their own political purposes'. The report was critiqued as 'an insult to history and our intelligence' (*Daily Mail* 11 October 2000). This response suggests the destabilising potential of claims to reimagine Britishness. The report's argument that those who have hitherto been a marginalised presence on the edges of the British identity should be placed at its centre prompted a passionate defence of particular notions of Britishness and whiteness. The strength of the uproar was an indication of just how unsettling it can be for those who have occupied normative subject positions to have those positions questioned or challenged. The argument that 'race' has nothing to do with white people, or with Britishness, remains a deeply felt conviction on the part of many white people. Gordon Brown's call to 'move on' is likely to strike a chord with many.

The material presented in this book has shown not only that the collective identity of Britain remains raced, but also how processes of racialisation are deeply embedded within everyday practices and imaginaries. In this way, it has argued that it is unsustainable to argue that 'race' has nothing to do with even the most well-intentioned 'non-racist' white people. The white metropolitan subject is produced at least partly through racialised imaginaries and practices. Whiteness is not an identity that is often spoken of. However, this book has shown the ways in which whiteness is lived in the everyday. The ways in which white women's seeing, doing, talking and imagining performatively reinscribe racialised discourses. Through mothering practices, it is possible to see some of the ways in which children are constructed as racialised, classed and gendered. I have also shown how the women's sense of self was sometimes built around a racialised (and also classed) other.

It is a potentially dangerous political moment when white researchers start to 'discover' their own (and others') whiteness and capture grants, publish books and generally make careers out of writing about 'race' and whiteness. The danger comes, in part, from the creation of a 'field of studies' that is, yet again, dominated by white researchers and makes white experience central. There is also a risk that there emerges a notion of a unified 'white culture', in contrast to 'black' or 'Asian' cultures. Or, yet more problematically, the idea of a 'white race' is somehow confirmed. However, this latter problem is a risk that is inherent in any discussions of 'race'. David Goldberg argues that what is at issue in discussions of 'race' is a field of discourse made up of all racialised expressions. This would include the analysis involved in examining the historical formation or logic of racial thinking from a critical perspective, as well as different racisms: 'racism turns out to be one such object among possible others in the emergence and elaboration of racialised discourse' (Goldberg 1993: 42). Thus, he argues that '*race* is a discursive object of racialised discourses that differs from *racism*. *Race* nevertheless creates the conceptual conditions of possibility, in some conjunctural conditions, for racist expression to be formulated' (Goldberg 1993: 43, emphasis in the original). It is this point – that any analysis of, or even opposition to, concepts of 'race' involves utilisation or engagement with racialised discourses – that leads Alistair Bonnet to argue that:

> anti-racism cannot be adequately understood as the inverse of racism. [. . .] anti-racists have frequently deployed racism to secure and develop their project. The most characteristic form of this incorporation is anti-racists' adherence to categories of 'race', categories which, even when politically or 'strategically' employed, lend themselves to the racialisation process.
>
> (Bonnett 2000a: 3)

The continuing risks of engaging in racialised or racialising discourse, coupled with what he sees as a 'crisis in raciology', have led Paul Gilroy to call for 'the renunciation of "race" as a critical concept' (Gilroy 1998: 838). According to Gilroy, the crisis exists

> because the idea of 'race' has lost much of its common-sense credibility, because the elaborate cultural and ideological work that goes into producing and reproducing it is more visible than ever before, because it has been stripped of its moral and intellectual integrity, and because there is a chance to prevent its rehabilitation.
>
> (Gilroy 2000: 28–9)

For Gilroy, this offers the possibility of developing a radical 'non-racial humanism', which is also 'wilfully ungendered' (Gilroy 2000: 16). The prospect of being able to move beyond 'race' is not only attractive but must also be kept constantly in mind in writing about 'race' in general and whiteness in particular. However, I have suggested in this book that I do not believe that this moment has arrived. We are still too implicated in racialising processes simply to declare the end of 'race' as a category of analysis. Rather, I have argued that we need to attend to 'race' as a 'troubled' category in a way that denies its ontological status.

'Race' needs to be understood as produced within different formulations of power. I argued that 'race' can be fruitfully understood as 'performative' – existing only where it is reproduced through discursive recitation. 'Race' is, following Judith Butler's rendering of gender, 'constituted by the very "expressions" which are said to be its results' (Butler 1990: 25). One 'expression' that I argued was particularly important was a range of *perceptual practices* which construct concepts of difference that are then incorporated into discourses of 'race'. These perceptual schema are, as Gilroy makes clear, neither 'natural' nor inevitable, but are the product of a whole range of potentially conflicting discursive formations and practices (for example, see Goldberg's (1993: 149) discussions of western science and racial thinking). Questions of power, therefore, lie at the heart of the continual circulation and reformulation of racialising discourses. 'Race' is not the result of visual practices alone, but is conditioned by *who* is seeing and who has the ability to assert what is seen and how it is seen. Whiteness, occupying the position of the norm in racialised schemas, is therefore often asserted (particularly by white people) as invisible or as unmarked by 'race'. It is defined by what is excluded, by those who are racially 'marked' (visually and symbolically) and form whiteness's 'constitutive outside'.

The interviews have shown some of the anxieties that circulate around these acts of seeing, perhaps particularly for white subjects. As discussed in Chapter 5, mothers talked with some degree of trepidation about what they thought their children saw. As far as 'race' was concerned, there was no consensus about what children did see and what levels of racialised looking were 'innocent' or 'natural'. Some children were thought to 'see' neither race nor class, whereas others were expected to be relatively attuned to ethnic and racialised difference. For many, to notice racialised difference was to risk allowing racism to bubble to the surface and therefore the best option was not to see. Being colour blind might be understood literally, as in the case of their children who they often asserted did not see skin colour differences, or metaphorically, when children and adults are described as not being prejudiced. But this does not mean that 'race' did not register in their perceptual schemas, or that they did not have emotional responses to racialised differences. One result was the potential overvisualisation of racialised others. Black faces in school assemblies or photographs sometimes seemed to obliterate the white faces that were also there. In addition, young black men appeared to loom large in the social imaginary as a threatening presence on the racialised space of the street.

Discussions of difference were sometimes diverted from those of skin colour to that of 'cultural' difference, which was, however, often marked by visual signifiers (such as saris) or by language, names and accents. This produced a discourse of 'exposure' to difference which maintained the unexplored whiteness as the norm bounded by those who dress or name themselves differently. Thus, this shift from skin or 'race' to culture marked a recitation of racialised discourses, again often functioning around the visible, but on slightly different grounds. It was marked by a mixture of desire and unease, which appeared in different ways through many of the interviews. While whiteness was largely undiscussed, it was at the same time defined through difference. Some of these differences were constructed as things to be celebrated and embraced. In some cases, there was even a suggestion of envy that 'others' had richer and more interesting customs and cultures. Yet at the same time, difference could also produce a sense of risk and threat. In the case of the trope of the black male, as mentioned above, this might be a physical threat, whereas in the discussion of schools, friendships and Englishness, the threat was less directly to the body and indicated a vulnerability of the respondents' own, or children's, identities and sense of self. The normative nature of whiteness needed to be constantly protected. One way in which whiteness was constructed was through the summoning up of a gendered and racialised 'other', in the form of the threatened and/or desired black male. White femininity was produced through this imagining as under threat and also tempted.

Not only was *seeing* 'race' an anxious process, but this carried through to racialised and racialising *talk*. The material has shown how there is no single way to tell or narrate the white self. The production or non-production of a narrative of the self is the result of a complex interaction of classed, gendered and racialised processes. Not all white subjects have the same sense of agency or sense of coherence in their self-narratives, and some found available discourses of the self inadequate for describing their own experiences. Most of the interviewees displayed an awkwardness in talking about 'race'. Generally, 'race' was something that pertained to others and, in this way, it contrasted with class and gender, which could be, perhaps to different degrees, inhabited by the respondents. Unlike with class, and particularly gender, there are few culturally familiar narratives of the experience of becoming aware of (coming to terms with?) one's whiteness. However, in a similar way, talking about class was also avoided in many instances.

One response to the difficulty of knowing what areas of 'race' talk were permissible was to skirt around the issue with various discourses that served to recirculate and reiterate racialised concepts without being directly labelled as such. Thus, multiculturalism proved to be a flexible discourse as it could be used positively, in the idea of wanting children to have an 'exposure' to difference that might enrich their lives. However, this still ensured the fixity of the difference between 'them' and 'us', the norm and the other. But there was also a cautionary element to this idea of exposure, which emphasised the need to achieve the right 'mix' in order to ensure the best socialisation for children. The risk of 'overexposure' was perhaps always present. Class difference was also a shadowy presence in this discourse. Both class and race could also be alluded to through geographical location depending on the assumption of a shared understanding of areas having particular racialised and classed characteristics.

Other ideas of location and locatedness were expressed through discussions of national identity. By exploring imaginings of Englishness, Chapter 7 was able to examine how the women responded to and inserted themselves into public discourses of nationhood and belonging. At the level of national identity, it was possible to see how definitions and imaginings of the collective were produced through constructions of different 'others'. This was most straightforward in the case of those who took up a nostalgic, defensive imagining of Englishness, where it was contrasted to a negative construction of 'Britishness', to Americanness and to racialised others. Here, Englishness was posited as white, middle class and rural and under threat from difference, including the racialised urban space in which the women lived. For others, Englishness was an empty concept, much like whiteness, where other people had culture and exciting difference leaving Englishness empty and seemingly bereft. Finally, some interviewees saw Englishness as defined by nationalists and racists and therefore something to be evaded wherever possible. What was interesting was the limited extent to which the interviews made explicit recourse to public discourses of national identity of the kind that politicians and others promote. Rather, their narratives of identity and imaginings of belonging were formed around personal experiences and trajectories. This indicates the extent to which public, collective identities are read through the personal.

Ways of seeing and talking were not the only racialised practices that emerged through the interviews. The act of coming to London, settling down and being in a particular place was experienced as racialised as well as classed and gendered. In Chapter 6, I argued how practices involved in mothering can be understood as performative of 'race', class and gender. Not only is mothering an inescapably gendered activity, but the mothers also discussed the large extent to which they saw their work as *gendering*. That is, ensuring that their children were equipped to enter a social universe that was gendered. However, when it came to questions of 'race' and class, the women were far more equivocal about their input. They generally denied or downgraded their mothering in terms of 'race' and class – asserting that, in contrast to gender, this was something that they did not often discuss with their children (or perhaps even think about it). Nonetheless, through the interview material on the mother's own social lives, as well as their children's, the subtle and not so subtle processes of inclusion and exclusion that are part of everyday life became clear. This was both at the level of mothers meeting other mothers, where distinctions were made between others who were 'like-minded' and those who were not, but also, more significantly, around the question of children's schooling. A key concern for the women was to find a school for their children that had the 'right' social and racial 'mix' of students. It emerged that practices around choice of schooling were highly racialised, as well as classed. A school that was seen as being 'too black' or 'too working class' was also viewed as potentially disruptive to their children's education. This disruption concerned not merely questions of qualifications and gaining the right racialised and classed social capital, but also, I suggest, the desire for their children to become raced and classed subjects. While the women might at times engage in a discourse of celebratory multiculturalism, or what Gilroy terms the 'commodified exotica' of 'racialised glamour' (Gilroy 2000: 21), their practices as mothers were far from 'post-racial'.

Thus, through analysis of the interview accounts in this book, I have argued that we still need to understand how the everyday lives of white people are shaped by the reiteration of discourses and practices of 'race', despite the risks involved in dealing with racialised discourses. Importantly, we also need to be attentive to how this intersects with other social processes, as Vron Ware and Les Back argue:

> A new social movement that seeks to expose and dismantle the machinations of White Power requires more than emotional energy, and open mind, and a commitment to direct action; it also needs a constant flow of analysis and theoretical debate in order to comprehend the ways in which racism is intrinsically interconnected with other forms of social division.
>
> (Ware and Back 2002: 13)

But where does this leave the study of whiteness? What is the nature, and objective, of work on whiteness? Perhaps it would help to restate what it is not. I would not want this work on exploring whiteness to contribute to any attempt to recuperate the 'feel good' factor for the white subject. This is not a quest to find good things to say about whiteness (in the way that some are arguing for a positive British nationalism). I do not believe that the emotional fragility (if it exists) of the white subject should be given this kind of support. However, it is also important that critical attention to whiteness does not become a form of class struggle with sole attention focused on working-class (and often male) expressions of racism and prejudice. Middle-class and female performances of race are equally in need of scrutiny. If there is need for identities to feel positive about, the aim should be to find non-racialised (or at least less racialised) identities to affirm, while at the same time acknowledging the powerful impact of racialisation in the production of experience and identity. These more positive identities might revolve around different forms of locatedness, such as those of being a Londoner or even a radically revised idea of Britishness or Englishness. They are also likely to come from a recognition of the multiplicity and evolving nature of identities.

Nor is this work a 'me too' (or a 'we too') claim. It is not concerned with arguing that white people can do 'race' (and therefore somehow experience racism) just like black or Asian people. Rather than a call for 'we too', the objective is the critical examination of the 'we'. How is white experience constructed as white – what practices and imaginaries depend on its repetition? How is it that dominant ideas of the commonsense and normal come to be overlaid with racialised conceptions that centre around whiteness. This can be seen in the Conservative electoral slogan of 'Are you thinking what we're thinking?'. It can also be seen in the discussions of the reasonableness of looking for the right 'mix' in schools.

Finally, this examination on whiteness has not set the terms for a call for action. There is no anti-racist 12-step plan appended to this work. The book has focused on how things are done as a preliminary move towards working out how they might be undone. This hesitancy about action is frustrating, but perhaps a necessary pause for thought for the white subject who has for too long taken the power to define (rather than be defined) and to act (rather than be acted upon). There is no easy 'escape' from whiteness; rather, as Sara Ahmed argues

> race, like sex, is sticky; it sticks to us, or we become "us" as an effect of how it sticks, even when we think we are beyond it. Beginning to live with that stickiness, to think it, feel it, do it, is about creating a space to deal with the effects of racism. We need to deal with the effects of racism in a way that is better.
>
> (Ahmed 2004: 49)

Yet often the task of dealing with the effects of racism is left to those who suffer its impact most brutally. What I have argued in this book is that white people cannot evade 'race' by thinking that it has nothing to do with them. The white self is constructed through racialising practices and discourses, just as it is also constructed as classed and gendered. To return to the discussions with which I opened the book, I would argue that whiteness, and therefore 'race' and racism, are not only 'out there' in former colonial societies or in the minds of BNP activists. They are also 'in here' in the ways that white people talk and see, the ways they interact with others, their aspirations for their children and their sense of who they are, both as part of collectivities and as individuals.

Notes

1 Knowing 'whiteness'

1 The use of apostrophes or 'scare quotes' around 'race' in this book is to highlight its problematic and constructed nature. While I recognise that the same argument could be employed in the case of class and gender, in this book, it will be used only for 'race'.

2 There is a problem of language and terminology here. Although I recognise that it is not without problems and contestation (for a discussion, see Brah 1996: 98), I am adopting here the political usage of 'black' as employed for instance by Heidi Safia Mirza, writing in the British context: 'What defines us as Pacific, Asian, Eastern, African, Caribbean, Latina, Native and "mixed race" "others" is not our imposed minority status, but our self-defining presence as peoples of the post-colonial diaspora. At only 5.5 per cent of the population we still stand out, we are visibly different and that is what makes us "black"' (Mirza 1997: 3). The question of the notion of 'visible' differences will be taken up in the following chapter. In addition, I am aware that some black women thinkers would have reservations about the label 'feminist' (see Walker 1984; (charles) 1997). This points to the importance of not assuming that the category of either black feminists or white feminists is as homogeneous as it may appear for the sake of brevity in this discussion.

3 See Ware (1992) for a discussion of the sometimes difficult relationship between campaigns for female suffrage and abolitionism.

4 For a review of this literature, see Alexander (1996).

5 They are also mainly white, which has obvious significance. Anoop Nayak is an important exception (see his discussion in Nayak (1999)).

6 See for example Husband (1982), van Dijk (1991), Rattansi (1992), Goulbourne (1993), Cohen (1994), Macey (1995), Hesse (1997), Paul (1997), Waters (1997), Gabriel (1998), Carter et al. (2000).

7 See for example Morrison (1992), Wetherell and Potter (1992), Goldberg (1993), Dyson (1995), Gabriel (1994), Gabriel (1996), Aanerud (1997), Dyer (1997), Goldberg (1997), Muraleedharan (1997) and Neal (1999).

2 Troubling 'race'

1 It is now generally agreed by scientists that race has no biological meaning. Genotypical differences (differences in genetic make-up) do not map onto so-called racial groups, largely defined by phenotypical differences. As Steve Jones (1993: 247) argues: 'Modern genetics does in fact show that there are no separate groups within humanity'. However, as argued above, this does not

mean that the term race is not frequently used, either explicitly or implicitly, in a biologically essentialist manner.

2 Vikki Bell (1999a) makes this argument strongly in considering Judith Butler and anti-semitism, but there is a risk here that race and ethnicity are being used as interchangeable/identical terms. The argument Bell makes for ethnic identity may hold less strongly for 'race', which generally fails to escape biological essentialist articulations. It is less easy to change or reject a racial identity than a religious affiliation and less easy to be intelligible without a racial identity.

3 In *Excitable Speech* (1997b), Butler examines legal and political responses to hate speech, including race hate. In this work, she explores the performativity of racialised speech, rather than of 'race' itself.

4 This aspect of Butler's work has often been misunderstood, particularly in response to *Gender Trouble* (1990), which prompted studies embracing the idea of 'stylised' performance and, in particular, the subversive potential of drag. Sara Ahmed, in noting the later re-emphasis of Butler's work on performativity, and considering the case of racialised 'passing' (where those normally positioned as non-white are able to 'pass' for white), questions discourses that tend 'to position "passing" as a radical and transgressive practice that serves to destabilise and traverse the system of knowledge and vision upon which subjectivity and identity precariously rests' (Ahmed 1999: 88). She goes on to argue that 'I do think that there is a failure to theorise, not the potential for any system to become destabilised, but the means by which relations of power are secured, paradoxically, through this very process of destabilisation' (Ahmed 1999: 89).

5 For a discussion of borderlands, see Anzaldua (1987).

6 This accounts for the phenomenon of racial 'passing' (see Derricote 1997; Twine 1997; Ahmed 1999).

7 Gilman also traces how, with the development of aesthetic surgery, attempts were made to modify these 'different' looks.

8 See for example Vron Ware's discussion of literary representations of the 'foolhardy' colonial woman whose muddled thinking on race often results in tragedy or even death (Ware 1992: 232).

9 For reviews of the literature within 'race studies', see Solomos and Back (1994); Bulmer and Solomos (1998); Bonnett (1999); Back and Solomos (2000).

3 Talk, tea and tape recorders

1 Initially, I was open to talking to 'parents', i.e. both mothers and fathers. But it quickly became clear that fathers as primary carers (which was who I wanted to speak to) were hard to come by. It is likely that accounts of men and fatherhood would have produced different results.

2 Census information is used here only as a very rough guide, in that there are many problems with the way the information is elicited, particularly in the case of racial identity. See Ifekwunigwe (1997) for a discussion of the 1991 census's failure to accommodate mixed-race identities.

3 An additional ten interviews were carried out with women in the pilot stage of the research who either were not white or did not live in the two areas. These interviews proved useful and have been drawn on in the study (and this chapter).

4 One o'clock clubs are run by local authorities and provide a room with toys, books and art equipment and also an open space with toys and equipment where parents can come with their children to play. The clubs are free and drop in (i.e. do not require regular attendance) and parents must stay with their children.

5 Class position is notoriously difficult to capture, particularly if class is understood to reach beyond economic position (Bourdieu 1994). Classifications of

'middle' or 'working' class in this research are intended as broad brush designations based on a combination of economic position, educational and social background and cultural outlook.

6 See Domínguez (1986), Cohen (1988), Allen (1994), Ignatiev (1995), Haney López (1996), Squires (1997) and Bonnett (1998).

7 See Tizard and Phoenix (1993), Ahmed (1997), Ifekwunigwe (1997) and Twine (1997).

8 All names have been changed to provide anonymity.

9 In quotations from interviews, pauses or gaps in speech are donated by '. . .' and, where speech has been omitted, this is in square brackets: '[. . .]'.

10 While several white interviewees said that it was interesting to be offered the opportunity to think about things that there wasn't usually time or motivation for, this contrasted with Claudia, a 'mixed-race' respondent who said 'the questions were fine. It just made me think about things I just think about all the time anyway' (Interview 6).

11 See Appendix 2 for general areas for discussion.

12 Chapter 4 examines the question of the production of narrative in detail.

13 This will be illustrated more fully in Chapter 6, 'In search of a "good mix"'.

14 See Acker *et al.* (1991) for a discussion of some of the problems of including research subjects in analysis.

15 This concept will be discussed further in Chapter 5.

4 Narrating the self

1 See Byrne (2003) for further discussion of narrative.

2 This phrase is from Gayatri Chakravorty Spivak quoted in Butler (1993a: 122).

3 See S. Hall (1992) and Weedon (1997) for a fuller account of the challenges to the Enlightenment subject.

4 This contrasts with other interviewees who cited their mothers as an important influence on them. See for example the following extract from Teresa: 'I have a very strong mother who was a wonderful mother and there was a very strong sense of security through our childhood, and I guess I would want to replicate that' (Interview 18). Even for those who were more ambiguous about their parents, they often did provide a benchmark for comparison, for instance their styles of mothering – see for example Madeleine later in this chapter.

5 See also Chamberlain (1997).

6 See Chapter 6 for a further discussion of the significance of music as a signifier of class.

7 Chanfrault-Duchet also suggests that a narrative may not be produced because of the 'attitude of both members of the interaction'. In my own research, there were cases where it was clear that the interviewee did not want to tell her life story, perhaps particularly to me.

8 Part of the reason for the difference between the interview with Rosemary and that with, for example, Sally or Madeleine must surely lie in the ways in which they responded to me as an interviewer. It is likely that Sally related to me more or less as a peer, someone who at least had similar interests and whom she felt had a broadly similar social position, in terms of gender, class, race and perhaps even economic status. She said that she enjoyed the interview, and it was clearly a style of encounter – where you explore aspects of your life with an empathetic listener – with which she was familiar. Rosemary must have been conscious of the class difference between us. Here before her was a middle-class woman (who had been introduced to her by a middle-class parent at her daughter's school), who was in further education and wanted to ask her personal questions. It may

be that Rosemary's reticence to talk came from an unwillingness to divulge personal details to me – as a form of resistance even. Certainly, she may have felt slightly uncomfortable with me and, conscious of these differences, I may also have been less at ease. However, we were both more relaxed in the second interview than we had been in the first (helped by the absence of her children).

9 See Cohen (1996) for work on racialised narratives of local areas.

5 Seeing, talking, living 'race'

1 Ruth Frankenberg prefers to use the terms colour or power-evasiveness rather than colour blindness because the latter 'deploys and judges negatively a physical disability, and in part because it is misleading in that this discursive repertoire is organised around evading difference or acknowledging it selectively rather than literally not "seeing" differences or race, culture and color' (Frankenberg 1993: 272, n. 2). While acknowledging the problems with the term, I would suggest that the concepts of both 'colour' and vision or 'blindness' are central to the discussion.

2 See Dyer (1997: 46–8) on white as a colour.

3 Thanks to Naomi Hossein for discussion on this point.

4 There is a serious problem in finding the appropriate terminology to refer to different racialised positions. This problem becomes particularly clear when discussing those who are positioned as 'mixed race' or of 'mixed parentage'. The term 'mixed race' gives further credence to ideologies of 'race', whereas reference to 'mixed parentage' as a particular position denies the fact that we are all mixed in terms of being the product of a combination of our parents' genes. Jayne Ifekwunigwe proposes the term *metis* (Ifekwunigwe 1997), but I am hesitant to use a term to describe people that they would not use themselves or even recognise the meaning of.

5 See Rattansi (1992) and Yuval-Davis (1992) for discussions of multiculturalism.

6 See particularly Yuval-Davis (1992) for a discussion of the dominance of religion within multicultural education and the racialisation of religion.

7 For further discussion of the imaginary, see Laclau (1990), Bhabha (1994) and Hesse (1997).

8 See Bonnett (1999) for a review of the relationship between geography and race studies.

9 Ruth Frankenberg discusses how some of her interviewees had 'apparently all-white' childhoods, which in fact turned out to be populated by many people who were not white (Frankenberg 1993: 46).

6 In search of a 'good mix'

1 It could also be argued that there is also gendered exclusion, in the form of fathers. During the fieldwork, I did not encounter any full-time fathers or men acting as primary carers. Those that did exist would perhaps have felt uncomfortable in the social situations that are discussed in this chapter. In the following extract, Deborah is discussing one full-time father who used to live locally: 'I was always very very conscious of trying to involve him as much as anybody else, you know, any woman, but then there's always this sort of, um, I mean, I didn't . . . I don't know if he came across it, I'm sure he did, um, a certain amount of caution . . . It was certainly different talking to him. I'd talk to him on a completely different level to the way I'd speak to my female friends' (Interview 17).

2 It is not within the scope of this chapter to consider fully the implications of

social mobility. Steph Lawler emphasises the pain and sense of estrangement associated with movement from a working- to a middle-class position (Lawler 1999).

3 Inevitably, the material and discussion in this chapter rely on the accounts of the mothers. I did not have access to wider family discussions in which, no doubt, fathers would participate and where they might provide a very different perspective. It is interesting to note, however, that while the interviewees referred to discussions that they had had with other mothers, relatively few references were made to their partners taking part in decision-making around schooling.

4 The names of the schools have been changed.

5 See also Reay (1999) for a discussion of working-class women's sense of intimidation in dealing with school authorities.

6 This is a similar case of the overvisualisation of black children to that of Liz in the last chapter, who realised when she examined a school photograph closely that her daughter's class had far fewer black students than she had previously thought.

7 Teresa's protestation that she was not suggesting something 'unreasonable' and my attempt to occupy a non-judgemental position show that Teresa knew that this was a politically sensitive area.

8 In 1997, according to Lambeth educational statistics, 60.8 per cent of school pupils were Christian, another 18 per cent had 'no religion' and 10.9 per cent were unclassified. The largest religious minorities were Muslims (at 7.2 per cent) and Hindus (at 1.2 per cent).

7 How English am I?

1 This title is adapted from the title of an article by James Donald, which is in turn an adaptation of the title of the novel *How German is it?* by Walder Abish (Donald 1993).

2 See for example Nairn (1981), Wright (1985), Colls and Dodd (1986), Crick (1991), Kearney (1991), Colley (1992), Cohen (1994), Jones (1998), Paxman (1998) and Kumar (2003).

3 The interviews took place between June 1997 and March 1998.

4 See Binnie and Skeggs (2004) for a useful discussion of cosmopolitan spaces.

5 See in particular C. Hall (1992), Ware (1992) and McClintock (1995).

6 Except in the instance of linguistics where black English or 'Blinglish' is a more familiar concept.

7 This reference to 'the gypsies' was prompted by reports in the newspapers in the week of the interview about Roma asylum seekers fleeing discrimination in Eastern Europe – or coming as 'economic migrants' and seeking benefit payments, depending on which interpretation was followed.

8 See for example Roger Hewitt's accounts of racist jokes (Hewitt 1996).

9 See also Dyer (1997: 75–6).

10 See Cohen (1988).

11 See Bhabha (1990a).

8 Conclusion

1 http://news.bbc.co.uk/1/hi/programmes/newsnight/4347369.stm (downloaded 2/04/05).

2 See the newspaper article in defence of the report 'Get your facts right first please' by Runnymede Trust Chair, Samir Shah, in the *Guardian* (20/10/00).

Bibliography

Aanerud, R. 1997. 'Fictions of whiteness: speaking the names of whiteness in US literature' in Frankenberg, R. (ed.) *Displacing Whiteness. Essays in Social and Cultural Criticism*. Durham, NC: Duke University Press.

Acker, J., Barry, K. and Esseveld, J. 1991. 'Objectivity and truth. Problems in doing feminist research' in Fonow, M.M. and Cook, J. (eds) *Beyond Methodology: Feminist Scholarship as Lived Research*. Bloomington, IN: Indiana University Press.

Adkins, L. 2002. 'Reflexivity and the politics of qualitative research' in May, T. (ed.) *Qualitative Research in Action*. London: Sage.

Ahmed, S. 1997. '"It's a sun-tan, isn't it?" Autobiography as an identificatory practice' in Mirza, H.S. (ed.) *Black British Feminism. A Reader*. London: Routledge.

Ahmed, S. 1999. '"She'll wake up one of these days and find she's turned into a nigger". Passing through hybridity'. *Theory, Culture and Society* 16: 87–106.

Ahmed, S. 2002. 'Racialised bodies' in Evans, M. and Lee, E. (eds) *Real Bodies. A Sociological Introduction*. Basingstoke: Palgrave.

Ahmed, S. 2004. 'Declarations of whiteness: the non-performativity of anti-racism'. *Borderlands ejournal* 3 (2): 1–16.

Alexander, C.E. 1996. *The Art of Being Black. The Creation of Black British Youth Identities*. Oxford: Clarendon Press.

Allen, T.W. 1994. *The Invention of the White Race. Vol. 1. Racial Oppression and Social Control*. New York: Verso.

Amos, V. and Parmar, P. 1984. 'Challenging imperial feminism'. *Feminist Review* 17: 3–20.

Anderson, A. 1991. *Imagined Communities. Reflections on the Origin and Spread of Nationalism* (rev. edn). London: Verso.

Anthias, F. and Yuval-Davis, N. 1983. 'Contextualising feminism – gender, ethnic and class divisions'. *Feminist Review* 15: 62–75.

Anzaldua, G. 1987. *Borderlands/La Frontera. The New Mestiza*. San Francisco: Aunt Lute Books.

Aziz, R. 1995. 'Feminism and the challenge of racism' in Blair, M., Holland, J. and Sheldon, S. (eds) *Identity and Diversity: Gender and the Experience of Education*. Milton Keynes: Open University.

Back, L. 1994. 'The "white negro" revisited: race and masculinities in South London' in Cornwall, A. and Lindisfarne, N. (eds) *Dislocating Masculinity: Comparative Ethnologies*. London: Routledge.

182 Bibliography

Back, L. 1996. *New Ethnicities and Urban Culture: Racisms and Multiculture in Young Lives*. London: UCL Press.

Back, L. 1998. 'Inside out: racism, class and masculinity in the "inner city" and the English suburbs'. *New Formations* 33: 59–76.

Back, L. and Solomos, J. 2000. *Theories of Race and Racism: A Reader*. London: Routledge.

Barrett, M. and McIntosh, M. 1985. 'Ethnocentrism and socialist-feminist theory'. *Feminist Review* 20: 23–48.

Bauman, G. 1996. *Contesting Culture. Discourses of Identity in Multi-ethnic London*. Cambridge: Cambridge University Press.

Bell, D. 1993. *Daughters of the Dreaming*. St Leonards, NSW: Allen & Unwin.

Bell, V. 1999a. 'Mimesis as cultural survival. Judith Butler and anti-semitism'. *Theory, Culture and Society* 16 (2): 133–61.

Bell, V. 1999b. 'On speech, race and melancholia. An interview with Judith Butler'. *Theory, Culture and Society* 16: 163–74.

Bhabha, H.K. 1987. 'Interrogating identity' in Appignanesi, L. (ed.) *Identity. The Real Me. Postmodernism and the Question of Identity*. ICA document no. 6. London: ICA.

Bhabha, H. K. 1990a. 'Introduction: narrating the nation' in Bhabha, H.K. (ed.) *Nation and Narration*. London: Routledge.

Bhabha, H.K. 1990b. 'DissemiNation: time, narrative and the margins of the modern nation' in Bhabha, H.K. (ed.) *Nation and Narration*. London: Routledge.

Bhabha, H.K. 1994. *The Location of Culture*. London: Routledge.

Bhabha, H.K. 1996. 'The other question' in Mongia, P. (ed.) *Contemporary Postcolonial Theory: A Reader*. London: Arnold.

Bhavani, K.K. and Coulson, M. 1986. 'Transforming socialist-feminism: the challenge of racism'. *Feminist Review* 23: 81–92.

Billig, M. 1995. *Banal Nationalism*. London: Sage Publications.

Binnie, J. and Skeggs, B. 2004. 'Cosmopolitan knowledge and the production and consumption of sexualized space: Manchester's gay village'. *Sociological Review* 52 (1): 39–61.

Bonnett, A. 1998. 'Who was white? The disappearance of non-European white identities and the formation of European racial whiteness'. *Ethnic and Racial Studies* 21: 1029–54.

Bonnett, A. 1999. 'Constructions of "race", place and discipline. Geographies of "racial" identity and racism' in Bulmer, M. and Solomos, J. (eds) *Ethnic and Racial Studies Today*. London: Routledge.

Bonnett, A. 2000a. *Anti-racism*. London: Routledge.

Bonnett, A. 2000b. *White Identities. Historical and International Perspectives*. Harlow: Prentice Hall.

Borland, K. 1991. '"That's not what I said": Interpretive conflict in oral narrative research' in Gluck, S. and Patai, D. (eds) *Women's Words. The Feminist Practice of Oral History*. London: Routledge.

Bourdieu, P. 1994. *Distinction*. London: Routledge.

Brah, A. 1996. *Cartographies of Diaspora, Contesting Identities*. London: Routledge.

Bulmer, M. and Solomos, J. 1998. 'Introduction: re-thinking ethnic and racial studies'. *Ethnic and Racial Studies* 21: 819–37.

Butler, J. 1990. *Gender Trouble. Feminism and the Subversion of Identity*. London: Routledge.

Butler, J. 1993a. *Bodies that Matter. On the Discursive Limits of 'Sex'*. London: Routledge.

Butler, J. 1993b. 'Endangered/endangering: schematic racism and white paranoia' in Gooding-Williams, R. (ed.) *Reading Rodney King. Reading Urban Uprising*. New York: Routledge.

Butler, J. 1995. 'For a careful reading' in Benhabib, S., Butler, J., Cornell, D. and Fraser, N. (eds) *Feminist Contentions. A Philosophical Exchange*. New York: Routledge.

Butler, J. 1997a. *The Psychic Life of Power. Theories of Subjection*. Stanford: Stanford University Press.

Butler, J. 1997b. *Excitable Speech. A Politics of the Performative*. London: Routledge.

Byrne, B. 2003. 'Reciting the self'. *Feminist Theory* 4: 29–49.

Cannon, L.W., Higginbotham, E. and Leung, M.L.A. 1991. 'Race and class bias in qualitative research on women' in Fonow, M.M. and Cook, J. (eds) *Beyond Methodology: Feminist Scholarship as Lived Research*. Bloomington, IN: Indiana University Press.

Carby, H.V. 1992. 'White women listen! Black feminism and the boundaries of sisterhood' in Center for Contemporary Cultural Studies (ed.) *The Empire Strikes Back. Race and Racism in 70s Britain*. London: Routledge.

Carr, B. 1998. 'At the thresholds of the "human": race, psychoanalysis and the replication of imperial memory'. *Cultural Critique* 39: 119–50.

Carrington, B. 2000. 'Double consciousness and the Black British athlete' in Owusu, K. (ed.) *Black British Culture and Society. A Text Reader*. London: Routledge.

Carter, B., Harris, C. and Joshi, S. 2000. 'The 1951–55 Conservative government and the racialization of black immigration' in Owusu, K. (ed.) *Black British Culture and Society. A Text Reader*. London: Routledge.

Cathcart, B. 1999. *The Case of Stephen Lawrence*. London: Viking.

Chamberlain, M. 1997. *Narratives of Return and Exile*. London: Macmillan Press.

Chanfrault-Duchet, M.-F. 1991. 'Narrative structures, social models and symbolic representation in the life story' in Gluck, S.B. and Patai, D. (eds) *Women's Words. The Feminist Practice of Oral History*. London: Routledge.

(charles), H. 1993. '"Queer nigger": theorizing "white" activism' in Bristow, J. and Wilson, A.R. (eds) *Activating Theory. Lesbian, Gay, Bisexual Politics*. London: Lawrence and Wishart.

(charles), H. 1997. 'The language of womanism. Re-thinking difference' in Mirza, H.S. (ed.) *Black British Feminism*. London: Routledge.

Childers, M. and hooks, b. 1990. 'A conversation about race and class' in Hirsh, M. and Keller, E. (eds) *Conflicts in Feminism*. London: Routledge.

Coates, J. 1996. *Women Talk*. Oxford: Blackwell Press.

Cohen, P. 1988. 'The perversions of inheritance: studies in the making of multi-racist Britain' in Cohen, P. and Bains, H.S. (eds) *Multi-Racist Britain*. London: Macmillan Education.

Cohen, P. 1993. *Home Rules. Some Reflections on Racism and Nationalism in Everyday Life*. London: University of East London.

Cohen, P. 1996. 'All white on the night? Narratives of nativism on the Isle of Dogs' in Ruston, M. (ed.) *Rising in the East*. London: Lawrence Wishart.

Cohen, P. 1997a. 'Laboring under Whiteness' in Frankenberg, R. (ed.) *Displacing Whiteness. Essays in Social and Cultural Criticism*. Durham, NC: Duke University Press.

Cohen, P. 1997b. *Rethinking the Youth Question. Education, Labour and Cultural Studies*. Basingstoke: Macmillan.

Cohen, R. 1994. *Frontiers of Identity. The British and the Others*. London: Longman.

Colley, L. 1992. 'Britishness and otherness: an argument'. *Journal of British Studies* 31: 309–29.

Colls, R. and Dodd, P. 1986. *Englishness. Politics and Culture 1880–1920*. London: Croom Helm.

Costera Meijer, I. and Prins, B. 1998. 'How bodies come to matter: an interview with Judith Butler'. *Signs: Journal of Women in Culture and Society* 23: 275–86.

Crick, B. 1991. 'The English and the British' in Crick, B. (ed.) *National Identities. The Constitution of the United Kingdom*. Oxford: Blackwell Publishers.

Cross, M. and Keith, M. 1993. 'Racism and the postmodern city' in Cross, M. and Keith, M. (eds) *Racism, the City and the State*. London: Routledge.

Davies, J. and Smith, C.R. 1999. 'Figuring white femininity: critique, investment, and the example of Princess Diana' in Brown, H., Gilkes, M. and Kaloski-Naylor, A. (eds) *White Women. Critical Perspectives on Race and Gender*. York: Raw Nerve Books.

Derricote, T. 1997. *The Black Notebooks. An Interior Journey*. New York: W.W. Norton and Co.

Disch, L. 1999. 'Judith Butler and the politics of the performative'. *Political Theory* 27: 545–59.

Domínguez, V.R. 1986. *White by Definition. Social Classification in Creole Louisiana*. New Brunswick: Rutgers University Press.

Donald, J. 1993. 'How English is it? Popular literature and national culture' in Carter, E., Donald, J. and Squires, J. (eds) *Space and Place. Theories of Identity and Location*. London: Lawrence and Wishart.

Dyer, R. 1997. *White*. London: Routledge.

Dyson, L. 1995. 'The return of the repressed? Whiteness, femininity and colonialisation in *The Piano*'. *Screen* 36: 267–76.

Edwards, R. 1990. 'Connecting method and epistemology. A white woman interviewing Black women'. *Women's Studies International Forum* 13 (5): 477–90.

Entine, J. 1999. *Taboo. Why Black Athletes dominate Sport and Why We're Afraid to Talk about It*. New York: Public Affairs.

Fanon, F. 1967. *Black Skins, White Masks*. New York: Grove.

Fine, M., Powell, L.C., Weis, L. and Wong, M.L. 1997. *Off White: Readings on Race, Power, and Society*. London: Routledge.

Flax, J. 1993. *Disputed Subjects. Essays on Psychoanalysis, Politics and Philosophy*. New York: Routledge.

Fonow, M.M. and Cook, J. 1991. *Beyond Methodology: Feminist Scholarship as Lived Research*. Bloomington, IN: Indiana University Press.

Frankenberg, R. 1993. *White Women, Race Matters. The Social Construction of Whiteness*. London: Routledge.

Frankenberg, R. 1997. 'Introduction: Local whiteness, localizing whiteness' in Frankenberg, R. (ed.) *Displacing Whiteness: Essays in Social and Cultural Criticism*. Durham, NC: Duke University Press.

Frankenberg, R. and Mani, L. 1993. 'Crosscurrents, crosstalk: race, "postcolonial-ity", and the politics of location'. *Cultural Studies* 7: 292–310.

Fraser, M. 1999. 'Classing queer. Politics in competition'. *Theory, Culture and Society* 16: 107–31.

Gabriel, J. 1994. *Racism, Culture, Markets*. London: Routledge.

Gabriel, J. 1996. 'What do you do when the minority means you? *Falling Down* and the construction of "whiteness"'. *Screen* 37.

Gabriel, J. 1998. *Whitewash. Racialized Politics and the Media*. London: Routledge.

Garvey, J. and Ignatiev, N. 1997. 'Towards a new abolitionism. A *Race Traitor* manifesto' in Hill, M. (ed.) *Whiteness. A Critical Reader*. New York: New York University Press.

Gilman, S.L. 1985. *Difference and Pathology: Stereotypes of Sexuality, Race and Madness*. Ithaca: Cornell University Press.

Gilman, S.L. 2000. 'Putting a new face on it: German Jews, American Jews, Israeli Jews and the origins of aesthetic surgery' in *German Research Colloquium*. Brighton: University of Sussex.

Gilman. S. 2001. *Making the Body Beautiful. A Cultural History of Aesthetic Surgery*. Princeton: Princeton University Press.

Gilroy, P. 1992a. *The Black Atlantic. Modernity and Double Consciousness*. London: Verso.

Gilroy, P. 1992b. 'The end of antiracism' in Donald, J. and Rattansi, A. (eds) *'Race', Culture and Difference*. London: Sage Publications.

Gilroy, P. 1993. *Small Acts. Thoughts on the Politics of Black Culture*. London: Serpent's Tail.

Gilroy, P. 1998. 'Race ends here'. *Ethnic and Racial Studies* 21: 838–47.

Gilroy, P. 2000. *Between Camps. Race, Identity, Nationalism at the End of the Colour Line*. London: Allen Lane, The Penguin Press.

Goldberg, D.T. 1993. *Racist Culture. Philosophy and the Politics of Meaning*. Oxford: Blackwells.

Goldberg, D.T. 1997. *Racial Subjects. Writing on Race in America*. London: Routledge.

Goulbourne, H. 1993. 'Aspects of nationalism and black identities in post-imperial Britain' in Cross, M. and Keith, M. (eds) *Racism, the City and the State*. London: Routledge.

Hall, C. 1992. *White, Male and Middle-class. Explorations in Feminism and History*. Cambridge: Polity Press.

Hall, S. 1987. 'Minimal selves' in Appignanesi, L. (ed.) *Identity. The Real Me. Postmodernism and the Question of Identity*. ICA document no. 6. London: ICA.

Hall, S. 1992. 'The question of cultural identity' in Hall, S., Held, D. and McGrew, T. (eds) *Modernity and its Futures*. Cambridge: Polity Press.

Hall, S. 1995. 'Negotiating Caribbean identities'. *New Left Review* 209: 3–14.

Hall, S. 1996. 'Introduction: who needs identity?' in Hall, S. and du Gay, P. (eds) *Questions of Cultural Identity*. London: Sage.

Hall, S. 1999. 'From Scarman to Stephen Lawrence'. *History Workshop Journal* 48: 187–97.

Hall, S. 2000. 'Old and new identities, old and new ethnicities' in Back, L. and Solomos, J. (ed.) *Theories of Race and Racism. A Reader*. London: Routledge.

Haney López, I.F. 1996. *White by Law*. New York: New York University Press.

Hernstein, R.J. and Murray, C. 1994. *The Bell Curve. Intelligence and Class Structure in American Life.* New York: Free Press.

Hesse, B. 1997. 'White governmentality. Urbanism, nationalism, racism' in Westwood, S. and Williams, J. (eds) *Imagining Cities. Scripts, Signs, Memories.* London: Routledge.

Hewitt, R. 1986. *White Talk Black Talk: Inter-racial Friendship and Communication amongst Adolescents.* Cambridge: Cambridge University Press.

Hewitt, R. 1996. *Routes of Racism. The Social Basis of Racial Action.* Stoke-on-Trent: Trentham Books Ltd.

Hill, M. 1997. 'Introduction: Vipers in Shangri-la. Whiteness, writing and other ordinary terrors' in Hill, M. (ed.) *Whiteness. A Critical Reader.* New York: New York University Press.

Hill Collins, P. 1990. *Black Feminist Thought. Knowledge, Consciousness and the Politics of Empowerment.* Boston: Unwin Hyman.

hooks, b. 1990. *Yearning. Race, Gender and Cultural Politics.* Boston: South End Press.

hooks, b. 1992. *Black Looks. Race and Representation.* Boston: South End Press.

hooks, b. 1997. 'Representing whiteness in the black imagination' in Frankenberg, R. (ed.) *Displacing Whiteness. Essays in Social and Cultural Criticism.* Durham, NC: Duke University Press.

Husband, C. 1982. *Race, Identity and British Society.* Milton Keynes: Open University.

Ifekwunigwe, J.O. 1997. 'Diaspora's daughters, Africa's orphans? On lineage, authenticity and "mixed race" identity' in Mirza, H.S. (ed.) *Black British Feminism. A Reader.* London: Routledge.

Ifekwunigwe, J.O. 1999. *Scattered Belongings. Cultural Paradoxes of 'Race', Nation and Gender.* London: Routledge.

Ignatiev, N. 1995. *How the Irish became White.* London: Routledge.

Ignatiev, N. and Garvey, J. 1996. *Race Traitor.* New York: Routledge.

Jacobson, M.J. 2000. 'Looking Jewish, seeing Jews' in Back, L. and Solomos, J. (eds) *Theories of Race and Racism. A Reader.* London: Routledge.

Jones, E. 1998. *The English Nation The Great Myth.* Stroud: Sutton Publishing.

Jones, S. 1993. *The Language of the Genes.* London: HarperCollins.

Kearney, H. 1991. 'Four nations or one?' in Crick, B. (ed.) *National Identities. The Constitution of the United Kingdom.* Oxford: Blackwell.

Kristeva, J. 1982. *Powers of Horror: An Essay on Abjection.* New York: Columbia University Press.

Kuhn, A. 1995. *Family Secrets. Acts of Memory and Imagination.* London: Verso.

Kumar, K. 2003. *The Making of English Identity.* Cambridge: Cambridge University Press.

Laclau, E. 1990. *New Reflections on the Revolution of our Time.* London: Verso.

Lawler, S. 1999. '"Getting out and getting away": women's narratives of class mobility'. *Feminist Review* 63: 2–24.

Lawler, S. 2002. 'Narrative in social research' in May, T. (ed.) *Qualitative Research in Action.* London: Sage.

McClintock, A. 1995. *Imperial Leather: Race, Gender and Sexuality in the Colonial Context.* New York: Routledge.

Macey, M. 1995. '"Same race" adoption policy: anti-racism or racism?'. *Journal of Social Policy* 24: 473–91.

McNay, L. 1999. 'Subject, psyche and agency. The work of Judith Butler'. *Theory, Culture and Society* 16: 175–93.

McNay, L. 2000. 'Habitus and the performative: Bourdieu and Butler on gender identity' in *Sussex SPT Graduate/Faculty Seminar Series*. Brighton: Sussex University.

MacPherson, W. 1999. *The Stephen Lawrence Inquiry*. Report on an inquiry by Sir William MacPherson of Cluny advised by Tom Cook, The Right Reverend Dr John Sentamu, Dr Richard Stone. Presented by the Secretary of State for the Home Department by Command of Her Majesty. London: The Stationary Office.

Martin Alcoff, L. 1999. 'Philosophy and racial identity' in Bulmer, M. and Solomos, J. (eds) *Ethnic and Racial Studies Today*. London: Routledge.

Mirza, H.S. 1997. 'Introduction: mapping a genealogy of black British feminism' in Mirza, H.S. (ed.) *Black British Feminism. A Reader*. London: Routledge.

Modood, T. 1997. 'Difference, Cultural Racism and Anti-Racism' in Werbner, P. and Modood, T. (eds) *Debating Cultural Hybridity. Multi-cultural Identities and the Politics of Anti-Racism*. London: Zed Books.

Mohanty, C.T. 1988. 'Under Western eyes: feminist scholarship and colonial discourses'. *Feminist Review* Autumn: 61–88.

Mohanty, C.T., Russo, A. and Torres, L. 1991. *Third World Women and the Politics of Feminism*. Bloomington, IN: Indiana University Press.

Morrison, T. 1992. *Playing in the Dark. Whiteness and the Literary Imagination*. London: Picador.

Muraleedharan, T. 1997. 'Rereading *Gandhi*' in Frankenberg, R. (ed.) *Displacing Whiteness. Essays in Social and Cultural Criticism*. Durham, NC: Duke University Press.

Nairn, T. 1981. *The Break-up of Britain*. London: Verso.

Nayak, A. 1999. '"Pale Warriors": Skinhead culture and the embodiment of white masculinities' in Brah, A., Hickman, M.J. and Mac an Ghaill, M. (eds) *Thinking Identities. Ethnicity, Racism and Culture*. London: Macmillan.

Nayak, A. 2003. *Race, Place and Globalization. Youth Cultures in a Changing World.* ⟵ Oxford: Berg.

Neal, S. 1999. 'Populdarist configurations of race and gender: the case of Hugh Grant, Liz Hurley and Divine Brown' in Brah, A., Hickman, M.J. and Mac an Ghaill, M. (eds) *Thinking Identities. Ethnicity, Racism and Culture*. London: Macmillan.

Oakley, A. 1981. 'Interviewing women, a contradiction in terms?' in Roberts, H. (ed.) *Doing Feminist Research*. London: Routledge and Kegan Paul.

Ofsted. 1995. *Crooms Hill Infants. Inspection Report*. London: Ofsted.

Owusu, K. 2000. 'Introduction: charting the genealogy of black British cultural studies' in Owusu, K. (ed.) *Black British Culture and Society. A Text Reader*. London: Routledge.

Parekh, B. 2000. *The Future of Multi-Ethnic Britain*. London: Profile Books.

Parker, I. and Burman, E. 1993. 'Against discursive imperialism, empiricism and constructionism: thirty-two problems with discourse analysis' in Burman, E. and Parker, I. (eds) *Discourse Analytic Research. Repertoires and Readings of Texts in Action*. London: Routledge.

Patai, D. 1991. 'US academics and third world women: is ethnical research possible?' in Gluck, S. and Patai, D. (eds) *Women's Words. The Feminist Practice of Oral History*. London: Routledge.

Paul, K. 1997. *Whitewashing Britain. Race and Citizenship in the Postwar Era*. New York: Cornell University.

Paxman, J. 1998. *The English. A Portrait of a People*. London: Penguin.

Phoenix, A. 1991. *Young Mothers?* Cambridge: Polity Press.

Phoenix, A. 1995. 'Young people: nationalism, racism and gender' in Lutz, H., Phoenix, A. and Yuval-Davis, N. (eds) *Crossfires. Nationalism, Racism and Gender in Europe*. London: Pluto.

Polkinghorne, D.E. 1991. 'Narrative and self-concept'. *Journal of Narrative and Life History* 1: 135–53.

Pratt, M.B. 1984. 'Identity: skin blood heart' in Bulkin, E., Pratt, M.B. and Smith, B. (eds) *Yours in Struggle: Three Feminist Perspectives on Anti-Semitism and Racism*. Brooklyn: Long Haul Press.

Rattansi, A. 1992. 'Changing the subject? Racism, culture and education' in Donald, J. and Rattansi, A. (eds) *'Race', Culture and Difference*. London: Sage Publications.

Reagon, B.J. 1983. 'Coalition politics: turning the century' in Smith, B. (ed.) *Home Girls. A Black Feminist Anthology*. New York: Kitchen Table, Women of Color Press.

Reay, D. 1996. 'Insider perspectives or stealing the words out of women's mouths: interpretation in the research process'. *Feminist Review* 53: 57–73.

Reay, D. 1999. 'Linguistic capital and home–school relationships: mother's interactions with their children's primary school teachers'. *Acta Sociologica* 42: 159–68.

Ribbens, J. 1989. 'Interviewing – an "unnatural situation"?'. *Women's Studies International Forum* 12 (6): 579–92.

Ricoeur, P. 1991a. 'Life in quest of narrative' in Wood, D. (ed.) *On Paul Ricoeur. Narrative and Interpretation*. London: Routledge.

Ricoeur, P. 1991b. 'Narrative identity' in Wood, D. (ed.) *On Paul Ricoeur. Narrative and Interpretation*. London: Routledge.

Roediger, D.R. 1994. *Towards the Abolition of the White Race*. London: Verso.

Roediger, D.R. 1998. *Black on White. Black Writers on What it Means to be White*. New York: Schocken Books.

Rutherford, J. 1997. *Forever England. Reflections on Masculinity and Empire*. London, Lawrence and Wishart.

Saeed, A., Blain, N. and Forbes, D. 1999. 'New ethnic and national questions in Scotland: post-British identities among Glasgow Pakistani teenagers'. *Ethnic and Racial Studies* 22: 821–44.

Samuel, R. 1989. *Patriotism*. London: Routledge.

Samuel, R. and Thompson, P. 1990. 'Introduction' in Samuel, R. and Thompson, P. (eds) *The Myths We Live By*. London: Routledge.

Savage, M., Barlow, J., Dickens, P. and Fielding, T. 1992. *Property, Bureaucracy and Culture. Middle Class Formation in Contemporary Britain*. London: Routledge.

Schwarz, B. 1996. 'Introduction: the expansion and contraction of England' in Schwarz, B. (ed.) *The Expansion of England. Race, Ethnicity and Cultural History*. London: Routledge.

Skeggs, B. 1997. *Formations and Class and Gender. Becoming Respectable*. London: Sage.

Skeggs, B. 2002. 'Techniques for telling the reflexive self' in May, T. (ed.) *Qualitative Research in Action*. London: Sage.

Smith, S.J. 1993. 'Residential segregation and the politics of racialization' in Cross, M. and Keith, M. (eds) *Racism, the City and the State*. London: Routledge.

Solomos, J. and Back, L. 1994. 'Conceptualising racisms: social theory, politics and research'. *Sociology* 28: 143–61.

Squires, C. 1997. 'Who's white? Television talk shows and representations of whiteness' in Fine, M., Weis, L., Powell, L.C. and Mun Wong, L. (eds) *Off White. Readings on Race, Power and Society*. New York: Routledge.

Stoler, A.L. 1997. 'Making empire respectable: the politics of race and sexual morality in twentieth-century colonial cultures' in McClintock, A., Mufti, A. and Shohat, E. (eds) *Dangerous Liaisons. Gender, Nation and Postcolonial Perspectives*. Minneapolis: University of Minnesota Press.

Thompson, P. 1988. *The Voice of the Past. Oral History* (2nd edn). Oxford: Oxford University Press.

Tizard, B. and Phoenix, A. 1993. *Black, White or Mixed-Race? Race and Racism in the Lives of Young People of Mixed Parentage*. London: Routledge.

Twine, F.W. 1997. 'Brown-skinned white girls: class, culture, and the construction of white identity in suburban communities' in Frankenberg, R. (ed.) *Displacing Whiteness. Essays in Social and Cultural Criticism*. Durham, NC: Duke University Press.

van Dijk, T.A. 1991. *Racism and the Press. Critical Studies in Racism and Migration*. London: Routledge.

Walker, A. 1984. *In Search of Our Mother's Gardens*. London: The Women's Press.

Walkerdine, V. and Lucey, H. 1989. *Democracy in the Kitchen. Regulating Mothers and Socialising Daughters*. London: Virago.

Ware, V. 1992. *Beyond the Pale. White Women, Racism and History*. London: Verso.

Ware, V. 1997. 'Island racism: gender, place and white power' in Frankenberg, R. (ed.) *Displacing Whiteness. Essays in Social and Cultural Criticism*. Durham, NC: Duke University Press.

Ware, V. and Back, L. 2002. *Out of Whiteness. Color, Politics and Culture*. Chicago: University of Chicago Press.

Waters, C. 1997. '"Dark strangers" in our midst: discourses of race and nation in Britain, 1947–1963'. *Journal of British Studies* 36: 207–38.

Weedon, C. 1997. *Feminist Practice and Poststructuralist Theory* (2nd edn). Oxford: Blackwell.

Werbner, P. 1999. Conference paper, *Representations of Migrants and Multiculturalism in Britain, 1933–present*. Brighton: Sussex University.

Wetherell, M. and Potter, J. 1992. *Mapping the Language of Racism. Discourse and the Legitimation of Exploitation*. London: Harvester Wheatsheaf.

Williams, P.J. 1997. *Seeing a Colour-Blind Future. The Paradox of Race. The 1997 Reith Lectures*. London: Virago.

Winant, H. 2000. 'The theoretical status of the concept of race' in Back, L. and Solomos, J. (eds) *Theories of Race and Racism. A Reader*. London: Routledge.

Woodward, K. 1997. 'Motherhood: identities, meanings and myths' in Woodward, K. (ed.) *Identity and Difference*. London: Sage.

Wright, P. 1985. *On Living in an Old Country: the National Past in Contemporary Britain*. London: Verso.

Young, H. 2000. 'The inclusiveness of "Britain" cannot be challenged'. *The Guardian*. London.

Young, R.J.C. 1995. *Colonial Desire. Hybridity in Theory, Culture and Race*. London: Routledge.

Yuval-Davis, N. 1992. 'Fundamentalism, multiculturalism and women in Britain' in Donald, J. and Rattansi, A. (eds) *'Race', Culture and Difference*. London: Sage Publications.

Newspapers

Anon. 2000. 'What an insult to history and our intelligence'. *Daily Mail*, 11 October 2000.

Anon. 2000. 'Prescription for harmony. But race report is spoilt by a bad idea'. *Guardian*, 11 October 2000.

Anon. 2000. 'London life'. *London Life*.

Chandran, R. 2000. 'An insult to all our countrymen'. *Daily Mail*, 11 October 2000.

Appendix 1
Interviewees

Interviews 1–6, 10 and 19 were either pilot interviews conducted outside the fieldwork areas or with interviewees who are not included in the main list because they were not white.

Sally (Interviews 7 and 22)
Single parent in her early 30s, living in Camberwell. Grew up in a rural working-class family. Two daughters (described as 'mixed race'), one at primary and one had just started secondary school. Working part time.

Louise (Interview 8)
Working-class woman in her late 30s living in Camberwell. Grew up in Australia, with English parents, had been in London since she was 18. One son and one daughter, both at primary school. Working as a cleaner in private houses.

Madeleine (Interviews 9 and 44)
Single parent in her late 20s living in Camberwell. Grew up in a middle-class family in the Far East and suburban London. One daughter (described as 'mixed race'), at primary school. Working as a freelance consultant.

Stephanie (Interviews 11 and 31)
Woman in her mid-30s, living in Clapham. Grew up in a middle-class family in the south of England. One son and one daughter, both preschool. In the process of applying for primary school for son. Not in paid employment, had worked in administration.

Helen (Interviews 12 and 26)
Woman in her early 30s, living in Camberwell. Grew up in a working-class rural family. Two daughters (described as 'mixed race'), preschool. Working in administration.

Barbara (Interview 13)
Woman in her mid-40s, living in Camberwell. Three sons (described as 'black'), all at secondary school. Grew up in a middle-class family in the Midlands. Working as a child carer.

Rosemary (Interviews 14 and 32)
Working-class woman in her late 30s, born and still living in Camberwell. Three daughters all at primary school. Working as a sales assistant.

Heather (Interviews 15 and 27)
Middle-class woman in her early 30s living in Camberwell. Grew up outside London, in the south of England. One daughter, preschool. Not currently employed, had worked in arts administration.

Emma (Interviews 16 and 45)
Woman in her late 20s living in Peckham. Grew up in a middle-class family, outside London, in the south of England. Two daughters, one at primary school, one preschool. Working in childcare.

Deborah (Interviews 17 and 40)
Middle-class woman in her mid-30s, living in Clapham. Grew up in London and overseas. One son at primary school. Working in publishing.

Teresa (Interviews 18 and 35)
Woman in her mid-30s, living in Clapham. Grew up in London. One son at primary school. Not currently employed, had worked as a manager in the commercial sector.

Rosalind (Interviews 20 and 36)
Woman in her mid-30s, living in Clapham. Grew up in a middle-class family in a rural area in the west of England. One son and one daughter, both at primary school. Working in publishing.

Emily (Interview 21)
Working-class woman in her mid-30s grew up and living in Camberwell. Two children (son and daughter), both at primary school. Working in childcare.

Eve (Interview 23)
Middle-class woman in her mid-30s living in Clapham. Grew up in South Africa. One daughter at primary school. Not currently employed. Had worked in management.

Phillipa (Interview 24)
Middle-class woman in her late 30s living in Heathley. Grew up in London. Two children, one son about to enter primary school, daughter preschool. Not currently employed, had worked in publishing.

Jennifer (Interview 25)
Middle-class woman in her late 30s living in Clapham. Grew up in the Midlands. Two children, one son and one daughter, both at primary (private) schools. Not currently employed. Had worked as a designer.

Jan (Interview 30)
Middle-class woman in her late 30s living in Clapham. Grew up in London. Three children, two daughters, one son, all at primary school. Not currently employed, had worked as a teacher.

Irene (Interview 33)
Working-class woman in her early 40s, living in Clapham. Grew up in London. Four children, two at secondary and two at primary school. Not currently working.

Sue (Interview 34)
Middle-class woman in her early 40s, living in Clapham. Grew up in the north of England. One son, preschool. Teaching in higher education.

Hilary (Interview 37)
Middle-class woman in her late 20s, living in Camberwell. Grew up in the south of England, outside London. One son, preschool. Not currently working. Had been an actress.

Karon (Interviews 38 and 46)
Working-class woman in her late 20s, living in Clapham. Grew up in London. One son, about to enter primary school. One daughter. Working as a child carer.

Melanie (Interview 39)
Middle-class woman in her late 20s living in Camberwell. Grew up in Wales. One son (described as 'mixed race') preschool. Not currently employed, artist.

Jessica (Interview 41)
Middle-class woman in her mid-30s living in Clapham. Grew up in the north of England. One daughter, preschool. Currently working in administration.

Beverley (Interview 42)
Working-class woman in her mid-30s. Grew up in London, living in Clapham. Two sons. Not currently working, had worked as a sales assistant.

Liz (Interview 43)
Middle-class woman in her mid-40s. Grew up and living in Camberwell. Two daughters both at primary school. Working as a writer.

Appendix 2
Interview questions

First interviews

The interviews were conducted in an open-ended manner. They did not follow a strict list of questions. Depending on the relevance of the questions, some of these individual questions would lead to extensive discussions, which would include several follow-up questions from me. However, in general, all interviews would include versions of the following questions, although not necessarily in the order given.

How many children do you have?
  Boys or girls?
  How old are they?

Has having children had an impact on your sense of identity?
  Has it changed the way you see yourself, the way you think others see you? In what ways?
  What other changes has it brought?

Do you have many other friends who are mothers?
  How did you meet them?
  Did you set out to meet other mothers in the area?

Do you see much of your family?

How long have you lived in the area?
  Why did you move here?
  Will you stay here?

Has being a mother changed your relationship to the area?

Does having children make you think about your own childhood?
  How does your childhood differ from your children's?

Do issues of race, gender and class come up with your children?
   In what ways?
   Do your children ever talk about differences of class, race and gender?
   Do you talk to your children about any of them?
   Does it affect how you choose toys, books, etc. for them?
   Do they have friends across differences of race, class and gender?
   Are friends who they meet in school different from those they meet through you?

How did you (or will you) go about choosing a school for your children?
   What were you looking for?
   What criteria did you use?
   How did you find out information about the different schools in the area?
   What are the schools (primary and secondary) like in the area?

Does your child go to after-school activities? (or to a nursery or playgroup)?

Do you often have your children's friends round to play?
   How are these arrangements made?

How would you describe your nationality?
   Is there a reason you said English and not British (or vice versa)?
   Do you think that the nature of being British or English has changed since you were a child?
   Do you have a sense of bringing up your children as English or British?

Second interviews

In the second interview, I would begin by briefly summarising some of the things that we discussed in the first interview and asking the interviewee if they had thought about the interview since, had anything to add or any reflections on it. I would then say that I was seeking in this second interview to look at aspects of their life that were less to do with children, perhaps to fill in some of the gaps in terms of finding out about life before children. I would then ask them to talk about any significant 'turning points' in their lives. The interviews would generally flow from here, with interviewees selecting what areas to talk about. I would try and ensure that the interviews covered the following areas: leaving home, education and working life. I would also prompt them to consider whether questions of class, 'race' or gender had arisen in different parts of their lives.

Index